The Men in Blue

Larry R. Gerlach

The Men in Blue

Conversations with Umpires

With a new afterword by the author

*To Margie,
who, like the umps,
calls 'em as she sees 'em.
With best wishes,
Larry Gerlach*

University of Nebraska Press
Lincoln and London

First Bison Book printing: 1994
Most recent printing indicated by the last digit below:
10   9   8   7   6   5   4   3   2   1

Library of Congress Cataloging-in-Publication Data
Gerlach, Larry R.
The men in blue: conversations with umpires /
Larry R. Gerlach; with a new afterword by the author.
p. cm.
ISBN 0-8032-7045-3
1. Baseball umpires—United States—Biography.
2. Baseball umpires—United States—Interviews.
GV865.A1G48 1994
796.357 '3' 0922—dc20   [B]
93-42576 CIP

Reprinted by arrangement with Larry R. Gerlach

Acknowledgments

Frank Music Corp.: From "Six Months Out of Every Year" by Richard Adler &
Jerry Ross. © 1955, 1957 Frank Music Corp. International Copyright Secured.
All rights reserved. Used by permission.

Sporting News and the Office of the Baseball Commissioner: From "Official
Baseball Rules." Used by permission.

All photographs courtesy of the National Baseball Hall of Fame and Museum,
Cooperstown, New York, except the photograph of Bill Kinnamon, which is
courtesy of *The Sporting News*, St. Louis, Missouri.

∞

*For Stan Layton and Mike Sorich, fellow bleacher bums
who understand that Derks Field is more than a ball park
and baseball is more than a game*

Preface

"Kill him! Kill the umpire!" shouted some one on the stand;
And it's likely they'd have killed him had not Casey raised his
hand.

> Ernest Lawrence Thayer
> "Casey at the Bat," 1888

You're blind, ump, you're blind, ump.
You must be out of your mind, ump!

> "Six Months Out of Every Year"
> *Damn Yankees*, 1955

One day the Devil challenged the Lord to a baseball game.
The Lord, smiling, proclaimed: "You don't have a chance.
I have Babe Ruth, Ty Cobb, and all the great players up
here." "Well," snickered Satan, "I've got all the umpires."

> Folktale

The umpires shall be responsible for
the conduct of the game in accordance
with these official rules and for
maintaining discipline and order on
the playing field during the game.

> *Official Baseball Rules*

If it is true, as Jacques Barzun, the Columbia University philosopher, once observed, that "whoever wants to know the heart and mind of America had better learn baseball," an appropriate corollary would be that whoever wants to know baseball had better learn about umpires. As every kid who ever tried to play a sandlot game with the honor system knows, it is the presence of an arbiter that transforms competitive chaos into organized baseball. In fact, baseball is officially defined as "a game between two teams [played] under the jurisdiction of one or more umpires."

It has always been so. The constitution and bylaws of the pioneer Knickerbocker Base Ball Club of New York provided for team captains to select an umpire whose judgment was indisputable. When on October 6, 1845, on the Elysian Fields of Hoboken, the Knickerbockers played the first officially recorded baseball game in history, one William R. Wheaton served as the umpire. Subsequent entries in Knickerbocker scorebooks reveal the predictable: The arbitrator brought order but not harmony to the game. Even Alexander J. Cartwright, the inventor of modern baseball, was once fined "for disputing the umpire." Teammate Ebenezer Dupignac, assessed six cents, was not the last player ever fined "for saying s--t" (to the umpire?). Although the relationship between arbiter and athlete has often been stormy, it is the former who makes it possible for the latter to "Play ball!"

Despite his central role, the umpire is the most neglected, least appreciated, and most misunderstood participant in the National Pastime. In the public mind he appears at best as a necessary evil, at worst as a nearsighted Neanderthal bent upon robbing the home team of its just deserts. How else to explain the singular propensity of umpires to blow calls obvious even to those sitting in the last row of the upper deck and to misinterpret rules known even to those who have never read a rule book? The image of arbiter as antagonist persists because neither the public in general nor sportswriters in particular pay much attention to umpires except when a controversial call or missed play seemingly exposes their incompetence, perfidy, or both.

The fan who can instantaneously recite a wealth of detail about players and games of this and yesteryear is hard pressed to provide substantive information about umpires or their profession. The *Official Encyclopedia of Baseball* merely provides an alphabetical listing of major league umpires, while the massive *Baseball Encyclopedia*, which contains career profiles of every man who ever played or managed in the major leagues, makes no mention of umpires. Although the *Baseball Register* has provided over the years biographical information about umpires, the data are often inaccurate and incomplete; except for 1964, the *Register* omitted umpire profiles from 1959 through 1969. During the early decades of this century every major daily newspaper included umpires in box scores with the deferential designation "Mr."; today not a single newspaper identifies umpires in box scores.

Given the general lack of recognition accorded umpires, it is not surprising that arbiters were first elected to the National Baseball Hall of Fame in 1953. And of the five umpires—William Joseph Klem, Thomas Henry Connolly, William G. Evans, John Bertrand Conlan, and Robert Cal Hubbard—currently enshrined in Cooperstown, Jocko Conlan alone did not hold a front-office position in baseball. As Furman Bisher has so poignantly remarked about umpires: "They're submerged in the history of baseball like idiot children in a family album."

Most baseball fans might think Sam Crane, an old-time player turned sportswriter, a bit extreme when he declared, "There never was a good umpire." They might even disagree with Dodger great Maury Wills, who in 1976 said: "Give or take a few, one-third of all the umpires in the National League are incompetent." But surely they would concur with Jimmy Dykes, a longtime manager and prominent umpire baiter, who told the Washington Touchdown Club in 1954: "Despite all the nasty things I have said about umpires, I think they're one hundred percent honest. But I can't for the life of me figure out how they arrive at some of their decisions."

Although those who officiate at athletic contests can hardly be expected to win popularity polls, baseball umpires have traditionally been the most abused and vilified of sports officials. The rhubarb, an especially emotive mode of discussion that usually terminates in banishment, is unique to baseball; in no other sport can participants come onto the playing area and argue so loudly for so long with an official. The puerile song "Three Blind Mice," ingrained in the mind of boo-birds by Gladys Goodding's Ebbets Field Wurlitzer, and the homicidal exhortation "Kill the umpire!" are reserved for the baseball umpire alone. As late as 1977 shortstop Frank Taveras, then with the Pittsburgh Pirates, remarked of umpire Ed Sudol: "I hope he drops dead. I hope he has a heart attack." The torrent of verbal abuse—not to mention the occasional physical assaults—directed at umpires speaks volumes not only about the nature of the sporting crowd but also about the character of those to whom it is directed.

Over the years a series of quotable quotes from arbiters themselves have formed the public's perception of the umpiring profession. Bill Klem's declaration "I never missed one in my heart" and Bill Guthrie's contention "Der ain't no close plays, me lad; dey is either dis or dat" suggest arrogant infallibility. Tim Hurst's admonition to "call 'em fast and walk away tough" and Larry Goetz's claim that "you can't be a good fellow and be a good umpire" connote a hard-nosed breed of autocrat. Guthrie's query in response to criticism of his deportment by American League president Ban Johnson—"No gentleman would ever be an umpire, would he?"—advances the stereotype of the arbiter as a rough-and-tumble, lower-class character. Bill Stewart's lament "I'm the loneliest man in town" conveys the dull existence of a social pariah, while Dolly Stark's complaint "I can't find time to quiet my nerves" alludes to the debilitating on-field pressures placed upon a man who, when behind the plate, makes more than 250 split-second decisions in two hours. Finally, Hurst's famous flippancy "You can't beat the hours" conjures up the image of a thankless job made tolerable by its brevity, whereas Klem's confession "Umpiring, to me, is a religion" testifies to a fanatical commitment to umpiring as a way of life.

To determine what manner of men become umpires and to learn more about the umpiring profession, I set out across the country to interview former major league umpires. The interviewees were selected because of their historical importance, contributions to baseball, or both. If American League umpires predominate, it is not because I am an inveterate Yankee fan; rather, it is because some of the National League arbiters I contacted declined to participate in the project.

The chapters that follow are edited and condensed versions of tape-recorded interviews which ranged in length from four to seven hours. In addition to eliminating my questions and comments, I have rearranged material to achieve topical and chronological unity. On occasion I have silently added the first names of individuals or provided dates of events for clarity. Similarly, I have made minor alterations in grammar and syntax to remove redundancies and "conversationalisms." Although expletives have occasionally been deleted, the texts have not been bowdlerized; I have merely distinguished between the purposeful use of a poignant epithet or adjective and its offhand use in informal conversation. Whenever possible I have checked the participant's recollections against newspaper accounts and baseball record books to ensure accuracy; the discrepancies were few and inconsequential, testimony to the umpires' amazing ability to recall events from the distant past with extraordinary precision. The repetition of some subject matter in various chapters is deliberate; I asked many of the same questions of each interviewee in order to determine disagreement or consensus on major points of interest.

The Men in Blue is designed to be read on several levels by baseball buffs and serious students of sport alike. Most simply, it is a collection of reminiscences of major events and personalities associated with baseball during the past half century by men who were on the scene. It is not, however, merely a mélange of anecdotes and yarns. Accounts and remembrances were selected for inclusion because they illustrate specific themes or provide special perspective, not simply because they were amusing or entertaining. The chronological arrangement of the chapters, determined by an individual's initial appearance in the major leagues, also allows the book to be read as an informal history of baseball and umpiring from the glory days of the 1920s to the era of continental expansion. Enormous social, economic, and technological changes occurred in baseball between the time Beans Reardon broke in in 1926 and Ed Sudol retired in 1977. Umpires speak herein with firsthand knowledge about important developments ranging from night games and television to racial integration and unionization. In addition, the diverse personalities of the umpires reflect the changes in the game from the flamboyance of the Ruthian age to the no-holds-barred Depression days of the Gas House Gang through the uncertainties and dislocations of World War II to the professional advancements and conservatism of the 1950s and 1960s. Moreover, because the book contains considerable technical information about the lives and duties of umpires, it serves as something of a handbook on the art of umpiring and the nature of the profession.

Above all, *The Men in Blue* should be read as a collection of autobiographies. Here a group of extraordinary men tell their life stories. Theirs is a story of exceptional ability and perseverance; after all, there are far fewer opportunities to advance from the bush leagues to the big leagues for umpires than for players. Theirs is also a story of remarkable courage and dedication; of men who endured ridicule, paltry salaries, and primitive working conditions because of a devotion to the game of baseball. The book reveals that if umpires are not the myopic miscreants of popular myth, neither are they saints or martyrs; that if they share certain personality traits and attitudes in common, they are also unique human beings with distinctive qualities. In the final analysis it is the individuality of the umpire—the intangibles of judgment, style, presence, and personality—that stands out in a game often dominated by cold statistics and calculated maneuvers.

This book does not, of course, do full justice to its subjects. The printed page cannot capture the personal vibrancy or the depth of character of each man. An umpire is a special breed—a natural leader in any endeavor. He is a powerful man, imposing in bearing and forceful in the manifestation of strongly held convictions. He is an extrovert who relishes both the publicity (albeit mostly negative) and the responsibility of his pressure-packed position. Dedicated, determined, egotistical, confident, authoritarian, honest, fair—these are the kinds of adjectives that describe an umpire. And he is a split personality—simultaneously a raging emotional volcano liable to erupt with awesome fury at the slightest provocation and a warm, sensitive, good-natured soul brimming with humanity. They are imposing, appealing, unforgettable men.

Preparation of this book has fundamentally altered my perspective on baseball, indeed on all sports. I now find myself, both unconsciously and by design, paying more attention to the officials than to the players. Therein lies the purpose of The Men in Blue. Organized baseball—professional and amateur alike—owes umpires, past and present, a debt that can never be repaid. I hope this book will help provide some of the recognition that is overdue the highly visible, yet invisible, men in blue. (Despite Ban Johnson's experiment with khaki-colored uniforms, the National League's brief use of white [or "ice-cream"] pants, and the American League's adoption of maroon blazers, the navy-blue suit remains the trademark of the umpire.) It is also my hope that the book not only will prove entertaining but also will provide greater empathy for umpires as individuals and as professionals.

The manuscript for this book was completed prior to the strike of the Major League Umpires Association at the start of the 1979 season. Although the strike brought unprecedented publicity to major league umpires, the characterization of arbiters as generally misunderstood and unappreciated remains valid. The strike made the public better aware of the tangible aspects of umpiring in the big leagues—salaries, pensions, travel schedules—but did little to publicize either the intangible dimensions of the profession or the realities of umpiring in the minor leagues.

During the eighteen months the manuscript was in the making, I incurred a debt to many people. First, I am indebted to Robert E. Warden, an amateur umpire in Salt Lake City, who accompanied me on several interviews, conducted initial interviews with Lee Ballanfant and Bill Kinnamon, and assisted with drafting the chapter on Emmett Ashford. Personal complications thwarted our design of collaboration, but without his encouragement I should not have undertaken the project in the first place. To Eugenia Reardon and Dolly Rue, my deepest thanks for their special interest and assistance. F. Ross Peterson, a shortstop-turned-scholar who is currently chairman of the history department at Utah State University, generously made available much needed secretarial assistance to transcribe the taped interviews. Craig Fuller, who personifies the word "fan," deserves numerous "assists" for facilitating completion of the manuscript. Don Avery of the National Association of Professional Baseball Leagues graciously assisted my search through minor league records; Cliff Kachline, historian at the National Baseball Hall of Fame, greatly aided my research in Cooperstown. Randy Marsh and Bill Lawson of the Pacific Coast League contributed valuable insight into the life and aspirations of minor league umpires. Augie Donatelli and Tom Gorman, former National League umpires, discussed candidly their careers as well as the current state of the profession. Thanks, too, to Max Stone, who, as an umpire in the old Class A Western League, initially aroused my interest in umpires and signed my first autographed baseball. Finally, my thanks to Gail for tolerating—even abetting—my obsession with sports in general and baseball in particular, and to T.J. for sharing my enthusiasm for the National Pastime. At the tender age of seven, my son exhibited keen perception by suggesting the title of this book about "empires." He is the only youngster I know who volunteers to umpire sandlot games.

It is said that an umpire is the only person who is expected to be perfect at the start of his career and to improve each day thereafter. Umpires are not perfect, and neither is this book about them. But just as every arbiter strives to avoid making mistakes that affect the outcome of a game, I have labored to avoid errors of omission and commission that would detract seriously from the quality of this book. If I have kicked a few, I admit sole responsibility and shall stoically endure the boos.

Contents

The Men in Blue

Beans Reardon explains to Boston Braves manager
Casey Stengel why Buddy Hassett was out at home in
a game against the Dodgers in 1940. Courtesy National
Baseball Library & Archive, Cooperstown, N.Y.

Beans Reardon

ᗧᗧᗧ

John Edward Reardon
Born: Taunton, Massachusetts, November 23, 1897
Height: 5' 8"
Weight: 145
Playing career: none
Umpiring career: Western Canada League (B), 1920–21; Pacific
              Coast League (AA), 1922–25; National League,
              1926–49
No-hit games: Clyde Shoun, May 15, 1944
All-Star games: 1936, 1940, 1948
World Series (games): 1930 (6), 1934 (7), 1939 (4), 1943 (5), 1949 (5)

Umpiring is as old as history itself. A home without an arbitrator or a game without an umpire is like a steam engine without wheels—always chugging away but getting nowhere. Somebody has to run things.

Some people say I was a tough umpire. I don't know if I was tough, but I had the guts to go out there and do the job. And to be a good umpire, you first of all must have guts because you're going to have trouble, no two ways about it. If the Pope was an umpire, he'd still have trouble with the Catholics.

I never pulled any punches. I let them know I was the boss. The main thing for an umpire is to make the ballplayers respect you. If they respect you, you won't have too much trouble. If they don't respect you, they'll run you right out of the league.

You have so many close plays, there's no way you can get away from kicking a few. I don't care how good you are, you're going to blow a play now and then. But you're not wrong too many times, or you wouldn't be out there. Nobody's perfect.

Umpiring is doubly hard because you have thousands of critics in the stands who do their own umpiring on every call. When they don't agree with you, which is every time you call one against their team, they treat you like a blind man who should be begging for alms.

Nobody can make you an umpire. Today they have schools for umpires. I don't know what the hell they tell them. Oh, you can tell them to hustle or move here or there, something like that. But you have to have guts to be an umpire, and you can't put guts in a guy. He's got to be born with it.

I was born in Taunton, Massachusetts, November 23, 1897. My father was born in Manchester, New Hampshire, but his parents came from Ireland. My mother's parents came from there, too; she was the only one of the children born in this country. My father was a foreman in one of the cotton mills and a partner in a saloon. My mother was a very strict nondrinker, so she soon made him sell the saloon. He died when I was just a kid. I had an older brother, Bill. He went to college, but I never graduated from any place but grammar school. I might have gone to high school for one day or something. I wasn't the best scholar who ever lived.

My mother had a big influence on me. She taught me never to tell a lie. That's the way I was raised. So as an umpire I didn't alibi when I missed a play. I just said, "Yeah, I missed it. So what? If you don't keep your mouth shut, you're not going to be here to find out why." I think that honesty helped me out in the long run. They used to say, "The little SOB won't lie to you."

I've always been a little thickheaded and quick to tell somebody to go to hell. I got sent home from school one time for calling a nun an SOB. I don't know why I'm like that. Maybe I'm just honest.

My life was anything I made it. I never allowed anyone to interfere. In New York I lived at the New Yorker Hotel. I was there when it first opened. Then some of the players started moving in on me because it was an easy subway ride to the Polo Grounds. Somebody asked me if I was going to move because in those days umpires and players were not supposed to stay in the same hotel. I said, "I am like hell. I was here before they were. I'm not going to move."

I've always liked sports. My father did, too. He was a back jumper; the Irish jumped backwards in the old days. I loved baseball but wasn't good enough to make any teams. I had a lot of fun playing by myself, just bouncing a ball against a barn or house or something. I'd go to Boston to see ball games every chance I got. I guess I never amounted to much as a ballplayer because I was so small. As a kid I was undersized and underweight. When I was full grown, I weighed only about 125 pounds—had to stand twice in the same spot to make a shadow.

When my father died, my mother married a fellow who had moved out to the Coast, so we moved to Los Angeles when I was about four- teen. I hated to leave Massachusetts because I was so crazy about baseball, but I told my mother I'd go wherever she went. We lived in Boyle Heights, which was a pretty rough section of the city. I went to work as a messenger boy, riding a bicycle. When I turned eighteen, I went to work as a boilermaker's apprentice in the Southern Pacific Railroad shops.

I still loved baseball, but since I wasn't very good as a player, I started to umpire. The church I went to, St. Benedict's, sponsored a ball team, and when the guys started complaining that they weren't getting a square deal from the umpires, I volunteered to officiate. Then, after I went to work for the railroad, I volunteered to umpire the shop games during lunchtime.

I got my nickname during one of those noon-hour games. When- ever people asked me where I came from, I told them Boston because I figured nobody in California knew where Taunton was. So one day, when I came up to bat, Lee Allen, a fancy Pullman car painter, yelled, "Come on, Baked Beans, old boy, hit one now!" The crowd picked it up, and from then on everybody called me Beans. Before then they called me Jack, but it was Beans Reardon ever since.

Harry Hammer, who worked in the blacksmith shop, really pushed me along to umpiring. He was the catcher for a semipro team spon- sored by Billy Cole's father's tailor shop over on Broadway. Hammer and the other players took a liking to me, so I'd travel with them to games. Harry paid my fare, and I'd carry his grip, hold his money during the game and things like that.

One Sunday we were up in Pasadena. Dan Tobey, a local fight an- nouncer, was the umpire. He was standing out behind the pitcher, so they were looking for another umpire. Hammer said, "Put in that kid with me. That kid can umpire." So I did. After the game we went to the Pasadena Athletic Club to change. Milton Murray, who had the Walk-Over shoe store, came over and said, "Kid, would you like to umpire every Sunday?" I said, "Sure, how much do you pay?" He said, "Three dollars." "And carfare," I told him. Carfare at that time was twenty-five cents round trip from Los Angeles to Pasadena. He didn't want to pay the carfare, but he fired Tobey and hired me. Every Sunday he'd put six half dollars right in the middle of my locker, and I'd say, "Another quarter." Always had to battle him for the other quarter.

I hung around with the ballplayers, and they'd help me get jobs in the semipro leagues. We used to hang around Donnie Oldfield's saloon at 530 South Spring Street or Jim Jefferies' saloon at 333 South Spring Street—Spring Street was the thing at the time. Abe Diamond was the tailor to all the ballplayers, and on the third floor of his building was a gymnasium where they held fights on Saturday nights. So I'd hang around there, and the guys would say, "Take care of the kid; the little SOB can umpire." Hell, pretty soon I was making more money umpiring than I was as a boilermaker.

When World War I came along, I went to the San Pedro shipyards as a boilermaker's apprentice and started umpiring for the shipyard team in the War Service League. That's when I umpired behind the bat for the first time. Before then I had always stood out behind the pitcher. I bought my first outfit then—a secondhand outfit for $11. I got $7.50 a game, but the league lasted only two weeks. Then I went back to umpiring shipyard games.

After the war I moved to Bisbee, Arizona. It was 1919, at the time of the Dempsey-Willard fight in Toledo. I was told I could umpire down there and get a soft job in the copper mines. Soft job, hell! They put me to work "mucking" on a "slope" 1,400 feet underground. We'd dig out the ore with a pickax and shovel it into a big shaft close by. The boss told us to be careful not to step in that hole because it was 200 feet deep. It was damned hard work. We worked stripped to the waist. Had to string up our lunches over a beam in the shaft to keep the rats from eating them. The rats were big as tomcats. You went down in the hole for eight hours. After three or four days I wondered what the hell I was doing there, so I went to the superintendent, who happened to be the mayor of Bisbee, and told him I wanted another job. He said, "That's the best job in the mine."

"Well," I said, "in that case you have to show me the way out." I already had my fare home, so I went back to Los Angeles, where I could enjoy the sunshine and have a clean bed.

One day [Wade] Red Killefer brought his Los Angeles ball club to Pasadena to play. I umpired back of the bat, and after the game he sent for me. He said, "Kid, did you ever think about going into umpiring?" I said, "Jeez, I'm too young, ain't I?" He said, "You got any guts?" "What do you think?" I said. "Well," he said, "you've got the

ability, and if you've got the courage, you don't need anything else."
So Killefer put the idea in my head to go and be a professional
umpire.

Sammy Beer, who had earlier pitched for the Angels in the Coast
League, was a favorite in Saskatoon, Saskatchewan. So they wrote up
to Canada, and he got me a job in the Class B Western Canada
League. I was only twenty-two at the time. I signed for $250 a month.
Had to pay my own expenses. But that was better than swinging a
sixteen-pound sledgehammer in the boiler shop fifty-four hours a
week for twenty-five cents an an hour.

When I got to Calgary, I went over to the office of this Dr. Birch
who owned the ball club. I sat around the waiting room for a while,
and then the nurse took me in to see him. I said, "My name is Reardon." I'll never forget this as long as I live. He said, "What did you
say your name is?" I told him again. He looked amazed. "You can't be
Reardon, the professional umpire. You're nothing but a schoolboy." I
said, "That's who I am, and I can umpire, doctor, don't worry about
that."

The night before my first game I went to see Joe Devine, the manager of Calgary, the home club, at his hotel. Devine was lying on the
bed talking to this guy. I said, "Which one is Devine?" He said, "I'm
Devine." So I said, "Mr. Devine, my name is Reardon. I'm going to be
the umpire tomorrow, and I don't want no arguments from anybody.
Do you understand?" He didn't say anything, just looked at me. I
could hear them laughing as I walked out. Hell, I was just a punk kid
who weighed about 135 pounds.

Nobody gave me any instructions. I just went out there and umpired. Hell, I was supposed to be a professional umpire, so they figured I knew how to umpire. So I went out there and ran the game.

The minors were rough in those days. You didn't have enough
money for food, so you just hustled, that's all. There weren't dressing
rooms at the ball parks, so you'd change in the hotel. I stayed in a
place in Moosejaw across the street from the railroad station; had to
run down the hallway to the bathroom. Umpires didn't get enough
money in those leagues to rent a place with a toilet in your room. But
when I went to the Coast League, it was a little different. I wouldn't
stay in a place if I couldn't have a room with a bath.

You had to be tough to survive. Hell, when I signed with the Western Canada League, they guaranteed my carfare home only if I lasted
the season. The president, Frank Miley, told me umpires had been
running out on him so fast that it was bankrupting the league's trea-
sury to pay their transportation home after a couple of days.

I had to fight my way out of tough situations in that league. There were some rough players up there who thought umpires were doormats. The fans weren't much better. They'd pick on me because I was a little guy. And when word got around that I'd been working in the boiler shops, they'd say, "The SOB used to work in the boiler shop, and now he's going to show us how tough he is."

Things were different in those days. Umpires didn't have the authority that they do now. I was a muscleman in the boiler shop, and as an umpire I was my own muscle, and that was it. I couldn't fight much, but I would fight. I never looked for a scrap, but I never ran away from one either. I didn't take any guff. You had to be the boss out there because you worked the games alone.

One day I caught all kinds of hell from both teams and the fans. After the game a crowd started gathering around the clubhouse. A policeman came in and said he'd show me how to sneak out of the park. I said, "I didn't sneak in, and I won't sneak out."

The same thing happened once in the major leagues. We had some trouble one day, so after the game this policeman came out on the field. I said, "What the hell are you doing out here?" He said he was supposed to protect us. I said, "Get the hell out of here. I don't need protection."

I could have gone from Western Canada to the big leagues, but by the time the majors contacted me I had already been picked up by the Coast League. That was probably the best thing that ever happened to me. If they had put me in the big leagues with only two years of experience, I never would have lasted.

I went to the Pacific Coast League in 1922. A fellow by the name of Bob Connery, the chief scout for the New York Yankees, traveled through western Canada looking for prospects. He asked me who looked good, and I'd tip him off. As it turned out, he was scouting me, too. He recommended me to his good friend [William H.] Dewey McCarthy, the president of the Pacific Coast League. When I reported, McCarthy said, "Now I'm going to tell you something, Beans. We want umpires in this league, we don't want fighters."

It was better in the Coast League, but it was still tough. I had a fistfight with Paddy Siglin during a game in San Francisco. It just so happened that a photographer was on hand, and he took some great close-ups. The newspaper the next day carried three big pictures of the fight. One of them showed me landing a punch on Paddy's nose. Another one showed him beating on the back of my neck. The fight got more publicity than it deserved.

I also had it out with Charley Pick of Sacramento. Charley had this bad habit of lifting his leg off a base after a slide. One day he slid into second and lifted his leg as he got up. The Vernon second baseman tagged him, and I called him out. He jumped around, calling me all kinds of names, so I had to throw him out of the game. After that he kept making my life miserable until we settled it with our fists.

Yes, I had a reputation as a fighter. But I really wasn't a fighter. I had some fights, but I didn't enjoy them. They just couldn't be avoided. My record in the National League shows I wasn't a trouble-maker. I never had a fight in the major leagues. I almost did, though.

When I got to the majors, John Heydler, the president of the National League, told me I had a good reputation for umpiring but a bad one for fighting. He asked me to promise him I wouldn't fight any-more. I told him I couldn't do that because when you break in at my weight, you have to be ready to fight. He said, "Okay, but promise me you won't throw the first punch." A few days later in Pittsburgh, Chick Fewster of Brooklyn said something I didn't like. I grabbed him, spun him around, and if Rabbit Maranville hadn't grabbed my arm, I'd have punched him. Rab probably saved my job.

While I was in the Coast League, I had a chance to go to Holly-wood. I worked in a few movies. Mae West always treated me real good. She'd say, "Put Beans on the payroll." They tried to get me to quit umpiring and become a cameraman or something, but I wasn't too hot for the motion pictures. I liked baseball a lot better. I knew if I stayed in baseball, it might take me a while to get to the majors, but I knew I had a chance to make it and it was all up to me. Besides, the directors had all the power in the studio.

Hank O'Day, the umpire who made the famous Fred Merkle deci-sion, is the man who put me in the big leagues. He was a bachelor from Chicago. He used to winter in Los Angeles, at the Biltmore Hotel down on Sixth and Grand Avenue. I got acquainted with Mr. O'Day, and I found out he liked horse racing, so I'd drive him down to the track in Tijuana on Sundays in my Hudson Speedster. He told me a lot about umpiring, things to look for. He was big and tough; guys didn't fool around with him. He told me not to try to imitate anybody. "Never mind what anybody tells you; you just go in there and umpire like you've been umpiring all the time." He told me that players would give a young umpire coming into the big leagues all the rough-ness he could put up with, but he said, "You're the boss out there. Don't let them tell you anything." And he told me, "Hustle all the time. Be on the top of every play, so you're in position to make the decision." He liked my work, so he recommended me to the National League. I was very fortunate to be able to learn from a great umpire like Hank O'Day. He was the best. At least he had the greatest influence on me.

I broke into the majors in 1926 with Charley Moran and Ernie Quigley. Charley lived in Horse Cave, Kentucky, and was the football coach at Centre College. Quigley was a great official. I also worked with Charlie Rigler. He was big, and a tough guy, too. Later on I worked with George Magerkurth a little bit, but I didn't like to work with him, so I didn't. Mage was stubborn—always wanted to do things his way. Hell, I was the senior umpire; we were going to do things my way. Al Barlick was a very good umpire. He was tough and could run the game. Jocko Conlan was a fairly good umpire. When I first came in, Billy Evans was supposed to be the great umpire in the American League. Hell, they were all good. You can't brag about umpires because if you do guys will say, "What the hell did he give you?"

Bill Klem is supposed to be the greatest umpire who ever lived. That may be true. He was a good umpire, but I wouldn't say he was the best who ever lived. But he was the greatest at running the ball game. The players knew that if they said one thing out of line, Klem would run them out of the game.

Klem was an arrogant little guy. One day we were in Boston working the Braves and Giants. Klem called a close one, and this woman in the stands yells, "Bill Klem, if you were my husband, I'd put poison in your coffee!" Klem turned and yelled back, "Lady, if I was your husband, I'd drink it."

I wasn't too fond of Klem. I didn't speak to him, and he didn't speak to me. In 1970 I received the Bill Klem Award for service as an umpire. I told them I was glad to get it, but that I hated Klem's guts and he hated mine.

Larry Goetz was a hell of a good umpire. He was my partner. He was also my man. The truth is that I kept Larry in the National League. See, Goetz would get mad and disgusted about things. He lived in Cincinnati, so one day when he was driving Babe Pinelli and me from the ball park to the Netherland Plaza Hotel, he said, "I'm going to quit this racket. I ain't going to umpire anymore." When we got to the hotel, he pulled over to the curb. Before I got out, I said, "Look Larry, I'm going to tell you sómething. You're always hollering about this, hollering about that. God damn you, you better not quit. What the hell are you going to do? Where are you going to get a job for two and a half hours a day that will do you like this one? Don't be a sucker. You be here to pick us up tomorrow at one-thirty, and don't you forget it." That was the last time Larry ever hollered about quitting. He later said if it hadn't been for me, he would have quit right then. I was glad he stayed with it because he was a very close friend and a great umpire. He was a tough guy who could really fight.

You know that painting Norman Rockwell did of the three umpires for the *Saturday Evening Post?* That's me in the middle with the chest protector and mask. The other guys are Larry Goetz and Lou Jorda. I've got it, autographed, in my den. It's my favorite picture.

When I had Babe Pinelli and Larry Goetz, people said we were the best team of umpires in baseball. When Jocko Conlan came into the league in 1941, he wanted to work with me. Jocko came out of Chicago, had played with the White Sox, and had pretty good drag with some of the owners. So they took Babe and sent him to another crew to spread the cream around and gave me Conlan. I hated to see Pinelli go because we had been friends from World War I, when he was working in the Los Angeles shipyards and playing ball.

Anyway, Jocko used the outside chest protector like I did. Goetz tried it for a while. In fact, my whole crew was using it. But then I think they called Larry in and talked him into using the inside protector. Conlan never did change, but they also called him in and told him to quit trying to be like me.

That's one of the reasons I didn't get along too well with Bill Klem. He wanted all the umpires in the league to do things his way. He tried to put through a rule that all the National League umpires use the inside protector, but President Ford Frick knew I would never use it. You do have an advantage with it because you can move around better than with that big mattress. But I didn't like it because it was dangerous. They only reason I wore the outside protector is that it gave me more protection from injury than the inside one. They told me nobody ever really got hurt, but I said, "That doesn't make any difference. I might be the first one, and I'm not going to wear it." That's all there was to it. Nobody could change me. I was the only one in the league who wore the outside protector until Conlan came in.

I also didn't believe in switching around in back of the bat. The National League umpires—again Klem started this—would work on the inside between the catcher and the batter just over the catcher's shoulder, so they would have to shift depending on whether there was a left-handed or right-handed hitter. I never did that. I stayed right over the top of the catcher, looking just over his left shoulder. I figured that was as good a way as any. Hell, you might miss one anyplace you looked. Besides, I always felt that working over the catcher's right shoulder, you were too close to his throwing arm with a left-handed hitter up there, and I didn't want to be responsible for a guy getting to second base who shouldn't have been there.

By wearing the outside protector and standing behind the catcher, I was using the American League style. Ford Frick used to smart-crack me once in a while, but he knew it wouldn't do him any good. Klem didn't like it either, but I didn't like Klem too well, so I didn't care what he said. I just did what I wanted to do.

See, there was a lot of rivalry between the two leagues because of Klem and Connolly trying to outdo each other. We didn't have the money the American League did. They outdrew us quite a bit, and if you don't get people in the ball park, you're not going to make money. The National League was tougher than the American to umpire. For some reason our players and managers always screamed and yelled more than the guys in the other league. Maybe it was because of the front office. Mr. Heydler was always very nice to me, but he wasn't as tough as Ban Johnson, the president of the American League. Ban Johnson was a very tough man; he backed up those umpires. Boy, you couldn't do anything over in the American League.

When I came up to the National League, most umpires stood back of second with a man on first base. I wouldn't do it. I stayed on the infield. I always figured that was the best position because when a guy went to steal, the minute he passed me I'd be in back of him and could catch him any way he went into the base. When Quigley and Moran saw I wasn't having any trouble with it, then they were on my side. Of course, Klem tried to tell me where to stand, but I didn't pay any attention to him.

They also tried to keep me from fraternizing, but they couldn't stop it. I wouldn't allow it. I've always liked people and couldn't help saying hello to my friends in the stands. I'd go over and shake hands, or tip my hat, or something. Mrs. Philip K. Wrigley later told me that she used to wait for me to come out in Chicago and say hello to her and Mr. Wrigley. One time a ballplayer told me that a guy in the outfield was really going to give me hell. I said, "What did I do to him?" "He says he's the only guy in the ball park you haven't said hello to."

I even said hello one time to Mr. Fred Vinson, the Chief Justice of the United States Supreme Court. He was at the ball park in St. Louis one day. The last out of the game was a pop foul near his box, so after I made the call, I went over and shook hands. I told him that umpires had more authority than Supreme Court judges: "It takes nine of you to make a decision, but I make my own." He said, "That's true, but I can sit here and boo your decision. You just try to come into my court and boo me." I said, "Yeah, but when I make a ruling, it stays made. Ain't nobody going to change it."

I got along with the fans real good. People got a big kick out of watching me bless myself when I walked on the field. They liked my bow tie, too. It was my trademark. Even the sportswriters wrote about it. Most of the other guys wore black four-in-hands, but I loved my little blue and white polka dot bow tie. That tie is more famous than I am; it's in the Hall of Fame.

I've always liked people, liked to be around them, liked to talk to them. My motto was: "Never too busy to say hello." See, the main thing in life is to make friends, and to make friends, you gotta treat people right.

I always tried to treat players fairly. Sure, I had my favorites. Umpires are human. A lot of guys were my friends, and we'd go out drinking at night. But I never gave them anything on the ball field. Oh, I might let them go on a little longer with an argument, but that's about it. Beans Reardon gave everybody an even break.

Frankie Frisch was one of my best friends in baseball. We were buddies, but on the field we were always arguing. One time Frisch was giving it to me pretty good, and it finally got to me. I whipped off my mask and headed for the Pirate dugout. "What was that you hollered, Frisch?" Frankie said, "You've been guessing all day. Guess what I said." I said, "I can't guess, but I can imagine what you said. You're out of the game."

Another time, after I threw him out for cussing, he invited me down to the hotel bar for a drink. Not only did the ruckus cost him a $50 fine and five rounds of beer, but I borrowed his car that night—made him call down to the garage and have the tank filled before I took it.

Casey Stengel was another one. Casey and I would fight like hell on the ball field, but once that game was over we were great friends. One day he was giving me hell behind the plate, and he kept it up the next day when I went to third base. He was out there giving it to me when a ground ball came down the third-base line. I was thinking more about Casey than the game, so I just reached down and fielded the ball. Stengel said, "It's a fair ball." I said, "Ooops!" and threw the ball down. After the game the press came in and said, "That's a good one, you fielding the ball." I said, "What the hell, they never went anyplace on it, did they?"

It was okay to go out nights and have a few beers with the good guys like Frisch, Stengel, or Hack Wilson. But if the player was too bad, I didn't want to be around him at night because he might say something I wouldn't forget or he might think I shouldn't throw him out because we'd been drinking.

Leo Durocher was the worst manager I ever worked with. He even made a habit of protesting half swings. Hell, if a guy wiggled his bat, Leo came out protesting. One day I told him he was coming out so much it was getting to be a joke. He said he was going to keep coming out on everything that moved, so I went to Ford Frick about it. Frick sent out an order stopping protests on half swings.

The best manager I ever worked with was Bill Terry. Rogers Hornsby was the only one who was even close to him as far as being fair to umpires. Terry would raise hell when he thought he had a beef, but many times he'd come out and defend the umpire's decision and tell his players to get away and play ball. I'd take Terry over anybody on the field, but if I was going out some night to have fun, I'd pick somebody like Casey Stengel or Charlie Grimm.

Grover Cleveland Alexander was my favorite pitcher. Alex was a good one. With a pitcher like Alex out there you really had to stay on your toes because you knew damned well he was going to be around that plate somewhere.

The first time I had him was in a spring exhibition game my rookie year. In his prime, he had been maybe the best pitcher in baseball, and here I was, just a punk. Alex threw the first two pitches right down the pipe, but I called them balls. Well, he walked toward the plate a few steps and said, "Young man, what's wrong with those pitches?" I said, "Not a thing, Mr. Alexander. I know I missed them. I'm just so nervous I can hardly see." Do you know what he said? "Don't worry about it, son. Settle down. I'll get the next one over." He did, too. And I never missed another one on him.

Bob Brown, who pitched for the Braves in the thirties, was the fastest pitcher I ever saw. I saw Lefty Grove and Bob Feller in their prime, but they couldn't match Brown for speed. Too bad he couldn't get his fastball over the plate.

We started to rub the gloss off the baseballs in 1929. You had to be careful not to get too much mud in the seams because the ball would sail if you got too much mud on one side. I really don't know whose idea it was, whether it was Mr. Heydler in our league or Ban Johnson in the American League. They stopped hitting home runs after we did that. The next year we had the so-called jackrabbit ball. Hack Wilson had 190 RBIs that year. To tell you the truth, I don't know whether it was a jackrabbit ball or not. I don't believe in that too much. It's the same old story: If a guy's hitting a lot of home runs, they rap the baseball. Why don't they give the guy credit for being a pretty good hitter? Rabbit ball or otherwise, you have to be able to hit it. A rabbit ball wouldn't do 60 percent of the hitters any good.

The batter I respected most was Stan Musial. A great hitter and a guy who'd never give you a beef. He had a great eye. When he turned around and looked at me after I had called a strike on him, I felt worse than after tangling with Durocher.

There were a lot of good players in the American League, but I only had them in the All-Star game or the World Series. I really liked Ted Williams. Williams wasn't very friendly with a lot of people, but he was good with umpires. The first time I saw him was in the All-Star game in St. Louis in 1940. He came out, knelt in the on-deck circle and said, "Hi ya, Beans." I looked over and said, "You're the California kid, aren't you?" He said, "That's right. That's me." I had never seen the guy before, and he says "Hi ya, Beans." You gotta like a guy like that.

The good players were like that. They didn't give you a bad time. You could call strikes on them wrong, and they'd just get in there and hit. The ones who weren't so good would yell, "The goddamn thing's a foot outside." It was a pleasure to work with the good players.

The only ballplayer I really didn't like was Eddie Stanky. He was a good competitor, but he didn't like the way I ran the game because I wouldn't put up with his kicking. We'd meet on the street, and he'd say, "Hello, Mrs. Reardon. How are you?" He always made a fuss over my wife, but he wouldn't speak to me. Of course, I wouldn't speak to him either. It was mutual. He was tough. But what the hell, you gotta have guys like that in the game.

There was never any problems when Negroes came into the major leagues. I never had any problems because I used to umpire games for the colored ball teams in Southern California. I was the regular umpire and never had any trouble because I'd tell them how far they could go and then chase them. We never got any special instructions when Jackie Robinson and the others came in, although Ford Frick did call in some of the guys and tell them not to call them nigger or something like that.

Hell, nicknames like that were part of baseball. You'd call guys dagos or polacks or whatever and nobody would think much about it. It all depended on the way you handled it. One time in St. Louis somebody in the dugout hollered at me, so I turned around and yelled, "Shut up, you polack SOB." There were a lot of Polish players on that team, so it got real quiet.

Then one of them yelled, "Hey, Beansie, which one of us did you mean?"

Anyway, there were only a few Negroes in the league when I was there. Jackie Robinson was all right. He was a good competitor. He took chances. He was kind of a fresh guy, would call balls and strikes from second base, things like that. But I never had any trouble with the guy; Jackie never made it tough for me, and we got along fine. Roy Campanella was a nice guy. Everybody liked Campy. Boy, he was a dandy catcher.

I was a fresh guy, but I never got on ballplayers and managers too much. You can knock guys off any time you want to when you're an umpire, but the thing is to figure the temperament of ballplayers and handle them each differently, just like the manager does.

Take Hack Wilson. He was a good hitter. He'd swing at pitches over his head—and hit them, too. Hack still holds the home run record [56] in the National League. Hack and I were good friends, but he was the kind of guy who never wanted any strikes called on him. If you threw Hack out of the game every time he kicked on a strike, he'd never have finished a ball game. But Hack was sincere. He really believed he never let a good pitch go by, so anything he didn't swing at must be a ball. You know, he wasn't one of those guys who'd kick to alibi.

But, boy, Hack would get mad if you made a decision against him. One afternoon at the Polo Grounds Rogers Hornsby gave Hack the take sign. That made Hack mad, so he stood there taking pitches till I called him out on strikes. As he went back to the bench, he said something to me and flipped his bat in the air. I said, "Oh, Hack, if the bat hits the ground, you're out of the game."

I had a funny run-in with Tommy Henrich in the 1949 World Series. In the first inning of the fourth game the Dodgers pulled off a double play by trapping Phil Rizzuto off third and Henrich off second. Tommy, who had a lot of family in the stands, came running over waving his arms and yelling about what had happened. I told him it didn't make any difference; he was out. He said, "I know it, but I'm embarrassed." So I told him he could talk awhile if he thought it would take the heat off. We chatted for a few minutes, but the crowd was going wild because it looked like he was giving me hell. Finally, he said, "Thanks, Beansie," and went back to the dugout.

One time in Philadelphia I called one of the Phillies out at second base trying to steal. Jimmie Wilson, the manager, came out wanting to know why I called the guy out. I said, "What the hell, Jimmie, I called him out because he was out." He says, "You know something, Beans. There are fifty thousand people in the ball park and you're the only SOB who thinks he's out." I said, "Yes, but I'm the only SOB who counts." He went back to the bench, laughing so hard he started shaking. The ballplayers kept asking me, "Did you really tell him that?" They got a kick out of it. That's the kind of little thing that keeps the game going and adds a little color to the game.

I never chased very many ballplayers. I didn't believe in chasing them. I didn't see any object in chasing too many guys because the people paid to see their favorite players. Besides, I didn't like to make out the reports and all you have to do after you chase somebody. Sometimes Mr. Frick would hear about a ruckus, and he'd ask me, "Beans, why didn't you chase him?" I'd say, "Didn't want to take up your time."

Instead of chasing them, I'd give it back to them a little better than they gave it to me. I could use profanity, and I blasted them pretty good. They'd get upset and tell the manager. Then he'd come out and ask if I called so-and-so this and that. I'd say, "Yeah, I called him that, and he's still in the game. If you don't like it, I'll chase him." Sometimes they'd tell Mr. Frick that I cussed them. Then Mr. Frick would say, "Did you call him a son of a bitch?" And I'd say, "Sure, I called him an SOB. I didn't know what else to call him, Mr. Frick." Mr. Frick never got on me about that. He was a good guy to work for.

I didn't like rhubarbs. Hell, no. I didn't want to be involved in them. I just wanted to finish the game and get out of there. Rhubarbs are bad if they take too much time. Most rhubarbs come from a misunderstanding by a player or manager. If a guy had a little something to say, I'd listen. But if he started going on too long, I'd say, "I've listened to you. Now get the hell away from me, or I'll chase you." They'd mumble and grumble, but they'd go back to their position and play ball.

People think an umpire stands out there just waiting for a player to kick so he can send him to the showers. What we really try to do is call them so nobody can argue. The best umpire is the guy who has the least arguments, and runs the ball game, and gets along with the boys on both clubs. Players, managers, and owners don't want a guy who can't run his business without a lot of fuss.

You can't allow the players to take control of the game. You've got to lay down the law. When guys get out of hand, you just show them that your job is to run the ball game and that you're going to run it. You don't go looking for anybody. That's bad. You give everybody an even break. You don't have to chase too many. Ballplayers are fighting for the pennant, so they don't want to get chased. Once they know you'll run them, they'll behave. They learn real quick.

The main thing an umpire has to do is make the ballplayers respect you. You do that by controlling the game. I let them know when I walked on that ball field that I was in charge, and if they didn't like it, I'd give them a ticket out of there. There are lots of ways to convey the message. Sometimes I'd go out on the field and a guy would say, "Hey, Beans, old boy, how's everything?" I wouldn't answer, so they'd say, "Look out, he's mad today." Sometimes, before a tough series or after the home team had given us a rough time the day before, I'd meet with the managers at home plate before the game and say, "Just a minute. Go back to your bench, and tell them I'm not taking any kicks today. The first son of a bitch who opens his mouth is gone. I'm going to keep this game under control today." Hell, they can't say anything. It's like arguing with a policeman. You've got the authority just like the policeman on the beat. If they don't do what you tell them, you run them.

I was always a hustler. I was small and quick and always tried to be right on top of plays. You couldn't get there all the time, but if you hustled, the players would give you credit for it. You just had to hustle. In any line of work you have to hustle, you have to work. You can't sit down and relax and say, "Well, bring it to me." Hell, no. You gotta go get it if you want it.

We worked with three men in those days. Never had four unless it was an All-Star or World Series game. It was tough for two men to cover the bases. Sometimes you couldn't get over there fast enough to make the call; sometimes you could get blocked out of the play. When that happened, you just had to guess at the play. I know damned well I had to guess at a few. If I was wrong, I caught hell; if I was right, they never said anything, that's all. Today with four umpires it's a much different situation because they're in better position.

Beans Reardon missed some—maybe called plenty of them wrong. Naturally it bothered me when I kicked one because I didn't want to do anything to hurt a guy. I just wanted to run the game and give them the best I had. But once a decision has gone wild, the damage has been done, and no amount of arguing can change it. When the play is over, you've got to forget it—right or wrong. It would be fatal otherwise.

When you see an umpire answer a player's squawk before the player can get it out of his mouth, you know the umpire knows he is right and is willing to go ten rounds. But if you see an umpire backing away and acting like he wasn't invited to the party, it's a sure sign that he is admitting to himself that he might have missed one.

The ballplayers never bothered me. A little talk now and then is all in a day's work. But the bird in the stands who starts riding you real good can sometimes wear a sore spot.

Yeah, the crowd bothered me. Some guys say you don't pay any attention. That's a lot of bull. The crowd can get on you, make no mistake about that. You'd have 50,000 people in the stands, and 49,000 would be against you. Naturally it makes you mad when they're calling you names. But there's no way you can get back at them. The only way would be to be crooked and call plays against the home team, but you couldn't do that.

Nobody likes to be hollered at. You can't do anything with the people in the stands; you've got to take it out on the players. If the fans are hollering and some guy picks it up and gets obnoxious, you knock him off and let him know who the hell is the boss out there. But mostly I figured: What the hell, let them yell. It's an aggravating thing, but if the crowd's going to hurt you, you might as well quit because you're going to be in trouble all the time.

Pittsburgh and Philadelphia had the worst fans in the league. They were pretty crazy over in Brooklyn, too, but they were fun. The whole damned Brooklyn Sym-Phonie would give us "Three Blind Mice" when we walked on the field. The organist, Gladys Goodding, started that. You can't play it in ball parks anymore; I complained to the Brooklyn club and they put a stop to it. That Hilda Chester was something. She'd sit there in Ebbets Field ringing that bell and yelling at the umps all the time. One time I asked her what she yelled at us. She said, "Open your other eye, joik; you got noive like a toothache."

Anyway, Larry Goetz hated the hollering. And it ate up Babe Pinelli. Me? Hell, I thought it was fun. I'd ignore them or growl back at them. The fans got a kick out of it when I'd growl at them.

The only time the fans like umpires is on a rainy day. The ballplayers don't want to play, of course, but the fans want to see the game, so we'd get a big hand when we walked out on that wet field. It was like music to my ears. Of course, they'd boo the hell out of your first call.

I like that rule about not selling beer in bottles in the ball parks. In my day bottles would come flying out of the stands. They should never have let fans have bottles—it was like putting weapons in the hands of imbeciles.

It's hard to say what was the most difficult call for me to make. A late, high tag on a slide is tough because you know the crowd is not going to agree with you. But I guess the most difficult call for me was the three-and-two pitch with men on bases when the batter takes a pitch that just nicked the plate so you have to give him the old out sign. That's such an important pitch, you really have to bear down so you don't take the bat out of his hands.

They used to call me old three-and-two. Early in my career I called a guy out at the Polo Grounds on strikes. He looked at me so surprised and said, "I'm not out, Beans. It's only the second strike." I told him, "No, that was the third strike." He was upset. "If I'd have known that, I wouldn't have taken it because it was a real good pitch." Well, I said to myself, nobody else will ever forget it. From that time on I made it a point to say, "Three and two now," or, "Two strikes now," or something like that to let the batter know he had only one more strike coming.

Working the plate is rough. I didn't like it, but I had to do it to keep my job. It's the hottest place in the park. You have to call about 250 decisions a day with the sun beating down on the back of your neck and nobody to hand you a sponge and no time in the dugout. You can't fool around back there. You just have to take a little pride in your work back of the bat. When the catcher says, "Nice going. You didn't miss a pitch all day"—well, then you're a pretty big shot.

I missed a few back there. Sometimes you'd get blocked out, and then there wasn't much you could do but guess. Sometimes you'd just miss one. One time in the World Series I missed one right down the middle of the plate. I called it a ball. Bill Dickey, the Yankee catcher, turned his head and said, "What's the matter with the pitch?" "Nothing," I said, "it was right down the middle." "Then why isn't it a strike?" he asked. "Because I called it a ball," I told him.

My greatest thrill in baseball was working my first World Series in 1930. I still wear my ring from that Series. The league gave you a ring for your first Series; you could be in ten World Series, and you'd never get another one unless a new president came in. I had never seen a World Series game before. I was behind the bat in the fourth game, when Jesse Haines of the St. Louis Cardinals put on the best pitching performance I ever saw. He beat Lefty Grove and the Philadelphia A's, 3–1. He gave up only four hits, and two of them were in the first inning. It was a masterpiece.

I was behind the plate the day [May 25, 1935] Babe Ruth hit three home runs in Forbes Field. He was with the old Boston Braves then. One of them went out over the third deck. I had never seen that before, and after the game they said it was the first time a ball had been hit out there. I didn't know at the time that it was the last game he'd get a hit in. He played only four more games. The Babe could have played a little while longer, but you could tell he didn't have much left.

The day before, the Babe and I had had a little discussion. I called him out on a play, and as he ran by me at first base, he started to give me a little trouble. I told him to get away or I'd chase him. He said, "You umpires don't like me in this league." I said, "Look, Babe, I'll give you a tip. We like you. We're just not going to give you anything."

I had a play one day in Brooklyn that was unbelievable: Babe Herman hit a triple that turned into a double play. The Dodgers had the bases loaded. Hank DeBerry was at third, Dazzy Vance on second, and Chick Fewster on first. "Turkey Neck"—that's what I always called Herman—hit one off the fence in right-center field. DeBerry scored. Vance should have, too, but for some reason he stopped and went back to third. Fewster, figuring Vance would score, went on to third. Herman, seeing the ball bouncing around out there, rounds second and comes into third. Now I got three men standing on third, and every one of them is being tagged. I said, "Damn it, wait a minute. I got to figure this out." Finally I said, "The bag belongs to Vance, so Fewster, you're out, and so are you, Turkey Neck, for passing a runner on the baselines. That's it. The side's out. Let's play ball, fellas."

I was in Detroit the day Judge Landis ordered Joe Medwick out of the final game of the 1934 World Series. Joe was a good player, a pretty rough player, too. In the sixth inning he went charging into third base. I don't know whether he pushed Marv Owen, the Detroit third basemen, or what, but there was quite a little action down there. So the fans started throwing bottles and everything when Medwick went out to left field. I was umpiring at first base. Judge Landis called me over to his box and said, "Bring that fellow in here." So I went out and told Joe that Landis wanted to see him. When we got over there, Landis said, "Who took the first punch?" Medwick said, "I did." Landis said, "You're out of the ball game." I'll never forget Frankie Frisch, the Cardinals' manager, saying, "That old son of a bitch. I'm going to take him." I told him to forget it. They were leading 9–0 at the time; only a miracle could have beaten them. St Louis finally won, 11–0.

I was behind the bat in the second game of the 1939 World Series when Monte Pearson of the Yankees had a no-hitter going. Ernie Lombardi, the big Cincinnati catcher, ruined it with a hit in the eighth inning. I knew Pearson had a no-hitter going, and it increased the pressure. I had to bear down as much as I could because I didn't want to beat the poor SOB out of a no-hitter.

Ninety percent of the ball games didn't mean a hell of a lot. I might be out there just waiting for the game to get over with, but they always got an honest day's work from me. Now when you'd have a big game or something like the World Series, I'd feel the pressure. I never exactly got nervous, but I'd get tense because there was so much at stake.

I didn't exactly like those big games because they always gave me the jitters. The night before the game I'd get to thinking how a fraction of a second could mean the difference between winning and losing, how I'd hate to call one wrong when so much was riding on every pitch and slide. I'd crack a few jokes or something to take a little edge off, but to be an umpire, you just have to take the pressure. I figured: What the hell. When I went on that ball field, I was the boss. If I did what was right, nobody was going to bother me.

After a game I'd relax by drinking some beer. I've never tried to hide the fact that I liked to drink. A lot of umpires didn't like to go into bars because they were afraid ballplayers or somebody would see them. I always said, "To hell with them. It's my life, and if I want to go into a bar, I'm going in there. I don't care how many ballplayers are there; I'm going to have my beer, and that's that."

I had lots of favorite joints. The Coal Hole in St. Louis was a good place. My favorite was this restaurant and bar run by Oney McManus in Pittsburgh. His joint was right through the alley from our hotel, so after a game eight or ten of us would go to Oney's and have our beer and tell stories. Oney was a likable guy. He posted the baseball scores in the bar, but when the Pirates lost, he refused to tell anyone the score. When we were in Cincinnati, we had to go over to Kentucky on Sundays because they didn't sell beer in Ohio. If we didn't feel like going over, we'd buy some beer on Saturday and tell the bellcap to ice it up.

Now, I've never had a drink of hard liquor in my life. My father had a saloon, but my mother couldn't stand alcohol. One day, when she thought she was going to die, she asked me to promise that I'd never drink. I said, "Ma, I can't do that. I'm drinking a litte beer right now." "Well," she said, "make me a promise that you'll never drink whiskey." I promised her I'd never take a drink of whiskey, and I haven't.

But I've always liked my beer. I could drink a case, case and a half, two cases of beer a night. I could *drink*. One time Ford Frick, the president of the league, asked me how much I drank. I said, "Well, some nights one, some nights one and a half, some nights two." "Oh," he said, "is that all?"

My beer drinking got me with Anheuser-Busch. Budweiser was my favorite beer; I'd walk out of a place if they didn't have it. The Budweiser people heard that I drank their beer, so they sent for me one time in St. Louis and asked if I'd work for them. I did some ads and in the winter did some public relations work. I continued to do that after I retired. I'd go talk baseball to groups all over the country—Indiana, Alaska, Hawaii, wherever they had Budweiser. I was obligated to speak only ten times a year, but I went as high as forty-three one year. I wouldn't go anywhere, though, unless they were going to have at least 250 in the crowd.

In 1946 I bought the Budweiser distributorship in Long Beach, California. The business started going real good, so the brewery wanted me to quit baseball. They used to tell me that I couldn't umpire and take care of my beer, too. I told them the hell I couldn't and that I got my mind made up that I was going to quit after a certain time.

I quit after the 1949 World Series. I was fifty-one years old, the highest paid umpire in baseball, making $11,500 a year. Ford Frick told me I had a good ten years left in me, but I told him I had a lot of money invested in my Budweiser distributorship and wanted to spend all my time with it.

See, the business was going pretty good, so I was in a position to tell everyone in baseball to go to hell. I had been working ever since I was fourteen years old—in cotton mills, in the Reed and Barton silver shop in Massachusetts, in boiler shops and copper mines, and for thirty years in umpiring. My last year in baseball every cent of my salary went for income taxes. I didn't get to keep my umpiring money. I didn't need it anyway. I made a lot of money off that agency. I sold it in 1967 to Frank Sinatra for a million bucks. Anyway, I had my own business and was my own boss.

After I retired I wrote a column called "The Umpire" for NEA for a while. It ran in newspapers all over the country and stirred up a lot of fireworks. Blow one, and the letters come pouring in. They'd write to me in care of the National League, ball parks, saloons, anyplace they'd think I might be known. The amateur and semipro umpire was the worst. Anyone who has ever umpired thinks he's a big league ump. They're jealous because you made it and they didn't, so they try to make you look bad with trick questions.

Hank O'Day used to fix them. When a guy came to him with a booby-trap question, he'd say, "Did you see it happen?" The guy'd say yes, and then Hank would say, "Well, then, get the rule book. The rule book will cover it." That shut them up every time.

Baseball was good to me. It made my connection with Anheuser-Busch that I wouldn't have had otherwise, and it gave me lots of friends and enjoyable moments. The thing I missed most was going from town to town, seeing my friends. I put in thirty years in baseball, and I can truthfully say there were only a couple of guys I didn't have any use for.

Umpires today have the best of it with their association and pensions. I put in twenty-four years in the National League and get $200 a month. The game has changed a lot. We used to have fun, you know. Now it's business, big business. And it seems the umpires now are getting more respect from the players. You don't see many guys being chased today like you used to in the old days.

I have great respect for baseball and the umpires. I still go to the ball park regularly. I've got a lifetime gold pass to major league baseball, but I never walk through that damned pass gate. I pay for my season tickets. The front office says, "We'll give you tickets. Take them." I tell them, "I don't want your tickets. I'm buying my own, and if I want to say anything about you or your ball club, I'll say it." You've got to have integrity.

Lee Ballanfant, in a picture taken during 1936 spring
training, his first season in the majors. Courtesy
National Baseball Library & Archive, Cooperstown,
N.Y.

Lee Ballanfant

ΘΘΘ

Edward Lee Ballanfant
Born: Waco, Texas, December 27, 1895
Height: 5' 8"
Weight: 150
Playing career: minor leagues, 1920–25
Umpiring career: Texas Association (D), 1926; East Texas League
(D), 1927; Lone Star League (D), 1928; West
Texas League (D), 1929; Texas League (A),
1929–35; National League, 1936–57
No-hit games: Fred Frankhouse, August 27, 1937 (7⅔ innings)
All-Star games: 1938, 1942, 1949, 1954
World Series (games): 1940 (7), 1946 (7), 1951 (6), 1955 (7)

I never thought I'd be an umpire. The only thing I knew about umpires was to give them hell. When I played, I was a real bad boy. I was never out, never. That third strike could be right down the middle, and I'd argue about it. That's the type of kid I was. I thought everybody picked on me because I was so small. It's still in my craw about being little.

When I got into umpiring, I forgot all about playing. Umpiring is like stealing. An umpire ought to back up to get his check. All you have to do is go out on the field and go to work. I can truthfully say that I never did like umpiring. I stayed with it because I had to eat. I had no education; it's all I knew. Besides, I loved baseball. I couldn't play the game, so I umpired. Even after I quit umpiring, I stayed in the game as a scout. I've been in the business sixty years. I've been fooling somebody.

I was born in Waco, Texas, December 27, 1895, the youngest of five kids. We were a poor family. My father was a carpenter and a good drinker. I can remember as far back as 1904, when Teddy Roosevelt came to town running for president. So many people turned out at the depot that they decided to move across the street to the old Katy ball park; Roosevelt climbed up on the roof of a dugout to give his speech. I remember the San Francisco earthquake of 1906, too, because the guys at the fire station used to tell me that the red glow of the setting sun was San Francisco burning.

As a kid I was the mascot of the fire station next door to my house. I'd hang around there shining shoes, doing 'most anything to make a nickel or a dime. When I got older, I started riding horses at the track—damn near became a jockey. But I really loved to play baseball. My father wanted me to be a preacher; my parents didn't know which was worse, being a jockey or a ballplayer.

My brother, who was a real good curveball pitcher with the fire department team, got me interested in baseball. It got so I would rather play ball than do anything else. We moved to Dallas in 1907 and had no sooner got the furniture out of the van when I took off for a ball game down the street. I was always very small, so I just watched the kids play. After a few innings they took a break and I started tossing knuckleballs to this guy. I had learned about knucklers hanging around Katy park, but these kids had never seen one before. I was the only kid around who could throw one, so even though I was the smallest guy on the block, I became the star pitcher.

When I was fifteen or sixteen, I decided I wanted to be a professional ballplayer, so I left home. The Central Texas Trolley League had been organized around the interurban train line between Dallas and Waco, so I packed a little pasteboard suitcase and hopped the train headed for Hillsboro, Waxahachie, Corsicana, Ennis, or someplace. I got off at Waxahachie and headed for the ball park. I introduced myself to the manager, Dee Poindexter. He told me he had already picked his club. I told him I didn't care, that I was a ballplayer and could outrun, outthrow, and outhit anybody on the club. He had a big laugh at this ninety-six-pound, five-foot-eight-inch kid. He said, "Well, young man, you come see me tonight."

I said I would but forgot to ask where he'd be. I made the rounds of the pool halls and finally found a guy who could tell me where I could find Poindexter. When I knocked on the door of this house in a pretty rough neighborhood, a woman opened the door. Poindexter was sitting on the divan, drinking a bottle of beer. He had a big belly laugh when he saw me. I told him again how good I was. He asked if I could hook slide, so I took off across the parlor and hooked left around a big brass cuspidor in the corner. I got up and did it again from the right side. He had another good laugh and then called a Miss Manning, who ran the boardinghouse for the players, and told her to give me a room with Earl Smith, later known in the big leagues as Oil Smith. I didn't realize it at the time, but I had my first tryout in a house of assignation.

I stayed with the club only two weeks. Those big guys just threw the ball right by me. The sheriff was one of the big stockholders in the club, and one day, after I struck out for the fourth time, he yelled from the stands, "Who are you waving at?" I yelled back, "At your mama, you SOB." They turned me loose that night.

In all I took off three times as a kid to play ball. One time I was driving a truck for a cleaning and pressing outfit, when I met some guys heading for Royse City to play ball. I left the truck setting there full of clothes and went with them; we were gone three weeks.

When World War I came, I enlisted in the Army in January 1917. During the war I came to realize how I had missed out on a good education. After the armistice, my outfit, 133 Field Artillery, 36th Division, was laid up in France waiting to go home. To pass the time and pick up a few francs for my buddies, I raced guys from other outfits. I was a skinny kid, but I could run the hundred in under ten seconds. One of the officers, an alumnus of the University of Virginia, offered me a full scholarship and money to go to his school. I was embarrassed, so I made up some excuse why I couldn't go. But then after I got home, Texas Christian University came after me. I finally had to confess that I didn't finish high school.

After the war I started playing semipro ball. I belonged to the Ranger club in the West Texas League, but the $25 and expenses a day was more than I could make playing professional ball. We were booked, just like a theatrical group, all over Texas, Oklahoma, and Arkansas. I was mostly a shortstop, but I played everywhere. I went back into pro ball in 1921 with Ardmore in the Texas-Oklahoma League, but something I didn't like came up, and I retired in July. I played for Sulphur Springs in the East Texas League in 1923 and the next year moved over to Paris.

The next year I wound up managing the Greenville club in the East Texas League. Roy Eichord from Dallas got me and a bunch of the local boys to play for his team. I was living at the time with my wife's folks in Cooper. We finished last the first half of the season, and then they asked me to take over as manager. I thought they ought to get somebody older with more experience, but finally, I agreed to do it until they could get someone else. I called a team meeting and changed the signs for hit-and-run and bunt. That's all I did, but that club finished second for the season. The players were kind of down on Roy because he didn't take his turn pitching and so on, but they played good ball for me.

My professional playing days came to an end in 1925, when I broke my leg sliding into home in Greenville. The Cardinals called up my roommate, Pepper Martin, while I hobbled around for the rest of the year. I played on a couple of clubs but was limping so badly I couldn't run. I played with Palestine for a while and then finished up at Austin in the Texas Association. Benny Brownlow, the Austin manager, needed a shortstop to finish the year. He said he didn't care if I couldn't run, just so I could stop the ball. Soon after I joined the club, somebody hit a perfect double-play ball to Benny, who was playing second. He kicked it, and as he hurried to toss me the ball, his glove came flying over. Well, to complete the double play, I grabbed the glove by the thumb and sailed it toward first base. It sailed into the grandstand, and I got fired for horseplay. That was all right with me. I was strictly a Class D ballplayer—good field, no hit.

It was rough playing in those D leagues. There were no lights then, so we played nine innings in 100-degree heat. I always played with a cabbage leaf under my hat to keep me cool; when one dried out, I put in another. There was a beer keg full of cool water in a hole by the dugout, and after every inning we'd stick our feet in there. Of course, it was damned hot at night, too. We stayed in those bowl-and-pitcher hotels where you could get a room for fifty cents. I slept naked on a soaking wet towel in the bathtub many a night, trying to keep cool; you'd wake up about midnight and the towel would be dry.

After getting fired, I went to work at a cotton compress in Corsicana. The superintendent was my first manager, Mr. Poindexter. Like most of the other guys, I worked at the compress from the end of October to the first of March and then played ball during the summer. The bookkeeper was Johnny Vann, who played with the St. Louis Browns. He and some of the fellows suggested that I ask the insurance inspector, Mr. Mark DeWitt, who was also president of the Texas Association, for a job umpiring. I didn't know anything about umpiring and didn't want to do it, but I thought it would be okay for a year while my leg healed, so I asked him for a job. He asked if I had any umpiring experience, and I lied a little—told him I worked some

amateur games around Dallas. Well, he agreed to give me a tryout—
$15 a day plus expenses to work fifteen exhibition games.

My first game was between Mexia of the Texas Association and
the St. Louis Cardinals' B team. The Cardinals had won the pennant
the year before, so that B club was a good one. Art Reinhart, one of
the regulars, pitched that day. Herb Hunter was one of the St. Louis
coaches, and as he passed by each inning, he'd say, "Young man, you
are a good umpire. You are going to be with us in this league." Finally,
in the ninth inning I said, "Mr. Hunter, for your information this is
the first ball game I ever umpired in my life." He was surprised, said I
was a natural umpire.

He told Doak Roberts, president of the Texas League, about me,
and Mr. Roberts came down to watch me work. I had good days each
time the old man came down, but he wouldn't hire me. He said, "Son,
you are a good umpire, but you are just too little. You can't see over
those catchers." I replied, "Yes, but I look around them." He wouldn't
give me a job, so I worked the Texas Association the rest of that year.
The next three years I worked the East Texas League, the Lone Star
League, and the West Texas League.

It was tough in those small D leagues, but that's where you get real
umpiring experience. I remember an incident in Corsicana, my first
year in the Texas Association. I called a guy safe at the plate on a
close play, and Bill Speer, a great big 215-pounder, who was on deck,
said, "You ain't got no guts." I said, "Hey, brother, when the ball
game is over, we will see who has the guts." I weighed only about 130
pounds, but as soon as the game was over, I tapped him on the shoulder and said, "What was that you said about having no guts?" He
turned around, and goddamn, I parted his hair with my mask. He
started bleeding like a stuck hog, and as I drew back to hit him again,
the catcher [Adolph] Dutch Krauss, grabbed the mask from me. Well,
I jumped on his back just like I was climbing a telephone pole and
started banging him on the jaw. Finally, a policeman pulled me off,
but in the process I tried to kick the big bastard's eyes out with my
spikes. I about lost my mind.

I had to report the incident to the league president. I thought sure I
was done for, but I didn't care because I had made up my mind that I
was going to whip that guy. I went downtown and bought a pair of
brass knuckles and waited for him the next day at the Western Restaurant. There were three or four ballplayers there. I told them that if
Speer even spoke to me, I was going to break his chin. He showed up
with two of his brothers, big guys. They went inside without saying a
word, and I followed them. They sat down on one side of the room,

and I sat down on the other. When they left, I quit eating and followed them. I followed them all the way to the ball park, vowing to break him in half if he so much as said hello.

Well, during the game that afternoon there was a play at second. The runner came sliding in, and Speer, who was the second baseman, tagged him. I called him out. Speer started off the field but then said, "Lee, how is everything?" I said, "All right. Everything is okay with me, Bill." That was the end of it. I didn't let him get away with anything, and I got his respect. In fact, I earned the respect of all the players. There were rough-and-tough guys in those days; some of them on his own team, guys I had played with, said they'd never speak to me again if I backed down from him.

I got along pretty good, but in 1929 I decided to quit umpiring. I had worked four years of Class D ball and had not missed a game. I worked all those games alone; you can imagine how tough it was calling balls and strikes, especially high curves, from behind the mound. I was getting only $275 a month and had to pay my own expenses. I got six cents a mile for driving my Model A, but since gasoline was eight cents a gallon, I filled half the tank with naphtha. The facilities were terrible. You had to change clothes at the hotel or in the two-hole room. The minor leagues forgot about umpires altogether; we got nothing.

I didn't stay out very long. During the summer I got a call from Mr. D. L. Snodgrass, president of the West Texas League. He was having trouble with umpires and wanted to know how much it would take to get me to go out there. I told him it would cost him $300. He laughed. "Hell, I can get two for that." I said, "Okay, get two. I'm not asking you for a job." The next morning he offered me the $300. I was supposed to work the play-offs, but I refused to do it. John King, one of the managers, and a kid named Harraway were both bad, and I wanted no part of it, so I quit.

Then I got a big break. After leaving the league, I did some bird hunting in West Texas and then visited Carlsbad Caverns. I had just checked out of the motel when a Western Union boy showed up with a telegram: Bill Ruggles, the acting president of the Texas League, wanted me to finish the year. I drove all night to get to Wichita Falls. Hell, the Texas League was the best minor league in the country. Whitlow Wyatt, Jo-Jo White, Birdie Tebbetts, Hank Greenberg, Jimmy Foxx, Zeke Bonura—man, I could name a hundred guys from the Texas League who made it big in the majors. And there were good umpires, too, like Ziggy Sears, Harry Kane, Steve Basil. We had two-man teams, the first time I had ever seen double umpires. The pay was real good, too—$500 a month and six cents a mile. That's $3,000; my starting salary in the major leagues was only $3,500.

Mr. J. Alvin Gardner, who took over as president of the league my second year, always thought I was too small to be an umpire. He advanced the other guys $100 or more to start the season but said he didn't have the money when I asked for $50. Then he was ready to pull me out after my first game.

I had trouble opening day in Fort Worth. In the ninth inning I had a very close play at first base; it went against the home club, and I had to run Frank Snyder, the manager. Fort Worth was a cow town, so most of the people in the bleachers were from one of the four big packinghouses in the town. Those pigstickers came after me as I headed for the dressing room. I hollered back at them, and then one of the Fort Worth club officials came over complaining about a lousy decision. I said, "You might think it was a lousy decision, but I thought it was a great one." He slapped me, and I went after him. A policeman finally broke it up and ushered me into the dressing room. The pigstickers hung around the dressing room for a while, and I talked back to them, saying they were acting like a bunch of cattle, that they didn't have the guts to start anything and so on. Finally, the policeman escorted me to the car.

When I called Mr. Gardner to make a report, he said, "Well, what do you think?" I asked him what he meant. He said, "Do you think I ought to move you?" I told him if he moved me, he better send me home. I stayed in Fort Worth and never had a bit of trouble after that. I showed the pigstickers and Mr. Gardner that I couldn't be intimidated and that I could umpire.

I don't care how good an umpire is, he can learn something every day. Hell, I learned something the very first game I umpired. A guy hit out of order, and the team was trying to get me to call two guys out. Well, I had sense enough to know that you can't call but one man out. I called one guy out but told both sides to protest because I really didn't know the rule. When I got to the hotel, I checked the rule book, and sure enough, I had made the right decision. I just guessed right, but I learned something.

Another thing I learned in the minors was never to prejudge a man or anticipate what's going to happen in a ball game. Harry Kane, an old-time left-handed spitball pitcher, one of the first in the American League, told me that Art Phelan, the manager of the Shreveport club in the Texas League, was a rat. He said he was really rough on umpires and cursed Ziggy Sears all the time even though they had been teammates. Well, the last manager I saw that spring was Art Phelan. I worked the plate in Shreveport, and after the game he said, "Hey, young man, you are a good umpire. I'm going to tell your boss when I get to Dallas." Now this is the guy I had been looking for. I had been all worked up about him being a bad guy, but he wasn't. I made up my mind right then that I'd find out about players and managers for myself.

From the very beginning I never hung around with newspapermen. I wanted no part of them. The worst freeloaders in the world are newspapermen. Besides, they'd always write what they wanted. Early in the big leagues, when I'd been in a jam, they'd come into the dressing room and ask about a play situation. I'd tell them my version of it; then they'd go right over to the ballplayers and then print what the players said. That's who they lived off. Finally, it got so bad, I'd say, "Go write what you goddamn please. Go over to the clubhouse, and write what they tell you because that's what you'll write anyway." I didn't mess with them.

I spent part of 1929 and six full years in the Texas League without missing a game. Then, on Christmas Eve, 1935, I got a call from Mr. Gardner telling me that my contract had been sold to the National League. Well, that's what I had been living for. I couldn't make it as a player, and now as an umpire I was going to see what the coffee was like up there. I stayed for twenty-two years. I went eleven and a half years before I missed a game because of arthritis; I worked 3,285 straight games—that's 1,000 more than the "Iron Horse," Lou Gehrig. In all I worked 4,517 games in the major leagues.

When I reported to spring training in Florida, the first day Mr. Ford Frick, the president of the National League, said, "Lee, if I'd known you were this small, I would never have brought you up." Now how do you think that made me feel? I've heard that crap about my size all my life. Well, I told him, "Where I come from rabbits outrun horses."

I broke in in April 1936 with Beans Reardon and George Barr, both good guys and veteran umpires. I had worked with Barr in the minors. Beans was one of the better umpires in the league. He would announce where each pitch was—ball outside, or whatever. He had a flat mask that would slip off every time a ball hit it; he never got it fixed, and I never understood why he didn't get killed back there. I worked with them for about a month. Larry Goetz and Ziggy Sears were working with Bill Klem, but since Goetz couldn't get along with Klem, we switched crews. I stayed with Klem for five years.

Klem was the king of umpires. He was a czar on that ball field. He made up his own rules. He tried to get me to draw the line on players like he did, but I said, "William, I can't umpire like you." Klem was good for the game. You needed a czar in those days. I enjoyed working with him; he was a fine old man. He was broke all the time, though, because he gambled a lot. He liked to bet the horses.

I had a real good tenor voice and called balls and strikes real loud, but Klem toned me down. He said, "Young man, people don't come out to see the umpires. They come to see the ball game. You take my advice: Walk in each day, have a good game, and walk out. The less notice you create, the better off you are." I thought that was pretty good philosophy, so I quieted down.

Klem always called me Joe Doaks. He picked it up from Goetz. I got that nickname playing semipro ball. C. K. Martin, the manager of the Royse City club, called me that one day, and it stuck. A few months later we were in a theater watching a song-and-dance act set in a graveyard scene; there was a big tombstone that read "Joe Doaks, 15 B.C." The guys let out a holler, and from then on it was "Joe Doaks." That's all they knew me by in the Army; I don't think my commander knew my real name. Even today, when I go to the ball park, someone I haven't seen for fifty years will yell, "Hey, Doaks." I've been called worse.

I also worked with [Albert D.] Dolly Stark. He coached basketball at Dartmouth during the winter. There wasn't a finer man who ever lived than Dolly. He was a good-looking fellow, a real gentleman, a favorite of all people. The man used to take care of his sisters and family. In my time umpires were *way* underpaid, and Dolly wanted more money. I guess he was the first umpire who ever held out. I took his place when he laid out a year and went into broadcasting. He came back but quit again. Dolly was a highly nervous umpire, and all the players knew it. If nobody hollered at him, he'd give you the greatest umpiring job you ever saw. But if they hollered at him, he'd get shook up and have a bad day.

Dolly just took the game too seriously; everything bothered him. You can't do that and be a successful umpire. The crap has to go in one ear and out the other. When I had a bad day, it didn't bother me. I went home with a clean conscience, went to sleep, and met the challenge of the next day. That's the way it has to be.

I broke in lots of good umpires. Tom Gorman, Al Barlick, Augie Donatelli were all outstanding. Barlick was the best I ever saw, a natural-born umpire. Everything he did on the ball field was natural. He had a knack for it; everything was easy for him. And he had good control—nobody ran over him.

He came in the fall of 1940 to replace Klem, who had had a hernia operation. I had a call from Ford Frick about ten days before the end of the season, saying that the new umpire was coming over to the Piccadilly Hotel, in New York, where Klem lived. I had never seen Al Barlick before, but I knew him the minute he walked in the door. He was only twenty-four years old, a big Hungarian-German kid just out of the International League. He was a coal miner from Illinois, and when the mines went on strike, he took up umpiring amateur ball for $1 a game. He just *looked* like an umpire. We talked for a while; then I took him up to Klem's room to meet the king of the umpires.

The old man was in bed, wearing one of those old-fashioned nightgowns that hang down to the floor. He was in his sixties at the time. He wore wooden shoes like a little Dutch boy; he had some kind of disease in his feet. There were always two buckets of water, one hot and one cold, by the bench for Klem to soak his feet in. I said, "William, this is my new partner, Al Barlick." Klem, who always talked real loud, shouted, "Who?" "Al Barlick," I said. The old man looked at the kid and roared, "Where did you come from?" "The International League, sir," Barlick replied. "I've never heard of you," the old man yelled. Barlick, who was sitting on the corner of the bed, sort of stuttered and said, "I don't doubt that, Mr. Klem."

We worked in Philadelphia the next day. Klem wanted the kid to work behind the plate his first day. It was the first major league game the kid had ever seen. Barlick used the mattress, but I could tell as he blew up the balloon that it was leaking. I said, "Al, you'd make a hit with the old man if you'd wear my inside protector." (Klem hated the mattresses they used in the American League.) He put it on, but then his coat wouldn't fit. I loaned him my jacket, which was made two sizes too big so it would fit over the protector. He had his minor league cap, so I loaned him one of mine. (I always carried along extra clothes so I'd look neat and clean; that's one way to gain respect.)

Well, Barlick really worked behind that plate. He called those balls and strikes real loud with that big, booming bass voice of his. The fans loved it; they'd scream every time he'd do it. Pretty soon they started giggling and laughing. Barlick came down to third base and said, "Mr. Ballanfant, I split my pants from squatting." I told him to wait till the inning was over. As soon as the side was out, he went to the clubhouse and put on one of my extra pants, which were also a little large so you could move around easily. I guess you could say I dressed Al Barlick for his first major league game.

I always had a lot of hustle. I was always real fast and liked to run. When I'd be on the bases and a guy would hit one in the hole, I'd pick him up at first base and holler, "Let's go for three." I'd take the inside cut and race him around the bases. I could outrun any of them. Of course, I had no business doing that because that's coaching. I used to race down from the plate to third to cover for Klem; the old man couldn't move too well toward the end.

The most frequent mistake an umpire makes is calling the play too quickly. I've seen guys call a runner out, and the next thing you know the ball is on the ground. I tried to discipline myself against that in the minor leagues. I never called a play on the run; I always came to a complete stop. And I never went through a lot of gyrations, just took my time and called it nice and easy.

I didn't think my size was a handicap to umpiring. The only advantage to size was that the players maybe wouldn't mess with you as much. George Magerkurth was a big man. He could whip any three men in the National League. He was tough, but he couldn't move. Same way with Cal Hubbard in the American League. A great big All-American football player, he'd bark and they'd shut up. But Klem, Reardon, Conlan, Donatelli, Barlick—they were small men, but they were tough, too.

I had to work down real low over the catcher's shoulder behind the plate because I was too small to see over them. Ernie Lombardi was real tough to work behind because he was so big. When I first started, I had some trouble with the outside curveball, but I soon learned to shift with the catchers. All the good catchers would shift for the outside pitch instead of reaching for it backhanded like they do today, and I'd go with them.

I preferred working behind the plate because you had to concentrate on the ball all the time. Hell, sometimes on the bases you'd be looking up in the stands at some gal or something, and the next thing you know there's a bang-bang play and you blew it.

It was easy to work a control pitcher, but God damn those wild ones. It was really bad in spring training. Those wild rookies would throw the hell out of the ball, hit you on the shins. I remember an exhibition game in Florida when Fred Haney tried to make Dale Long, the left-handed first baseman, into a catcher. Both teams had a couple of wild youngsters pitching; one kid walked six or eight guys in the first two innings. Haney sent out word for me to call anything close. I said, "Tell your little manager that I am having enough trouble trying to get them right, let alone give him some." With a left-handed catcher and two wild pitchers, I wasn't giving them *anything*.

The knuckleball was very hard to call. The best knuckleballer I ever saw was Hoyt Wilhelm. One day the ball got away from Wes Westrum and hit me right in the cup. Despite that steel cup, I was black and blue. The knuckler would really dance when thrown into the wind. I could throw a pretty good knuckler myself. In fact, I used to throw knucklers back to the pitcher; he'd get a big kick out of it.

Now that damned blooper pitch Rip Sewell used to throw was the hardest thing to judge. You're supposed to call the ball as it comes over the plate, but what do you do if it comes straight down? He just pushed it up there; wasn't hard enough to break a pane of glass. It was the damnedest thing you ever saw; I missed a lot of calls. He'd throw it fifteen, twenty times a game, especially if he didn't want to give a guy a good pitch. It sure looked big coming up there, and sometimes they'd pop it up because their timing was off. But if the batter was looking for it, it wasn't even a good batting-practice pitch.

All umpires have different strike zones. Mine was pretty big. I'd give them a strike if it nicked the corner or touched the black. That sidearmer Ewell Blackwell was good at catching the corner; by the time it got to the catcher it was way outside. I had a rule: Where the ball goes over the plate, that's what counts; it ain't where the catcher catches it. Of course, not a living soul could call the ball on the black consistently. All umpiring is common sense and judgment.

I saw a lot of spitballs in my time. After the major leagues banned the spitter, a spitballer could come to the Texas League and finish his career with it. I've seen them all. Preacher Roe said he threw a spitter, but he didn't. It was a fork ball. The old-timers would load up with Slippery Elm. I've seen them choke and start throwing up like a mad dog. Gaylord Perry doesn't throw a spitball either. If you've ever seen a ball break *straight* down, you'd know a real spitball.

In my day every club had four or five real good pitchers. There was only six or seven on the pitching staff. In those days that's all they needed because the starter usually finished the game; the manager didn't come out every time a man got to first base. There was better-caliber pitching before all the expansion, no question about it.

I saw some great pitchers in my time. Carl Hubbell, Freddie Fitzsimmons, Van Lingle Mungo, Lefty Grove, Guy "The Mississippi Mudcat" Bush, Robin Roberts, Warren Spahn, Ewell Blackwell, Lon "The Arkansas Hummingbird" Warneke. Bob Feller was the fastest I ever saw. Whitlow Wyatt was the best competitor. He went out there with blood in his eye and a frown on his face, and he never cracked a smile during that ball game—he was there to *beat* you. Whitey Ford had pinpoint control; he could throw the ball anywhere he wanted. Eddie Lopat couldn't splash water, but, oh, what a screwball.

Dizzy Dean was the best pitcher I ever saw. He was fast, had a good curve and great control. He could throw that ball right where he wanted. And he had more confidence than any pitcher I ever knew.

He'd yell to a batter, "Can you hit a curve?" Damn if he wouldn't throw a curve right by him.

I guess I knew Dizzy Dean as well as any living man. I knew him when he was in the Army before he went into professional ball. Our families were real close. I could tell stories about him all day.

I remember one time he went AWOL in the minors. He was pitching for Houston and getting only $250 a month. Every time he pitched the park was full, so he kept asking for more money. Old man [Fred N.] Ackerman, the club owner, wouldn't give it to him. (Hell, that's the sort of thing that ruined the reserve clause; the damned owners brought it on themselves.) Anyway, Dizzy took off. Nobody had seen him for two weeks. Then one night about midnight I was sitting in the lobby of the hotel in Houston where Dizzy lived when he came walking in with a big watermelon under his arm. I asked him where he'd been. He said, "Man, I've been out getting my money together." He'd been down to Old Mexico pitching every other day for $500 a game.

Dizzy always bragged about his quail hunting and threw lots of quail feeds during the winter. I did some bird hunting myself, and I kept asking when he was going hunting with me. He'd say, "Anytime," but then he'd always have an excuse not to go. Well, one day I ran across a guy who owned a quail farm. He told me that Dizzy always bought dressed quail from him for his dinners. All he had to do was put them in the pan. God damn me.

The next time I got an invitation to another quail feed—it was a big dinner with lots of family and some big wheels from Falstaff—I told a couple of guys about the quail before dinner. I said, "Look, we'll sit across from Dizzy, and while we're eating dinner, let's pretend we're spitting out buckshot." So we're eating and spitting away. Finally, Dizzy says, "What's the matter with you guys?" I said, "Dizzy, you shot up these birds too good. You put too much lead in them." That's the only time in my life I saw Dizzy Dean when he couldn't say a word.

Yes, I was one of those who almost quit when Jackie Robinson came in. I never had anything against colored people, but I had been brought up in the South and so didn't like it at first. Bill McKechnie, Dixie Walker, a lot of guys said they would quit if colored players came in, and I went along with them. I was just a little bit quick on the trigger. After I got to thinking about it, I figured why should I quit baseball and lose my pension on account of Robinson being a colored man? I mean the guy's a human being just like I am. What's the difference anyway?

We were given special instructions when Robinson first came up. We were told not to call him a nigger or abuse him in any way. But he could call you every dirty name in the world. I remember one time Herm Wehmeier of Cincinnati knocked him down a couple of times. I mean *knocked* him down—threw it behind him. Robinson came up blasting, "You white motherfucker!" You know, Wehmeier didn't say a goddamn word and didn't throw another ball at him. I lost all respect for that boy. I'd have knocked Robinson on his ass.

I didn't have any trouble with Jackie. He jumped on me a couple of times, but nothing serious. He was a mouthpiece for every colored ballplayer in both leagues. He was also very active in the NAACP. And he was a good ballplayer, a real good ballplayer.

Roy Campanella was the opposite of Robinson. He was a sweetheart. He never opened his mouth or gave you trouble of any kind. Campy was one of the greatest catchers I ever saw.

Gabby Hartnett, Clyde McCullough, Walker Cooper, and Hal Smith were also super catchers. They never bitched, not even on the close ones. They might say, "You owe me one," or something like that, but that's all. They could cover the low pitches real good. All of them liked to talk to the hitters, do anything to break their concentration.

Cooper could carry on a good conversation, but McCullough was the best at distracting hitters. McCullough drove Willie Mays crazy when he first came up. One time, when Willie came to the plate, McCullough said, "Hey, Lee, look at this SOB's fingernails. Those polished nails are cute, aren't they? I wonder if he can hit a curveball?" Then he tossed a little dirt on Willie's shoes.

Finally, Willie backed out and said, "Leave me alone." Here came the curveball, and Willie popped it up.

I had a call one time in the Polo Grounds that changed the game. It was July 15, 1939. In the eighth inning, with the Giants ahead, 4–3, Harry Craft of Cincinnati hit a drive into the stands in the left-field corner off Harry Gumpert. There was a big white pole on the foul line at the wall, but it was real hard to tell whether balls went foul in front or behind the pole. I was behind the plate, and I called it a fair ball. (Bill McKechnie, the Cincinnati manager whose word was indisputable, was coaching at third, and he stepped on the line and also called it a fair ball; I didn't know this until Ernie Quigley told me later.) Harry Danning, the Giants' catcher, gave me hell, so I had to run Harry the Horse. Ziggy Sears ran Joe Moore, the left fielder. Now Billy Jurges came running up to the plate. I told him he could get out, too, because there was no way he could see the ball from that angle at shortstop. At this point George Magerkurth came over from first base to help me out. Magerkurth was a big rough-and-tough SOB who was always chewing snuff and spraying saliva all over the place. Danning was scared of Magerkurth, so he left. But Jurges says, "What the fuck are you doing here?" Magerkurth got mad. "By God, what are *you* doing here? This boy is running this ball game, and you are out, and you are going to *go* out." All the time he is spraying Jurges with saliva. Jurges said, "Don't you spit in my goddamn face," and spit right in Magerkurth's face. George took a poke at him, and Jurges punched him back. They both got suspended for ten days and fined $150.

As it turned out the Giants put Lou Chiozza in at shortstop, and the next day he broke his leg. Ford Frick, the president of the league, asked me if I would rescind Jurges's ten-day suspension. I said, "I'll rescind nothing. I had nothing to do with the guy breaking his leg. I don't take the kind of abuse they were giving me." That incident led to the league requiring each park to put a three-foot screen on the foul poles so you can tell if the close ones are fair or foul.

I worked a lot of great World Series games, but I'll never forget the 1946 series between the Cardinals and the Red Sox. I was the senior National League umpire. In the very first game in St. Louis I had the damnedest obstruction play you ever saw. It was the bottom of the eighth, Boston ahead, 2-1, with two outs. Joe Garagiola hit a fly to left. Dom DiMaggio lost it in the sun but threw Garagiola out at second before Whitey Kurowski crossed the plate with the tying run. That would have ended the inning, but I said Kurowski scored because Pinky Higgins interfered with him as he came around third base. I was behind the plate, and I saw it—Higgins grabbed him. The American League club charged me, pushing and shoving. I said, "The first SOB who lays a hand on me is *through!*" Charlie Berry, who was umpiring at third, upheld me, said it was clear interference. That cooled them down.

After the first two games in St. Louis we took the train to Boston. We started playing poker at the depot. I was hot. I could draw to a flush and make it or draw to a straight open in the middle. I won about $550; stuck Dizzy for $150. We were nipping a little, and pretty soon I started saying, "It's a queen," when it would be a jack or, "It's an ace," when it was a deuce. Harry Caray, the Cardinals' announcer, kept telling me to "call the cards right." He finally got mad and left. We played all the way to Boston.

I had another big argument in the fifth game at Fenway. In the second inning Roy Partee scored on a close play at the plate after a hit by Don Gutteridge to put the Red Sox ahead, 2–1. Garagiola raised all kind of hell, claiming he blocked the plate. Said he had a cleat scrape to prove it. What happened was that Partee slid in head first, and when Garagiola dove at him, he fell across his legs and missed the tag.

In the seventh game I was at second base when Enos Slaughter scored in the bottom of the ninth on that mad dash from first base on a single. Dixie Walker hit one into the hole in left-center, and when Leon Culberson threw it in to Johnny Pesky, the shortstop, Pesky sort of banged the ball in his glove a little bit, and Slaughter scored the winning run. I guess he figured Culberson didn't have as good an arm as Dom DiMaggio, and Pesky never thought Slaughter would keep on running.

The 1951 Series between the Yankees and the Giants was another great one. I was behind the plate when Mickey Mantle got hurt in the second game. He stepped in a sprinkling system drain in center field, chasing after a ball. I saw him play his first game—it was an exhibition game in Phoenix in 1951. The first time Mantle came up to bat, he beat out a bunt; they didn't even make a play on him. He could *fly*. The average speed for a left-hander going down to first base is 4.1, but that guy could run it in 3.4 or 3.5. He was never the same after that injury. He was a great player, but who knows what he would have done if he had been healthy.

Same thing with Pete Reiser. He could do everything—run, throw, field, hit. He could go get that fly ball just like Willie Mays. But he kept running headlong into concrete walls. It's a wonder he didn't kill himself. He had the guts of a burglar; he wasn't scared of anything. There's no telling how good he could have been if he hadn't gotten hurt.

In the third game of the 1951 Series, Eddie Stanky was caught dead at second. A hit-and-run was on, but Yogi Berra called a pitchout and had Stanky thrown out by a mile. But Stanky kicked the ball out of Phil Rizzuto's hand into center field and went to third. That was Stanky. The little SOB would do anything to win. He'd step up to the plate and lean his arms way out over the plate. I'd say, "Hey, boy, get back there. Are you trying to steal your way on?" He wanted to get on so bad he didn't care how he got there.

Stanky was tough on umpires. One day, as he was coming up to lead off an inning, he picked up a ball that had been hit just once and looked at it. I asked to see it, but instead of giving it to me, he rolled it into the dugout. I said, "Young man, just follow the goddamn ball.

You are through for the day." He started foaming at the mouth. "You are taking my hard-earned bread away from me!" I told him to go to hell. I was the arbitrator, and *I* was running that ball game.

Stanky was a real competitor, but I could teach him something about the game. I used to kick or knock the ball away, too. One time in Texarkana I slid into second headfirst, grabbed the ball out of the guy's glove, and headed for third with it. The umpire called me back—said I couldn't do that. We had all kinds of tricks. Pitchers used to put those little scrapers you could buy in the five- and ten-cent stores on their belts and scraped the ball against it. That ball would soar. If you were the home team, you'd keep some balls in a freezer; then, if you were behind in the eighth inning or so, the manager would slip in a few frozen ones: it was like hitting wooden croquet balls. You can do lots of things to a ball. I've seen them put a phonograph needle between the seams to make it sink. One guy in the Texas League would loosen the cover of the ball by twisting it. A little spit and dirt would make a good mud ball, just a big enough piece of mud to make the ball drop. I've even seen them put gum on the ball. Of course, the gum doesn't come off, so that works only if it's the last pitch of the game and the catcher takes off real quick for the dugout. Hell, you can gash a new ball with your thumbnail and it will sink.

I was never a policeman as an umpire. I never asked to see the ball. Who cares if it's loaded? If somebody asked me to take a look, then I checked it. I think they ought to let pitchers throw anything they want. Most of the changes that have been made in the game take away from the pitchers and slow things down. They even make them come to a complete stop now before pitching; that's why there are so many stolen bases today. It makes Ty Cobb's stolen-base record all the more amazing.

I had trouble at first with a couple of veteran managers I won't name who got after me all the time. I got them out of there real fast—I had that "let-loose" trouble. One of them finally told Mr. Frick that I was a good umpire, but the other one said I was just trying to make a reputation. I finally got along with him, too.

I guess I had more trouble with Frankie Frisch than any other manager. We were good friends off the field, but we fought a lot on the field. You could run him one day, and he'd come back the next day with, "Hi, Slapnecker. How's your love life?" (He always called me Slapnecker; I don't know why. I called him that, too.) He'd never bring up something that happened last night, last week, last month, or last year. He was a great guy, one of my best friends.

Unfortunately I was involved in his getting fired in 1951. We were in Brooklyn. He had been run three straight days, and I told him before the game that I didn't want to run him anymore. He blew it, got on me from the first pitch. Hell, he didn't know what was going on. He was sitting in the corner of the dugout reading one of those lousy French girlie magazines. He'd be reading and yelling, "Where was it?" or "What was that?" on every pitch. Finally, I jerked off my mask. "Slapnecker, one more word from you, and you're gone." On the very next pitch he tossed that damned magazine out to the plate. That was it: He was through for the day. That night the Chicago club fired him. They were just tired of him being run out of the game all the time.

Some managers would try to get the psychological edge on you. Birdie Tebbetts, who was managing the Reds, tried that on me one time in Milwaukee when Lou Burdette was pitching. Lots of people thought Burdette threw a spitter, which he didn't, but Tebbetts came out, claiming there was something on the ball. I looked at it. There was nothing wrong with the ball, and I showed it to him. Pretty soon he came out a second time. I said, "No, I am not going to look at the ball." I'd known Birdie from the time he broke in as a catcher in Beaumont, but when he came out the third time, I said, "Now, look, little man, I'm in charge of this ball game, and you are killing time. One more time out here, and you are going to get a bath." He said, "Lee, I'm trying to use psychology on him." I said, "No, you are trying to use it on me." He didn't come out again.

I never had any problems with Leo Durocher because I never took anything from him. I got rid of him real fast. We all did. He was one of those guys who'd kick on every close pitch, a real nagging SOB. Leo didn't have a sense of humor; he'd always show up with a frown on his face. When Barlick, George Barr, and I would show up at the Polo Grounds, the players would say, "Leo won't be here all day." We finally broke him. But he was a good manager. Chuck Dressen made him a good manager.

Dressen was the best manager in the major leagues. He was aggressive, a quick thinker and played the percentages well. He could steal signs; he could even tell what pitchers were going to throw by the way they held the ball in their gloves. He pitched half the Brooklyn games from the dugout. He'd call the pitches. The pitcher picked up the sign and then shook off Campanella till he had it.

I caught his signs one time in Cincinnati. Johnny Corriden sat between Durocher and Dressen in the dugout. Dressen had a ball in his hands and would give the sign with it; the other two guys would do something to cover. I thought something was up, so I watched from third base. Pretty soon I figured it out. The next day I said to Dressen, "You pitched a hell of a ball game." He kinda grinned. "What do you mean?" I told him, but he said I was crazy. The next day I was at second base and picked up the same signs. So the next day I showed him the signs. But he still said, "I don't give no signs."

Umpires had signs, too. We had signs for the half swing, which was fine. But I don't like that new rule about appealing to another umpire on the play. Umpires don't like it either because you're passing the buck.

A sign came in handy on a call I made on Whitey Lockman at the Polo Grounds. Lockman was on second. I was on the inside between the bag and the mound. (That's the National League style; I always thought it was better to play behind the bag in the outfield like in the American League so you couldn't interfere with anything.) All of a sudden Connie Ryan, the second baseman, yells, "Hey, Lee. Look here." They had pulled the hidden-ball trick on Lockman. I turned around and called Lockman out. Whitey screamed, "You didn't see it." I said, "The hell I didn't. I have eyes in the back of my head." Here came Durocher. "You weren't looking." I said, "The hell I wasn't looking. I was looking with the eyes in the back of my head." I finally had to run them both. I asked Leo, "Didn't I get the play right?" He said, "Yeah, but you didn't see it." The hell I didn't. I never told them how I got that play. I wasn't asleep. I looked over to Al Barlick at third base, and he flashed the out sign. I saw it through Barlick.

I thought Rogers Hornsby was a hell of a good manager, but I didn't always like the way he handled some players. One time in Cincinnati Ted Kluszewski was playing first base when a pop foul came over by the stands. That ball was about five feet from the stands, but Kluszewski stopped and went fishing for it and missed. Hornsby, who was in the dugout, said something to him about it. Kluszewski turned and said, "If you think you can play any better, here's the glove." If I had been that manager, I'd have set him on the bench. I wouldn't give a damn if he was the greatest ballplayer who ever lived. Kluszewski was leading the league in home runs. That was Hornsby's last year, 1953.

I never had much trouble with ballplayers. Some umpires felt that players would try to throw you to the wolves, but I never thought that. I always found them pretty supportive of umpires even though they might get angry with you sometimes. I'd mix and mingle with ballplayers after the game, but only the old-timers. We'd have a few drinks in the cocktail lounge, but the next day you'd never know they knew you. You'd only get trouble from the young players coming up, the old ones who were just about washed up, and the .150 hitters. The good players like Stan Musial or Ted Williams never gave you any trouble on pitches—they knew where the ball was; that's why they were good hitters.

The only thing that I really didn't like was the alibiing or lying ballplayers. Same thing with the managers. Hornsby was one of those managers who wouldn't let his players alibi. He wouldn't let them come back to the bench complaining about a pitch. He always said, "If it's close enough for him to call it, it's close enough for you to hit it."

A good umpire is a guy who keeps the game going without running ballplayers. The easiest thing in the world for an umpire to do is run a player. Sometimes you have to do it, but you have to be a little tolerant. An umpire can be too quick. Now if you got a play absolutely right, you don't wait one damn bit. I'd tell them, "You done had your say, now get away from me. If you follow me, you run yourself." Then I'd walk away. Of course, after you told them that, you had to do it, or else you'd lose their respect.

Now sometimes they'd want an early shower. One time in Chicago I called Gabby Hartnett, one of the finest guys in the business, out on strikes in the fourth inning. That pitch was right down the middle. Gabby didn't say a word, just went back to the bench. As the next hitter stepped in, his glove came flying out of the dugout. I hollered, "Time." Now here comes a shin guard. Then another one. As I walked to the bench, out came the mask. He was *dead*. I said, "Young man, you are through for the day. Just gather up all your gear, take it on in, and get your ass wet." He just smiled. I found out later that he wanted to get out to Washington Park to see the horses run.

The next day I was working third base. Before the game Gabby came over and said, "I wish you were back of the plate today." I said, "Yes, I do too because you'd see the first race today instead of the second one." Judge Landis, who was sitting in the boxes with Ford Frick, called me over and asked what Gabby had said. I told them, and they just laughed.

The same thing happened with Frankie Frisch in the Polo Grounds. I ran him early one day. About two innings later a player came over to me with a little piece of paper. "Frisch sent this to you." I put it in my pocket until after the game. The note said, "Dear Slapnecker, I thank you very dearly for running me out of the ball game. I will be up on my veranda overlooking the bay eating boiled shrimp and

drinking a good cold beer while you are down there in that hot sun."
The next day, when he came up to bat, I said, "Mr. Slapnecker, you're
gonna stay in this damn game and suffer, too. I don't care if you sit on
home plate."

Whenever you ran somebody, you had to be honest in making the
report to the president. I never wanted to put the ax to anyone; I always waited until I cooled off to make the report. And then I told the
whole truth, even if it was embarrassing.

I ran Gene Mauch in Chicago one time because I thought he called
me a dirty SOB. I challenged him right there. I didn't run him out, I
took him out—took him clear up the steps to the dressing room. I had
blown my top, and when I got back down to the dugout, I realized the
ball game was waiting on me. When I made my report to Ford Frick, I
put every word in it—what he called me, what I called him, and that I
had challenged him to fight. And I said, "Mr. Frick, if you take this
boy's money, take mine, too. I gave it to him as good as he gave it to
me."

It just so happened that was my last year in the league, and after
the season I ran into Mauch in a hotel lobby. He told me he had read
the report I sent in on him. I said, "Didn't I tell him the truth?" He
said, "You had every word in there." I had only one question to ask
him: "Did he take your money?" He said he hadn't even heard from
him. Ford Frick wasn't much of an enforcer.

The front office makes all the difference in the world to an umpire.
The Texas League had the best president in minor league baseball,
Mr. J. Alvin Gardner. I guess Mr. Gardner and Judge [William G.]
Bramham were the two greatest minor league presidents who ever
lived. If you had presidents like them, mister, you would have a good
umpire staff because they would back you all the way so long as
you'd tell the truth. Now Warren Giles didn't back the National
League umpires. He had no guts. He was a politician. I don't want to
bad-mouth the man, but he was half-crocked all the time. I didn't like
the man. He had a recording machine in his office, and when you'd
call in your report, he'd tape it. I always told the new guys to write
out their reports and then read it over the phone. Both Frick and Giles
hired detectives to follow us. They never found anything wrong with
umpires, but they sometimes did with players. I've seen lots of players messing around in places where I didn't have any business being
either.

I liked Commissioner Chandler very much. Happy Chandler was
used by the major leagues. He was a Untied States senator when the
war came. They made him commissioner because they needed his

power; they thought that baseball would close down during the war. Chandler was a good man. He tried to raise the umpires' salary for the World Series from $2,500 to $3,000, but Will Harridge and Frick wouldn't stand for it. Ralph Kiner, Stan Musial, and four or five of the player representatives tried to get the umpires in the players' association, but Harridge and Frick wanted no part of it. Chandler would have gone for that. Chandler tried to get all the umpires under his control, but the presidents of the leagues didn't want that. I don't know much about Ernie Stewart getting fired, but you can bet all the tea in China some umpire stooled on him.

I resented that fact that umpires weren't paid more money. I still resent it. We were working for nothing while the National League carried the Philadelphia Phillies and the Boston Braves. The league paid those big salaries to Bob Quinn and Gerry Nugent for their front offices but couldn't pay the umpires a decent salary. I started for $3,500; my last year I got $18,000. After twenty-two years in the league, I get a pension of $300 a month.

Umpires are much better off today. The union has helped a lot. There is a good pension, and the salaries are much better. Augie Donatelli and Al Barlick were the two main guys behind the union. Jocko Conlan helped, too. On the other hand, the opportunities for a young umpire aren't as good today. Fewer minor leagues mean fewer jobs. If a young fellow has a family, he can't make it in the lower leagues for $500 or $600 a month; he can make more than that doing most anything. A major league umpire is set until he has to retire at fifty-five if he keeps his nose clean, so there's not much turnover. Now I don't think mandatory retirement at fifty-five is right. You can't beat experience. I worked until I was sixty-two.

I finally decided to quit in August 1957. Expansion to the Coast was one of the reasons I quit. I never did like to fly, and I didn't want to spend all my time on those damned planes crossing the country. Besides, I got tired thinking about all those doubleheaders coming up in the dog days. So I stopped off in Chicago to see Johnny Holland of the Cubs to see if the organization had anything that I could do down in my country. One of their scouts, a guy called McDowell, had just quit to coach at TCU, so they offered me $7,500 to scout. I scouted Texas and Oklahoma for them for two years and then caught on with Houston for awhile. Since 1972 I've been scouting for the Texas Rangers.

As a scout I see lots of baseball, and I don't like what I see. There are a lot more kids playing baseball today, but the caliber of ball isn't as good as in my time. The coaching isn't as good. I don't care whether you're talking about high school, amateur, college, or professional ball, the players just don't know the fundamentals of baseball. Look at the catchers. They reach instead of shift; they don't go down to block the ball; they catch low pitches with the palm down instead of up. Outfielders throw behind runners. You see all kinds of things today you wouldn't see in the major leagues twenty years ago. There aren't enough quality players for all these expansion teams. Guys who would have been too young or too old in my time are playing today; the quality is definitely down.

Another thing wrong with baseball today is not enough minor leagues. I can remember when there were seven minor leagues in Texas alone; now there are only two. The problem is money. In the old days there were independent leagues. A club would develop a player and sell him for good money to the majors. Now since the major leagues control everything, it's money down the drain if they don't get a player or two for the big club from each minor league team. The minors can't pay for themselves these days. Money is the problem with baseball. Getting rid of the reserve clause might ruin the game; I just don't think a player with a big salary and a multiyear contract will put out his best effort.

When I retired, Al Barlick said I was the best umpire in the business. I don't know about that. Being the best never bothered me. I just wanted to be known as a good guy, one who was always on the level. They say umpires don't have any friends, but I'll bet you any umpire who stayed in the major leagues for ten or fifteen years had more friends than any ballplayer could ever accumulate. I still get letters from people who want autographs, or ask about other umpires, or stop on their way through town. Guys still tell me that people in baseball ask about me.

I've had a good life. The only thing I missed is that education. To this day in the scouting business I don't like to sign a kid out of high school if he has a chance to go to college. In fact, I tell them to get their education because if they don't make the grade in baseball, there's nothing to fall back on. Baseball has given me a wonderful life, but there's no telling what I could have done if I had got that education.

Left to right; Paul Trout, Rudy York, and George
Tebbetts discuss a play with Joe Rue during a Detroit-
Chicago game in 1940. Courtesy National Baseball
Library & Archive, Cooperstown, N.Y.

Joe Rue

ⓈⓈⓈ

Joseph William Rue
Born: Danville, Kentucky, June 14, 1897
Height: 5′ 11″
Weight: 185
Playing career: none
Umpiring career: Western Association (D), 1921; American As-
          sociation (AA), April 1926; Piedmont League
          (C), April–September 1926; Virginia League
          (B), April 1926–27; American Association
          (AA), 1928–32; Pacific Coast League (AA),
          1933–34; American Association (AA), 1935–
          37; American League 1938–47
No-hit games: none
All-Star games: 1943
World Series (games): 1943 (5)

I've been mobbed, cussed, booed, kicked in the ass, punched in the face, hit with mud balls and whiskey bottles, and had everything from shoes to fruits and vegetables thrown at me. I've been hospitalized with a concussion and broken ribs. I've been spit on and soaked with lime and water. I've probably experienced more violence than any other umpire who ever lived. But I've never been called a homer.

It's really sinful the abuse umpires have had to take. Here is an important man representing millions of dollars, protecting the club owner by getting the game in and giving fans a good run for their money, and he is the most disrespected, despised person on the face of the earth. An umpire should hate humanity. But I never felt that way. What causes a man to go into such a screwy job? There is something that draws you to it—a love of the game.

I was born on June 14, 1897, in Danville, Kentucky. My father was a railroad man. We moved when I was young to Osawatomie, Kansas, and then to Kansas City. I had a good education. I went to school in Osawatomie, Northeast High in Kansas City, and St. Mary's College in St. Mary's, Kansas, where I got my B.A. degree in 1917. After graduation I enlisted in the Marines.

I loved baseball as a kid. We played in the backyard with balls made of wound-up string. My dear old mother couldn't keep glass in one window on account of all the foul balls. I wasn't good enough to play much ball myself, so I started umpiring for the town team at age fourteen. When my father was transferred to Kansas City, I started umpiring the sandlots there.

One day Dick Schmelzer, who owned a sporting goods company, got me a job umpiring in the Packer's League. The big packinghouses like Cudahy, Armour, and Swift had teams that played two games a week after work in the West Bottoms. I worked those games alone. I'd start behind the plate and then move behind the pitcher's mound when a runner got to first base; if a runner got to second base, I'd go back behind the plate so I could cover third. It was a pretty rough league. One night, after I had thrown a tough hombre out of the game, the head of the Armour Company, who was also president of the league, called a meeting in Schmelzer's sporting goods store. You know what they did? They elected me umpire in chief and president of the league!

But I got my real exprience umpiring for the Kansas City Monarchs in the old Negro League. (All the other umpires were white, too.) That was 1920. There were great players in that league who, had they not been denied on account of their color, would have been major league stars. The Monarchs had a wonderful ball club. They had a pitcher, [Wilbur] Bullet Rogan. Oh, he could throw that ball. Outside of Bob Feller and Walter Johnson, who I worked behind in an exhibition game, Rogan was the fastest pitcher I've ever seen. They had another pitcher, [Reuben] Currie, who had as good a curve as Tommy Bridges. And the manager of the Chicago [American Giants] team, [Andrew] Rube Foster, a big, heavyset fellow, was wonderful. He'd just give you the batting order—never argued about anything even though I was not a professional umpire. The Monarchs played barnstorming major leaguers each year—Casey Stengel, George Sisler, Zach Wheat, Hal Chase, those kinds of players—and beat them. Boy, I mean they'd *beat* them. There were ballplayers in that league. They were terrific. If Branch Rickey had been there, he would have gotten a handful.

John Savage, the business manager of the Kansas City Blues, got me my first professional job. It was 1921. I was selling paint for a living and umpiring amateur ball on the side. Savage saw me work and contacted George LaMotte, the president of the [Class D] Western Association. LaMotte offered me $300 a month, and I took it right away. I didn't know there was that much money in the world. Besides, I wanted to be an umpire so bad because I wasn't good enough to play baseball. When I told my father, who also loved baseball, what I was going to do, he said, "Well, son, there goes the money I spent on you for an education. It's gone down the drain. Go ahead and try it. You will be back in a week."

LaMotte was dumbfounded when I walked into his office. He was about five feet six inches, one-sixth Osage Indian, a smart, well-educated, fine gentleman. There I was, five feet eleven inches, 150 pounds, and all dressed up. He was expecting a big, tough character. He had a rough league—Oklahoma towns like Chickasha, Dumright, Enid, Henryetta, Pawhuska, and Okmulgee. He told me I'd have to work alone and then said, "Joe, I've had seventeen umpires down here. I'm going to wish you good luck now." He gave me $100 expense money and told me to report to Chickasha. I said, "How in the hell do you get to Chickasha?"

That night I took the train to Oklahoma City. There was a train out of there for Chickasha at eight o'clock the next morning, so I walked over to the railroad station and bought my ticket. On the way back to the hotel a guy jumped out of the dark, stuck a Colt .45 right against my heart, and said, "Stick 'em up, you son of a bitch." I put them up. He took all my money except sixty-nine cents and said, "Run your ass down that track, and if you look around, I'm going to blow you away." I thought about coming down on him—I was once a lightweight boxing champion—but that Colt got bigger and bigger, so I took off trotting down the tracks. When I finally stopped, he was gone. I sat up in the police station until 4:00 A.M., but they never brought the guy in. I called LaMotte, and he said he would arrange for the Chickasha club to advance me another $100.

The next day I began my career as a professional umpire. What a beginning it was. I had a rhubarb in my first game. Around the fourth inning, [L. Frank] Drap Hayes, the Chickasha manager, called me a

busher and an SOB, so I had to put him out. That night, while I was
eating dinner in the hotel with a kid, Ed Rafferty, from the Pawhuska
club, a fellow called Bad Bill pumped seven shots into a waiter right
outside the front door. Rafferty and I, who were on the end stools,
rushed to see what had happened; everybody else in the place headed
for the door and pushed us into the street. I looked up and there was
the cowboy standing over the waiter with his revolvers still smoking.
I got down on one knee, held the waiter's head in my arms, and called
for an ambulance. He died; Bad Bill did, too, a month later, of tuber-
culosis. That was my first day as an umpire.

The first time in Dumright, I had trouble when I stopped a game
because of rain. Everyone took cover, but I didn't have any place to
go. Those damned oil roughnecks wouldn't let me come into the
stands, and I couldn't go into the dugouts, so I just stood out on the
field and got soaked. Finally, the Dumright manager came out and
told me they would run me out of town if I called the game. His team
had just scored, and we hadn't completed five innings yet. He said,
"We ran Jim Bluejacket out over the center-field fence, and you'll go
the same way." (Bluejacket was an Indian who pitched in the majors
for a short time and then went to umpiring. He lasted only three
games in Dumright; the hotel manager told me that when the crowd
chased him, Jim jumped over the center-field fence and was never
seen again.) Well, I finally called the game on account of wet grounds.
The guy who had given me a ride to the ball park wouldn't give me a
ride back, so I had to walk to the hotel with the fans throwing mud
balls at me all the way. They even came into the hotel that night to
raise hell with me.

The hell of it was, the season wasn't a month old yet. Things didn't
get any better. I was mobbed in seven of the eight towns in the
league, every place but Springfield. I guess my father made an umpire
out of me. If he hadn't said I'd be back home in a week, I'd probably
have been the eighteenth umpire to leave that league. I went through
hell that summer.

I laid out the next few years. I loved umpiring, but I couldn't find
a job to get me through the winters. Nobody wanted to hire me for six
months, and I was too honest to lie about my desire to go off and umpire if the opportunity arose. So I went back to selling paint for the
Acme White Lead and Color company and working sandlot and
Negro League games in Kansas City.

Then it all started again in 1925. Jack Landrey, one of the American
Association umpires who was working with Frank Connolly, had too
much to drink the night before, so I was asked to umpire the Kansas

City–Louisville game. They were playing for first place. Boy, did I end that ball game! It was the last of the ninth, Kansas City behind, 1–0. But the Blues got a man on, and Dud Branom hit a ball between the pitcher and the first baseman. The pitcher covered first, and I called Branom out as the tying run crossed the plate. I didn't follow the play, just called him out and headed toward the dugout. I found out later that the ball hit the pitcher in the chest and fell to the ground: Branom was *safe*. They had to call out the police department. Connolly refused to reverse my decision, and all hell broke loose. Somebody kicked me down the dugout steps. I was going out to Swope Park after the game for a weenie roast, but instead I went to the hospital with two cracked ribs. I got mobbed in my own hometown.

Despite that experience [Thomas Jefferson] Tom Hickey, the president of the American Association, sent me a contract that fall. Actually, I got contracts from the Western League, the Three-I League, and the Association within two or three days of each other. I started to sign the Three-I contract, but when Hickey's came, offering me $400 a month, I took it.

I lasted only three days. I opened the season in Louisville with Frank Connolly, whose brother Tommy was the supervisor of umpires in the American League, and old Jim Murray. Jim couldn't read or write, but he was one hell of an umpire, a bullheaded Irishman if there ever was one, but boy, I loved him. Anyway, I was over at third base—Connolly and Murray kept me over there to break me in easy—when Nick Allen, the manager of the St. Paul club, called me a son of a bitch and pushed me. Well, I socked him. He just sat there on the ground and laughed. When I got back to the hotel, I got a call from Mr. Hickey asking me to meet with him in Chicago the next day. Tom, who was a great guy, said, "Joe, you're too young. I shouldn't have signed you to that. I'm going to send you down to the Piedmont League to Judge Bramham. He wants you, and he's going to use you as an extra umpire in the Virginia, Piedmont, and South Atlantic leagues. If you have a good year, I'll bring you back."

Now maybe I'm going to hell, I don't know, all the way to Durham, North Carolina. I rode a train for three days getting down there. Judge Bramham was the greatest. He and Ban Johnson were the same type of president. He *made* umpires, and he made ballplayers respect that umpire; brother, he ran those three leagues with an iron fist. He was finally made commissioner of the minor leagues, but he should have replaced Judge Landis as the commissioner of baseball.

I was born and raised right on the line of the southerner. When I was young, they used to say, "A nigger's a nigger." Not to me. I've never held anything against Negroes. That's why I never had problems umpiring in that old Negro League. Negroes are the greatest baseball fans in the country; the *greatest*. Many a ball club down South would have gone broke if those Negroes hadn't been at the ball park. They wouldn't be sitting in the grandstands either; they'd be by themselves in bleachers way down the foul lines. Umpires never had any trouble with the Negroes. It was always the white people who gave it to you.

I worked with some fine umpires in those leagues. Bramham assigned me to work with Larry Goetz, who later umpired in the National League, and Jack O'Toole in the Piedmont League. O'Toole, who was about sixty-five years old, walked funny because he had two clubfeet. But he was one hell of an umpire. He umpired that Southern League for years. He was a great character and did a great job with Goetz and me, two of the wildest bastards who ever drew a breath. I also worked with Fred Westervelt, a former National League umpire, over in the Virginia League. At the end of the season Bramham and Hickey thought I should return for another year, so I worked with Westervelt over in the Virginia League. The next year, 1928, I went back to the American Association and stayed for eight years.

In my very first year, I got hit with a whiskey bottle in Columbus, Ohio. We were in the last of the ninth, two men out. Goetz chased a couple of Columbus players off the bench. I didn't think Larry used good judgment because the last out was standing at the plate. There were only about 300 people in the stands, but they came out on the field after Larry. I was taught that if they go after your partner, you go with him, so I rushed in from first base and got within about five feet of Larry, who was swinging his mask to keep them away. All I remember is that somebody hit me in the back of the head with a bottle. (I was later told that it was a whiskey bottle.) That quieted everything. I was *out*. Goetz finished the game, and I went to Grant Hospital with a concussion. After four or five days I got tired of that hospital and the stiff neck and the pains in my head, so I put on that blue embalmer's suit, got a train, and joined Larry in Toledo.

One of the most embarrassing things that ever happened to me took place one night in Louisville. Mr. Hickey told me that a fellow in Louisville had invented a device for umpires to carry the baseballs in and that Bruce Dudley, the sports editor of the local paper, wanted me to demonstrate it. I agreed. Well, the fellow came to the dressing room with this U-shaped gadget, a tube that fit around the small of the back and fastened in front with a leather belt. It had a little trap on the right-hand side. I strapped it on, put in a dozen balls, and went out to work the game.

It happened in the first or second inning. I had taken out a couple of balls to replace fouls, and it worked okay. Then, with a runner on first base, the batter got a hit. As I went tearing off toward third base to cover the play, this thing started flopping up and down on my back. I knew balls were falling out, but I couldn't stop. By the time I got to third base there were baseballs all around me. As the runner slid into third, the throw got away from the third baseman, [Pelham] Ballenger, who then picked up one of the balls and tagged the guy. I called him out. Out came the manager just raising hell. I said, "I don't know where in the hell he got the ball; there are balls laying all round." They appealed to my partner. I don't remember whether we finally called him safe or out, but the gadget sure didn't last long. I took it off and threw it over the bench. That was the end of that thing. The fans went *crazy*.

There was one umpire in the Association who really got on my nerves because he was gutless. His name was [Zena] Zenie Clayton, a former player in the Texas League. I always felt he didn't have any business umpiring because he had to take aspirins before every game to calm down. I had to hold up the season opener in Columbus once for ten minutes while Clayton went back to the bathroom to get aspirins.

He was with me during a riot in Toledo involving Casey Stengel's club. Casey was one of the greatest storytellers ever; he could outtalk any man who ever lived and was great copy for the sportswriters and the fans. But on the ball field he was no good as far as umpires were concerned; for most of his life he just raised hell with umpires. Frank Connolly hated Stengel; if Casey even winked an eye, he was gone.

Well, Clayton and I were in Toledo for a big series with Minneapolis. Stengel's team was full of ex–major leaguers like Bob Meusel, Everett Scott, the Red Sox shortstop, and Jack Scott, the Giants' pitcher. Minneapolis had Bevo LeBourveau, who couldn't stick with the Phillies but was a great AA hitter. The stands were packed, maybe 16,000 fans.

It was the last of the ninth. Stengel's club was two runs behind but had two men on base with two outs. Jocko Conlan hit a drive into the left-field corner that hit the fence and went into a little alcove. There was a space of about six or eight feet between the stands and the fence down the left-field line; the ground rule was if the ball even momentarily went into that opening, it was an automatic two-base hit. Both runners scored, but I ordered one guy back to third and

Conlan back to second. As it turned out, that was the ball game. Stengel, who was coaching at third base, charged at me screaming, jumping up and down, and waving his arms like a madman. He really excited the fans.

Talk about riots. As soon as the game was over, the fans came out of the stands after me. In Toledo the umpires had to go *through* the stands to get to the dressing room. Wasn't that a hell of an arrangement? I was doing my best to control the mob when up came Le-Bourveau with a bat. He stood right next to me and said, "One of you lay your goddamned hands on this umpire, and I'll kill you with this bat." Jocko Conlan came running over to help also.

I finally got into the dressing room. It was really a shed; we didn't dress in there, it had no shower. The mob stayed right outside, raising hell. I thought they might tear the door down. Somebody went under the stands to where the grounds keeper kept his equipment, mixed a bucket full of lime and water, and threw it through the wide cracks in the dressing room. I got soaked; it was a real mess, lime all over everything. That damned Zenie Clayton wasn't in there; he hadn't followed me. Finally, the crowd disappeared, and he came in. I'm a mess, soaked, and mad as hell. "Where in the hell have you been?" He said, "I had to stop and pick up the rosin bag." "Well," I said, "that's just great. To hell with you, go on back to Texas where you come from." I was on *fire*. I always believed that partners stuck together: when one's in trouble, you're all in trouble, when one goes down, you all go down. That's the way I was brought up.

I made my report to President Hickey and thought that was the end of it. But a young fellow from Toledo, Slaven, a swell guy who wanted desperately to be an umpire, thought he would do us a favor by reporting the incident to Judge Landis's office. (I knew nothing about it; afterward I found out that Hickey didn't report it to Landis either.) Landis summoned us all to a hearing in Hickey's office. Landis asked me if Stengel had laid a hand on me. I told him no, just told the facts of how Casey had come over and raised hell. I'll never forget it. Judge Landis got up out of his chair, walked around the desk to Stengel, and said, "If you ever behave again like you did toward these umpires, I'm going to throw you out of baseball for the rest of your life. Now *get out!*"

My stay in the Association was interrupted by two years in the Pacific Coast League in 1933 and 1934. My sister, whom I hadn't seen for a long time, was living in Los Angeles, and I had never been on the West Coast, so I told Mr. Hickey that I wanted to go to the Coast League. There was an umpire in the PCL named McLaughlin, from

Philadelphia, who wanted to get back East, so we swapped leagues. I didn't care too much for the Coast League. It was a good league with lots of ex-major leaguers, but it was pretty much a Fountain of Youth league. But I enjoyed the Coast. I did a lot of sightseeing and came to love the state of California. I couldn't wait to get back.

They tried something in that league to dress up our uniforms. With those blue suits, white shirts, and black ties we looked like morticians. One year they had us wear white pants on Sundays. Now we looked like zebras. The players called us a bunch of sissies. They'd sneak up behind you and spit tobacco juice on your pants legs. Every time we'd see one of them walking by we'd say, "Get the hell away from me." I had to have those trousers cleaned every Monday morning.

When I started umpiring, I had only one thing in mind: to go to the American League. I was in the American Association so long I was beginning to think I would never make it. I know Fred Haney recommended me, but I wondered about it because I knew that Tommy Connolly and his brother didn't like me. Frank thought I felt I was too good for the other umpires because I wouldn't travel in their circle. But then I met Mr. Harridge, the president of the American League, one day in the Palmer House Hotel in Chicago, and he told me that he had received good reports about me. Finally, in 1937, he bought me from George Trautman for $4,000 to replace Brick Owens, a great old-timer. That was the highest Harridge had ever gone for a minor league umpire.

After all those years I made it out of the bush leagues. I say "bush leagues," but God love them. I enjoyed those days even though they were tough times for umpires. You'd have to stand at home plate and announce the batteries for the day's game. You'd work alone or with one partner. Conditions were primitive. In the Western Association games were literally played in fields; fans used to drive their horse-and-buggies along the foul lines to watch the games. The facilities were terrible. There were no dressing rooms; you had to dress at the hotel. There was no real money to be made. The salaries weren't too bad, but by the time you paid for your uniform and equipment, lodging and meals there wasn't much left. So umpires stayed in fleabag hotels full of whores and people who couldn't afford anything else. It turns my stomach when I think of how those umpires lived. It was disgraceful. You'd go into the president's office, and it would be: "Hello, Joe. How are you? You're looking fine." But they never did much to improve the lot of the umpire.

I was different. I always stayed in the best hotels because that was one way to gain the respect of your fellowman. I'll never forget meeting Ted McGrew and Jack Powell, one of the greatest umpires I've ever known, in this dump in Toledo. They were paying a buck a day; hell, I left them and stayed in the Waldorf for $2 a day. I did the same thing in the major leagues. I always stayed at the Bellevue Stratford in Philadelphia while the other guys looked around for a second- or third-rate place. In Chicago I stayed at the Palmer House, while the others stayed at the Congress. I went first class all the way. I still do. And I wouldn't just sit around all day talking baseball with umpires. I went out and met people. I was never lonesome. I had friends outside of baseball in every town in the league, people like the first executive vice-president of Anaconda Copper and that great opera singer, Miss Lily Pons. Harry Truman was a good friend from Kansas City, and I got to meet Vice President [John Nance] Garner once. Do you know what he said to me? "Well, by God, I've always wanted to meet one of you birds face to face."

How *well* I remember my first major league game. I opened the 1938 season in Boston with George Moriarty and Lou Kolls. Moriarty was rough and tough as a ballplayer (he was a third baseman), but one of the finest and most intelligent men I've ever met. He *ran* a ball game. You've never seen discipline like Moriarty had; a ballplayer wouldn't even *look* at him. While I was dressing before the game (he always came in ten minutes before it was time to go on the field), he said, "Joe, I hear a lot of good reports about you. I want to wish you a lot of good luck."

I needed it right away because in the third or fourth inning a Boston player hit a line drive to left field. If the ball hit the wire screen above that high left-field wall in Fenway Park, it's a home run; if it hit the ledge or facing where the screen is attached to the wall and came back on the field, it's in play. I was at third base, so it's my call. I ran halfway down the line and saw it perfectly: The ball hit the facing and dropped onto the field. Moriarty, who was behind the plate, thought the ball rolled down the wire, so he signaled a home run. Jimmy Dykes and the whole White Sox bench charged me. I'm like a child in the lion's den. Dykes said, "Rue, you saw where the ball hit. You know what the rule is." I didn't say a word because I was waiting to see if Moriarty would appeal to me for a decision. Finally, Dykes prevailed upon him to ask me. George came out, saw the players crowded around me, and shooed them away with a sweep of an arm. "Get the hell away from here, every damned one of you." He asked me, "Hey, kid, where did the ball hit?" "George, the ball hit the facing and dropped. The ball's in play." He said, "Thanks kid," turned around and walked back. That was the end of that. Later, in the dressing room, he said, "Well, you broke in with a bang. That's the first time I've been reversed in all my years in the American League. I tested you right quick, didn't I?"

The most difficult call I ever made was in Cleveland. Somebody hit a line drive into the left-field stands near the foul pole. It hadn't turned dark yet, and although the lights were on, it was hard to follow the ball in the dusk. I ran out there and called it foul. It landed in foul territory, but you couldn't tell for sure if it curved in front of the pole or behind it. One of the sportswriters sent a grounds keeper out there to ask the fans. You know, the fans said it was foul. That was the toughest decision I ever had to make, and I don't know to this day whether I guessed at it or I saw it at the last minute. But you just have to be right if you are going to be an umpire.

No one taught me to be an umpire. There was no such thing as an umpire school in those days. You learned umpiring in the school of hard knocks. You had to go out there and take the bumps, the bottles, the riots, and all the rest of it. You were on your own, and you either made it or you didn't on your own. I learned to umpire from experience.

And I never knew too much. As a young man I'd sit out in front of the old Majestic Hotel in Kansas City and talk with old-timers like Ollie Chill, who was umpiring in the American League. Those fellows were all honest-to-God he-men. They were rough, and they were tough. They even got me chewing tobacco because I was one of them. And in the American Association I talked about plays and situations with umpires like Dolly Durr and George Magerkurth. Magerkurth, who always called me kid, was really tough. One day I saw him go over to the hotel and beat up Ivy Griffin, the Milwaukee first baseman. I learned from them all.

Most people think Bill Klem was the greatest umpire, but he really wasn't so outstanding. Do you know what made Klem? He had a lot of trouble with Red Lucas, a pitcher for the Cincinnati Reds. When Lucas came down to tell Klem what he thought, Bill drew a line in the dirt with his foot and said, "You take one step beyond that line, and you're gone." Drawing the line gave Klem publicity, brought him to the attention of the fans. He was good, but he wasn't the greatest. All those old-timers were great umpires. They had to be in those days. I never saw a bad one. Emmett "Red" Ormsby, George Moriarty, Dick Nallin, Bill Dinneen, Harry Geisel—how could you improve on any of them? They all had poise, they were big men, they were impressive, and they *ran* their ball games. They were all great, or they wouldn't have been there.

To be an umpire, you must have good judgment, good eyesight, and confidence that you can do the job. You do not know or care to know who you are calling safe or out, and when the ball reaches home plate, you know only that it is either a ball or a strike. That's integrity; if an umpire loses that, he's lost everything. If players and managers know an umpire calls the play the way he sees it, they will respect him even if he might not be the best of umpires. You must take charge out there. I've always said an umpire is like an army officer: you can't fraternize with the troops, and you can't let them tell the lieutenant where to go. The umpire has got to be the boss. There isn't a player, manager, or club owner who likes a weak-kneed umpire. It isn't that you love to fight. You don't want to fight any more than a general wants to fight in a war, but without discipline you're not worth a damn as an umpire.

Nerves never got to me. In fact, the best ball game I ever worked was my first World Series game behind the plate. It was the third game of the 1943 Series. Al Brazle of the Cardinals against Hank Borowy of the Yankees. It was a real pitcher's duel until the Yanks got five in the eighth to win, 6–2. I was so confident I couldn't wait. I looked at it as just another ball game: It's either a ball or a strike; he's either safe or out. During that game I didn't have a batter or either catcher question me on a single call. My right hand to God, *not one.* I'll never forget it. After the game Commissioner Ford Frick came into the dressing room and complimented me: "Joe, you umpired one of the greatest ball games back of the plate I ever saw."

Dolly Stark was one of them who couldn't get control over his nerves. I knew Dolly pretty well even though we were in different leagues. He worked with Klem, but he and I would go out together when we were in the same town. (Nobody liked to hang around with Klem.) Dolly was a fine young man, well thought of as an umpire. But he would grieve if he missed a play or a call; he'd take it to heart and brood over it. He took two shots at umpiring. Klem brought him back after he quit the first time, but he just couldn't take it. That's why I say umpires are born and not made. I guess I was born an umpire.

Like Klem, I never missed one. I never missed one because the way I saw the play was the way I called it. Now, when I took a second guess, I might say to myself, "Rue, old boy, you sure kicked that one all to hell." I'd know that I kicked it, but at the time I made the call I didn't miss it. I always gave an honest decision. I didn't like it when I missed one, but I didn't brood because there was nothing I could do about it.

I was not a very colorful umpire; in fact, not colorful at all. I had a big, strong, heavy voice, but I'd never bellow like Bill Summers. My arms spoke for me. After all, I was there to call the balls and strikes, to call them safe or out, not to put on a show. Nobody goes to the ball park to see the umpires.

I was considered a hell of a ball-and-strike ump. But I was a horse-shit base umpire for the simple reason that I would loaf. I'd be lazy. But I could call balls and strikes with anybody. Even Birdie Tebbets, who got on umpires real good, once said I was the best umpire in the league on low balls.

I have always believed that the American League style of umpiring directly behind the catcher gave us a better view of the plate than looking over the catcher's shoulder like in the National League. If you're working over the inside shoulder and the ball is on the inside corner, sure, you'll get it. But if the ball is on the outside, there is no way you can see it. All we had to do was shift slightly to see perfectly. Everybody had trouble with the high strike—that is the most difficult pitch to call.

Of course, you had to work your tail off on spitters and knuckleballs. The first time I ever umpired a spitball pitcher, Stan Coveleski of Cleveland, in an exhibition game, I couldn't believe the things that ball did. And I remember one time Dutch Leonard of Washington, a real good knuckler, threw one way up high to Rip Radcliff of the White Sox. I called it a strike. Jimmy Dykes fell on the bench like he was dead, and the fans got a big kick out of it. (I didn't *miss* it; I just got the words mixed up.)

Sometimes you'd have trouble with those big catchers blocking you on low pitches. Bill Dickey used to raise up on you, but then he'd help you umpire. Whenever Dickey got a low pitch, he would come up with the ball. So if you lost a low pitch, you'd just wait a second to see if he'd raise up a little. Bill called all the low pitches for us; he never knew it, and we never told him.

Actually, the best ball-and-strike umpire I ever saw was Ted Williams. He would take a pitch *unbelievably* close. He always said, "I don't give a damn where the rest of them are but just look the last one over good." I asked him one time, off the field, why he never hit to left. He said, "I don't want to." Over a season he could have put thirty points on his batting average if he had hit to left field. I'll bet he would have had the highest batting average ever.

I firmly believe in that big balloon the American League uses. I was a smart aleck one time in the American Association and bought one of those inside protectors the National League used. A Spaulding, Bill Klem model, with football kneecaps for shoulder pads. In the very first inning I got hit *solid* with a foul tip. I want to tell you I thought my shoulder was torn loose. It really hurt, and, of course, the same old crap—the fans went wild. It's amazing. You get hit on the cup with a foul ball, and you're in pain, yet the fans cheer. It's sickening. Anyway, I called time and got my old balloon from the dressing room. Gave the other damned thing to one of the amateur umpires in Minneapolis.

It never bothered me to hear the crowd yelling insults and booing as I walked on the field. In fact, I used to smile at them. I'll make an honest confession: If you go through a ball game and everything is perfect, nobody says a word to you or questions anything, it gets kind of monotonous. You might say to the catcher or the batter, "Hey, it's getting dull as hell out here. Everything's going too smooth. I'm going to wake them up." And I have missed a pitch—called one nobody would question. But everybody in the stands would wake up. Then I'd apologize for calling the strike: "Now we're going, kid. I'm sorry."

Naturally you don't look forward to the rhubarb or chasing someone. I never permitted a ballplayer to curse me. If he was moving away, I ignored it. But if he said it to my face, he was automatically gone. I didn't permit them to curse me, and I never cursed them. Lots of times I wanted to, but I didn't. I've chased players for intentionally grandstanding on me. Now I have let a ballplayer get away with things that another player couldn't do. If a player never gave me any trouble or tried to show me up—players like Charlie Gehringer, Ted Williams, or Jimmy Foxx—I'd just walk away, never have rabbit ears. But I *would* hear a guy like Jimmy Weatherly of Cleveland. He always questioned the umpire's decision. A guy like that would go in a hurry.

Gehringer was a model. A delight for umpires. One day over in St. Louis he made a bunch of errors in the game. It was amazing; he was kicking them all day. Well, Don Heffner of the Browns stole second base. Charlie made the tag, but I called him safe. He was out a mile. I knew I'd kicked hell out of it. Gehringer looked at me, and all he said was: "Well, Joe, I guess we're both having a tough day." Can you beat that? He was a star, and I respected him all the more after that day.

Sometimes you'd get a rhubarb that was mostly show. That happened often in the American Association with Johnny "Red" Corriden, the coach of the Minneapolis club. Johnny was one of the nicest guys in the world, an old-time shortstop with the Chicago Cubs. Mike

Kelley, the owner and manager of the Millers, always wore street clothes on the bench like Connie Mack; so, according to the rules, he couldn't come on the field. So he'd send Johnny after us. He'd come out, waving his hands and screaming, "Joe, how the hell are you? Mike sent me out here, but you know what he's doing. I don't know whether you kicked it or not, but Mike wants you to bear down." He always woke up the stands real quick. He put on one hell of a show. Goetz and I would let him go through it up to a point. Then, I'd say, "You've done your job now, Johnny, so get your ass back on that bench, and tell Mike if he sends you out here again I'll chase you both."

That happened to me once in the majors. A service club in Kansas City, the South Central Businessmen's Association, came over to St. Louis one time to present me with a gift. Before the game they presented me with a beautiful Gladstone bag. During the game I called a guy out at second. He was out a mile, but here comes Fred Haney charging me. I said, "Fred, what the hell are you doing out here? All my friends are here. Are you trying to show me up?" He said, "No, you blind SOB, I'm going to step on your toes." I said, "Wrong, you little bastard. You're not man enough to step on my toes. But I'm going to step on you right now. Get the hell out of here." I chased him, and the Kansas City delegation stood and cheered. I later found out it was a put-up job and I was the only one innocent of it. Haney didn't give a damn: his ball club was in last place.

I was in the greatest riot the game has ever seen. It happened in Yankee Stadium on July 21, 1940. There were about 70,000 fans there for a doubleheader with the Detroit Tigers. The Tigers were in first place, but the Yankees, who were in fourth, had a big winning streak going. I was at first base in the opening game and had a lot of those bang-bang plays. You never have much trouble with those calls because you listen for the distinctive sounds of the ball hitting the glove and the runner's foot hitting the bag, but the fans sure give it to you anyway. Well, the Tigers won that game, 4–3, so the Yankees are now five out of first, and the fans weren't too happy.

I was behind the plate in the second game. Detroit was leading, 2–1, in the fifth inning. Joe Gordon had hit a home run, and Marius Russo and Red Rolfe had singled. With runners at first and second, Tommy Henrich hit a drive down the first-base line. The ball caromed off the glove of Rudy York, the Tigers' first baseman, but it was in foul territory by about two inches. I called it foul even before it caromed off York's glove. The runners had come around—Russo and Rolfe scored, and Henrich stopped at third—so I had to send them back.

Earle Combs, who was coaching at first, started raising hell. All of a sudden bottles, fruit, vegetables, and I don't know what else came pouring out of the stands. All *hell* broke loose. I just stood there at home plate. I made up my mind I wasn't going to retreat because they would have chased me all the way to the bleachers in center field. To be honest, I guess I was defying them because I knew absolutely that I was right. So I just stood there and never once looked at the stands. Oranges, tomatoes, and whatever hit the ground and splattered on my pants. Several bottles bounced off my shin guards, and a couple damn near hit my head. But nothing hit me directly. The good Lord was with me. Steve Basil and Harry Geisel were yelling at me to come out into the infield, but I'm thinking they could go to hell because they didn't stop those base runners. That's what caused the riot. It finally stopped when the cops came out; it took twenty minutes to clear the field of debris. When we started again, Henrich dribbled out to second base and the side was retired. That's always the way it works, it seems.

The next inning George Selkirk hit a drive down the line just like Henrich's. I called it foul. Selkirk walked from first base down to where the ball hit, looked at the spot for a minute, then turned around and trotted back to the plate. I was on fire. I mean, on *fire*. Oh, how I wanted to put that SOB out of the game for trying to show me up. He said, "Joe, I don't know about Tommy's ball, but mine was foul." I said, "Yes, and I should run your ass out of here right now, George, but that will start the bottles and fruit flying again. We are going to play this ball game, so get in there and hit." He flied out, and Detroit eventually won the game, 3–2.

When I telephoned Harridge to make my report, I told him the only reason I didn't run Selkirk was to avoid another barrage. The people had come to see a ball game, not to riot, and I didn't want to provoke something that might cause me to forfeit the game. Well, Harridge said, "Joe, I want to commend you for that. I want to congratulate you for using good judgment." The next day a sportswriter wrote a beautiful article about it. He called it the bravest thing he had ever seen on a ball field.

In September 1945 I got slugged by a player in Philadelphia. During the war there were a lot of players in the major leagues who never would have been there if the regulars hadn't gone into the service. The A's had one of them, Charlie "Greek" George. He was a habitual bellyacher, a real crybaby, a busher of the worst sort. The umpires in every league he had been in always had trouble with this fellow. Well, he was catching that day, jerking the ball, trying to fool me, and complaining. So I told him if he didn't shut up, I would run him. At the end of the tenth inning I was brushing off the plate when he hit me over the left eye. (He said I called him a Greek son of a bitch, but I never cursed a ballplayer in my life.) I staggered back but then went after him with my mask. I chased him all around in back of home plate until Charlie Berry and Cal Hubbard grabbed me—Hubbard wrapped those long arms around me. I'm yelling and cursing, and now I probably am calling him a Greek son of a bitch. It's a good thing I never caught him. If I'd have hit him with my mask, I might have killed him.

They finally got the Greek out of there. Blood was trickling from my eye, and the Philadelphia trainer told me I couldn't work anymore. I said, "The hell I can't. If that's his best punch, it's a good thing I didn't hit him." I finished the game and then called Harridge to make my report.

The next afternoon, before the game, I was called into the Philadelphia dressing room. Old Connie Mack, Lord have mercy on his soul, one of the great men and one of the great managers of the National Pastime, had also made a report to Harridge. Harridge then assigned Tom Connolly to hold a meeting. I didn't know anything about it. Well, there was Connie, his son Earl, the Greek, myself, and Connolly. I don't remember what Greek George said, but it was a very weak statement. My statement was emphatic: Mr. George was out of baseball for the rest of his life. I did all the umpires a favor.

There were also some humorous incidents. Like the time Cal Hubbard split his pants. We were working an exhibition game in Houston when all of a sudden everybody began to laugh—Cal, the catcher, the fans. I was out behind the pitcher, so I didn't know what was going on. Then Hubbard came out to me, carrying his protector and a great big mask. "Here, take it. I just split both cheeks." He had bent over to sweep the plate and split his pants. He was facing the grandstand, so the customers got the biggest laugh. I went behind the plate with his great big mask. If a foul ball would have hit me, I would have gotten killed.

Then there's the time Johnny Lindell ran over me in Yankee Stadium. Lindell hit a line drive that was caught. He was tearing around first base, going like hell, and I was standing there, telling him he was out. I tried to dodge him, and he tried to dodge me; but we both went the same way. The big bastard ran into me, and I went head over heels. When I came down, I was laughing to beat hell. He didn't hurt me. The Associated Press photo of that collision won the award for the best sports picture of the year.

One of the funniest things that happened to me took place in Boston. I was working third base and in the seventh inning called Bobby Doerr out on one of those real close plays; I was on top of the play, saw the tag clearly. But when Del Baker, the coach at third, and Doerr jumped all over me, those Boston fans went *crazy*. A woman sitting in the boxes got so excited she threw her shoe at me. It landed right at my feet; Jake Early, the Washington catcher, ran over and picked it up. I chased Baker, and that irritated them even more. Paper cups, everything, came flying from the stands. Out came Joe Cronin, who was managing the club. I could see that bulldog look on his face, his jaws flapping. I tried to move away from him, but he kept shouting. When he said, "You're a lousy umpire," I replied, "And you're a two-bit manager, so you get the hell out of here." That didn't help matters either. Well, Boston won the game, 1–0. As I started to walk off the field, this woman jumped out of the box to get her shoe. Early, who had taken the shoe into the dugout, knocked the high heel off it and stuck it in a bucket of water before throwing it out to her. When she picked up that shoe—I have never heard such profanity from a woman. The newspapers made a big thing of it. The next morning the headlines in the *Globe* said: INCENSED GIRL PARTISAN TOSSES SHOES AT OFFICIAL.

Two of the most important things that happened to baseball during my career were the beginning of night baseball and racial integration. And I worked historic games in each one of them.

I saw the beginning of night baseball. I worked one of the first night games, maybe the first, in the American Association. The owner of the Kansas City club was from Des Moines, Iowa, where the very first night game was played. He installed lights in Muehlbach Field, the biggest park in the AA. The lighting there and in other parks in the league was terrible. You could hardly see. It was great, though, for the people who had to work during the day; it gave them a chance to see a game now and then. Night ball began in the American League in 1939, and I worked the first one that was played in Chicago. I was working with Harry Geisel and Red Ormsby. Geisel, who was to be behind the bat, had never worked a night game before, and he was really worried about it. He kept asking me silly questions like: "Joe, will it blind you?" Finally, I said, "Harry, I'll umpire the damned game. You take my turn, I'll take yours." It was a great game, everything went fine. Edgar Smith beat Bob Feller, 1–0, in eleven innings.

The difference in the night games between the majors and the minors was unbelievable. The lighting was wonderful in Chicago. There were a few dark spots, but the engineers soon worked that out.

After the game I was asked about the lighting. I told them I had no trouble seeing the ball, none whatsoever.

I also worked the first night All-Star game in history. That was 1943, Shibe Park in Philadelphia. The Yankees had six guys on the All-Star squad, but the American League manager, Joe McCarthy, didn't play any of them because of criticism that he showed favoritism to his own players in other All-Star games. It didn't make any difference; the American League won, 5–3.

I retired from umpiring before there were many Negroes in the major leagues, but I was behind the plate the first game that Larry Doby played. We didn't get any special instructions from league headquarters about him. I had read that Bill Veeck signed him for Cleveland and that he was going to play this particular day [July 5, 1947] in Chicago. Doby came up to pinch-hit for the pitcher [Bryan Stephens] in the seventh inning against Eddie Smith. He swung and missed at three straight pitches—two of them were way high and the other a foot outside. In the pregame warm-ups he replaced Joe Gordon at second base. It was pathetic—looked like he belonged in the Western League. But he went on to be a pretty good ballplayer.

I was fined twice by the league office. The first time was in 1945, and it happened like this. Bill Summers and I were going to fly to Detroit after a series in Boston. The day before we were going to leave, we got a telegram from Harridge instructing us to accompany the Boston club to Detroit by train. Harridge wouldn't okay a plane trip unless it was an emergency. Summers decided to take the train, but I said the hell with that. We already had plane reservations, and I was planning to meet my wife in Detroit. Besides, you'd catch a train in Boston about six o'clock, travel all night, and arrive in Detroit about an hour before the game. Umpires are just like players: They don't feel like going on the field after traveling all night. So Summers went with the Red Sox on the train, and I flew. As it turned out, Summers and the Red Sox got to the ball park just before game time. A few days later I got a letter from Harridge reprimanding me for not following instructions and notifying me that I had been fined $200. Tommy Connolly, who lived near Boston, had told Harridge. So I asked Summers, "How the hell did Connolly know I took the plane?" "I told him," he said. "Thanks," I said.

The second fine happened after I put Bob Swift of the Tigers out of a game in Philadelphia in late September 1947. In the first game of a doubleheader, somebody hit a fair ball down the line—it wasn't even close. Swift started screaming, "Foul ball," so I tossed him. Steve O'Neill came out, complaining that he only had one catcher left. I told him that was his problem. Well, O'Neill worked on Bill Summers between games, trying to get him to let Swift go down to the bullpen in uniform for the second game. Earl Mack of the A's agreed to it, but I refused. As far as I was concerned, he was out for the day. But I told Summers that since he was going to be umpire in chief for the second game, he could do whatever he wanted. Wouldn't you know, Bill let him suit up. A few days later in Boston I got a telegram asking me to call Harridge immediately. Harridge was mad. He wanted to know why I let Swift remain on the field. I blew up. I told him that I was sick and tired of all the crap and that he could ask Summers, who had gone to Chicago, what had gone on in the dressing room. Harridge said, "I don't like your tone of expression. I don't like your answer. I'm fining you." Then he hung up on me.

That was the end of my career. I was scheduled to work the World Series that year. In fact, I had been sent to Boston to work with Bill McGowan and Bill Grieve because it was traditional to have the Series umpires work together the last few days of the season. But the call for the Series never came. And that winter I got a letter from Harridge informing me that I was not in his plans for the next season. That was the way I was released from the American League after eleven years. I had no recourse. Just like Ernie Stewart. He got a dirty deal. There isn't any question about it. And I got the same damned thing. That was the end. But I didn't really give a damn. I was fed up with it all anyhow.

It was absolutely disgraceful how umpires were treated during World War II. Salaries were frozen. I was making $8,000 to 8,500 plus $100 a month for expenses like hotels, meals, and cleaning uniforms. We didn't get one penny increase for expenses until Bill McGowan talked to Harridge and Connolly during the last year of the war. Then we got another $50 to $100 for expenses. Hell, all we got for working the All-Star game was a $25 government bond. Big deal. Yet all the ballplayers lived high on the hog; everything was paid for them.

The front office wasn't the best to work with. The umpire in chief, Tommy Connolly, was a tale carrier. I think Joe Cronin will probably go down as the worst president the American League ever had. I used to have all the respect in the world for him, and the umpires were tickled to death when he came in as president; but he turned out to be a horse's ass to the umpires. And with Harridge it was always favoritism and politics. When we were in Chicago, we had to go down to the league office and sit there waiting to see if Harridge wanted to talk to us. Sometimes we'd sit there until eleven-thirty, and he wouldn't even open the door to say good morning. We did that every morning for years. It wasn't necessary, and I skipped going down there quite a few times. It was just like me taking my dog out for a walk every morning.

The jealousy that existed between the umpires in the American League was the damnedest thing you could ever imagine. McGowan and Summers hated each other; those two caused a lot of turmoil. There were only a few umpires I didn't like. Steve Basil was always playing up to Connolly. Basil, who was a Catholic like I am, never went inside a church unless Connolly was in town, and then they would go together. And he'd run to Connolly and Harridge with everything like Bill Summers.

I got off on the wrong foot with Bill McGowan. After the first game I worked with him in Detroit he said, "You haven't asked me for any advice, Joe. I guess you're one of those kind who knows it all. You call your balls and strikes like some punk from the Eastern League." I said, "Bill, I want to tell you something. I've been umpiring for a good many years. I was purchased by this league for more money than you ever knew existed. I've been calling balls and strikes the same way wherever I've been, and I'm pretty goddamned good. You're supposed to be the ace of umpires; but to me you're a pain in the ass, and if I ever ask you anything, it will be over my dead body." But I have to say this: McGowan was the best umpire in the league.

It was also difficult for my wife, Dolly, to be married to an umpire. One time in St. Louis we were nearly attacked outside the park. You always had a rough day in St. Louis. The Browns didn't draw well, but their fans played, managed, umpired, did everything. One afternoon Dolly met Bill Grieve and me with the car after a ball game. As I started to drive off, this guy jumped on the running board and started giving us hell. Dolly, who was sitting in the back seat, hit his face and hands with her purse until he finally fell off. We got out of there right quick. That's the closest I ever came to having a fight off the field.

And it was hard for her to sit in the stands and hear the abuse directed at me. One time in Cleveland—it seems I was always in Cleveland—we were booed on every call. (I don't know why they sent me to Cleveland so much. It got so the Cleveland fans started booing the minute I walked on the field; they didn't have to wait for the announcer to give my name. Every time they'd boo me like that I'd just tip my hat.) Anyway, this particular day some fellow was really giving it to me—calling me an SOB and everything else under the sun. Finally, as I was walking off the field at the end of the game, he yelled, "Rue, you damned son of a bitch rat, why don't you go into your hole?" With that, Dolly yelled, "Don't you dare call my husband a rat." He turned around, amazed: "Why, lady, I didn't know that Joe Rue was your husband. Why didn't you tell me?" She just turned around and walked away.

On the other hand, umpires couldn't have been treated better than we were by an undertaker named Arthur Donnelly in St Louis. He was a great baseball fan and quite an umpire baiter, always yelling and screaming at the calls. One day there was a close play at third base that went against the home team. The fans started throwing bottles and stuff out of the stands at Red Ormsby. One of the bottles hit Red in the head. They had to take him to the hospital; he was in pretty bad shape.

Well, Mr. Donnelly went to the hospital to see Red and repented. He vowed he would never again yell at umpires. To show his respect for umpires, he arranged to have his chauffeur pick us up at the hotel in a big Packard and drive us to the ball park; after the game the limousine would be there to take us to the hotel. If your wife was with you, Bart, the chauffeur, would drive her around the city—he was at her disposal for shopping, whatever. He did that for both leagues, so Bart had almost a full-time job driving umpires. Donnelly felt so strongly about it that he put a provision in his will that the limousine service would continue after his death. Needless to say, we appreciated that very much.

After I left baseball, I did a lot of sales work. I was always a good salesman—whether for Du Pont, Acme White Lead and Color Works, or General Tire Company. Then I hit the jackpot in Las Vegas. I went there with the proverbial fifty cents in my pocket and turned it into a quarter of a million dollars. And umpiring helped me do it.

Las Vegas was in the old Sunset League. The league was having financial problems and couldn't afford to pay umpires to travel, so they went to hometown umpires to complete the schedule. I was new in town but had gone out to the ball games, so people knew who I was. The business manager of the Vegas team asked me to umpire. I figured it was a good way to get some publicity to help my business, so I agreed. I signed a contract for $1 a game. (When George Trautman, the commissioner of the minor leagues, saw that contract, he called to find out what was going on. I was probably the lowest-paid umpire in history.) I hired an outdoor artist to paint my Mayflower moving van. The body was green, for the grass, with a yellow playing field; at home plate there was a player sliding home, a catcher, and me as the umpire. I had a protector on one arm, a mask on the other, with my hands spread out wide. The sign said: YOU'RE SAFE WHEN YOU MOVE WITH RUE. It was one of the greatest business promotions ever.

There have been changes in the game since my day. Players today can't hit or field as well as the old-timers. The reason for it is overexpansion—too many minor league players are in the majors now. After they enlarged the leagues, ordinary ballplayers became superstars. And they're getting such big salaries now some clubs might go broke. I don't begrudge any man his money. I've always said a player is worth what he can draw at the gate, but hell, some of the guys today couldn't draw flies even if they had syrup poured on them.

I think it's good the umpires have started to get better salaries and have gotten away from that Klem-Connolly nonsense about equipment. Let them use whatever equipment or position they want so long as they can make the calls. And I'm glad to see them use four umpires. That gives more fellows a chance to umpire, although I wonder how umpires stay in shape these days since all they do is stand around. Of course, there are fewer rhubarbs today because there just isn't any reason for an umpire to be out of position anymore. But they also got accuracy with just three of us working. Umpires are more recognized now than in my time, and I guess that's all right. I guess I'm just an old-fashioned guy because I still believe that nobody ever paid to see an umpire perform and that the less you see of an umpire, the more successful he is.

I'm not as much of a fan as I was before I started umpiring. As an umpire you can't really appreciate a ball game. You have to concentrate so much on your job that you just don't enjoy the game. I said many times that when I got out of umpiring, I wouldn't go near a ball park as long as I lived. But I have. Still, I look at the umpires, not the ballplayers. I can't help it. I get a big kick out of watching the umpires, anticipating what they are going to do. And when I see a great young pitcher like Mark Fidrych, I think of how I'd like to stand behind the plate and see his stuff. I guess it's only natural. Once an umpire, always an umpire.

Umpiring has been good to me. I've been very fortunate. It even got me into the movies: I was the umpire in *The Stratton Story*—had to join the Screen Actors' Guild, got $175 a week. I gave between twenty-eight and thirty years, the most important time of my life, to baseball. When I think of the hard way I came up, I wonder how a man could go through all that. But really, I loved every minute of it, and I would do it all over again because I love the game. The only thing I would change would be working with a couple of umpires.

George Pipgras. Courtesy National Baseball Library &
Archive, Cooperstown, N.Y.

George Pipgras

⊗⊗⊗

George William Pipgras
Born: Ida Grove, Iowa, December 20, 1899
Height: 6′ 2″
Weight: 210
Playing career: minor leagues, 1921–22, 1925–26, 1935; American
　　　　　　League, 1923–24, 1927–34
Umpiring career: Eastern League, also known as the N.Y.-Penn
　　　　　　League (A), 1936–August 3, 1938; American
　　　　　　League, August 4, 1938–1945
No-hit games: Dick Fowler, September 9, 1945
All-Star games: 1940
World Series (games): 1944 (6)

I am as proud of my record as an umpire as my achievements as a
player. The thing I loved about umpiring was the honesty of it. The
fellows I worked with went out there every day and gave an honest
decision on every call. Like the umpire says: "I might have booted it,
but I called it like I saw it." Fans and players boo and abuse umpires,
but there isn't one umpire in the history of baseball who has ever
been proved guilty of being dishonest. I am very proud to have been
an umpire.

I don't go to ball games anymore. I haven't for years. I used to go
down to Tampa to see Bill Summers, and he'd say, "Come on, let's go
to the ball game." But I wouldn't go. I had no interest in the game. I

guess it's like any other profession. When you lose the active part of it, you want no part of it. I loved baseball. I enjoyed playing, and I went into umpiring to stay in it. But when it was over, it was over.

I was born on a farm outside Ida Grove, Iowa, on December 20, 1899. There were six kids in the family; I was number three. When I was seven, we moved to a very small town, Schleswig, where my dad went into the farm machinery business. I played baseball in high school. Baseball was the only sport we had in that little school. After graduating, I went to work in my dad's meat market, and then, in December 1917, I went into the Army. I was in the Army for the rest of World War I, spent nine months in Europe.

When I got out, I went up to Fulda, a little country town in Minnesota, to play semipro baseball. From there I went into professional ball. I was scouted in a strange way. Sometimes, when I was pitching, the train that ran on the tracks out behind center field would stop for a while. I didn't know it at the time, but a man by the name of Frank Flynn, who was the conductor, was scouting me. He loved baseball, so he'd stop that train to watch the game. I hope the passengers were baseball fans.

The White Sox signed me and farmed me out to Saginaw, Michigan, in the Class B Michigan-Ontario League in 1921. I had a good fastball, but I couldn't get it over the plate. I was wild throughout my career; I always walked a lot of batters. I was so wild Saginaw released me after a short time. Then Frank Flynn recommended me to Madison, South Dakota, an independent team in the Class D Dakota League. I finished the season there.

Then the Yankees bought my contract, but they transferred me to the Boston Red Sox, who farmed me out in 1922 to Charleston, South Carolina, in the South Atlantic League. That winter the Red Sox traded me back to the Yankees along with Herb Pennock for seven players. I had had a pretty good year in Charleston, so the Yankees brought me up. That was moving pretty fast—from the minors to the majors in two years.

When I got to spring training in 1923, I wondered how I was ever going to make the club. The Yankees had a great pitching staff—Bob Shawkey, Waite Hoyt, "Bullet" Joe Bush, Sam Jones, and, of course, Herb Pennock. I was with them in '24 and '25 and then was sent back down. I was farmed out to Nashville in the Southern League in 1925 and then went to St. Paul in the American Association in 1926. I went back up to the Yankees to stay in 1927.

In my opinion the 1927 Yankees were the greatest team ever assembled. I don't think any club in history could beat them. There

never was a one-two punch that could match Babe Ruth and Lou
Gehrig. Any team with those two had a big head start. We also had
Earle Combs, Joe Dugan, Tony Lazzeri, and Bob Meusel—every one
of them was a great ballplayer. The pitching was outstanding—Waite
Hoyt, Herb Pennock, Urban Shocker, Wilcy Moore. But it was the
hitting that was so great on that team. We'd be behind in the late innings and just know that Ruth or Gehrig or Lazzeri or somebody
would hit one out to win the game. It was a pleasure pitching for a
team like that.

Connie Mack had a real good ball club over in Philadelphia at the
same time. They had Jimmy Foxx, Al Simmons, Mule Haas, Mickey
Cochrane, Jimmy Dykes, Lefty Grove, George Earnshaw, and lots of
other great players. They won the league championship three years
[1929–31] and the World Series twice [1929–30]. The A's were very
good, but the '27 Yankees were the best I ever saw. There wasn't a
weak spot on that club.

Babe Ruth was the best ballplayer I ever saw. He was outstanding
at everything. Everybody knows how he could hit. But he could also
throw real well and could steal a base for you if you needed it. And of
course, he had been a great pitcher with the Red Sox before coming
to the Yankees. What more could you want from a ballplayer?

Bob Meusel was the most underrated ballplayer I know. He was a
real good hitter and an outstanding fielder. And he had the strongest
arm I ever saw. One time Ty Cobb was on third base with one out.
Somebody hit a fly ball to Meusel out in left. Meusel caught the ball
and held onto it, daring Cobb to go. Wally Schang, our catcher, yelled
down to Cobb, "Come on, Ty. Come in." Ordinarily Cobb would have
tagged up and scored on a fly like that. But he just stood there, glar-
ing. Nobody was foolish enough to challenge Bob Meusel's arm.

We won 110 games that year [.714] and finished 19 games ahead of
the A's. That was the year Ruth hit sixty home runs and Gehrig had
175 RBIs. Then we beat the Pirates four straight games in the World
Series.

The biggest thrill of my baseball career was pitching the second
game of the 1927 Series. I was surprised because I didn't think I was
going to start at all. But late in the first game Miller Huggins asked me
if I could pitch tomorrow. I told him, "Sure," so he said, "Okay, get a
good night's sleep." Well, I spent most of the night figuring out how I
was going to pitch to those big hitters in the Pirates' lineup—guys like
Pie Traynor and the Waner brothers, Paul and Lloyd. I was a little
nervous when I got to the ball park, and I got off to a shaky start.
Lloyd Waner hit a lead-off triple and scored to put the Pirates ahead.

We finally beat them, 6–2. I was real fast that day; I don't think I threw but about three or four curveballs the whole game.

My best year in the big leagues was 1928. I led the league with twenty-four wins. We won the pennant and swept the St. Louis Cardinals in the World Series. Once again I started the second game of the Series. I pitched against Grover Cleveland Alexander. Alex wasn't right that day. He was wild, gave up lots of hits, and went out in the third inning. Gehrig hit one of the longest home runs off him I ever saw—off the scoreboard in Yankee Stadium. We won, 9–3. I could tell when we got together for the pregame picture that Alex was either drunk or had a wicked hangover: I reached out to shake with him, and he missed my hand by about a foot.

We had a lot of guys hurt going into that Series. Combs and Pennock couldn't play, and Lazzeri was lame. But Ruth and Gehrig had an unbelievable series. Between them they had seven home runs [Ruth three, Gehrig four], thirteen RBIs [Ruth four, Gehrig nine], scored fourteen runs [Ruth nine, Gehrig five], and hit about .600 [Ruth .625, Gehrig .545].

The Yankees sold me to the Boston Red Sox in 1933 for $100,000. That was a lot of money in those days. I didn't much like the idea of going from a winning team to a losing one, but that's the way it goes. As it turned out, I broke my arm in August, and that was the end of my playing career.

It happened in Detroit. I had no balls and two strikes on Frank Doljack, so I thought I'd waste one on him up high. When I let go of the ball, my elbow snapped. I could feel it pop. A bone specialist in Chicago operated on me twice; he took seven pieces of bone out of my elbow. He told me that the muscles in my right arm had become so strong because of pitching that they just snapped the bone when I broke off the pitch. It sounds incredible: I broke my arm throwing a baseball.

I went on the inactive list for the 1934 season. My arm just wouldn't come around. I went down to Nashville in 1935, thinking the hot weather would help bring it around, but it didn't work. Three of the fingers on my pitching hand would always go dead on me. I could only pitch about two or three innings before the fingers would go numb. Of course, that would have been all right today; I could have been a relief man. But in those days they wanted starters, so I knew I was through as a pitcher.

I was kind of depressed. Baseball had been my whole life. I didn't know what to do now that I was finished. So one day, when I was hunting with Mr. Tom Yawkey, the owner of the Red Sox, at his plantation in South Carolina, I talked to him about it. Tom Yawkey was a fine man. He was a millionaire, but he was a regular guy who really cared about his players and the game of baseball. Anyway, he said, "How would you like to go into umpiring? You know the game. If you want to go into umpiring, I'll try to find a place for you." I told him I wouldn't mind it one bit.

With Mr. Yawkey's sponsorship, the American League signed me to a contract and sent me to the Class A Eastern League for the 1936 season. I got paid $300 a month for umpiring. I had made $12,500 as a ballplayer. The American League paid me a little extra. I think it was $40 a month. You couldn't live on that because you had to pay your own room and board. Of course, you couldn't afford to stay in very good places. But I didn't mind the money too much because I knew I would have to take a smaller salary in the minors.

There were several former major leaguers trying to make it as umpires at the time. Charlie Berry and Eddie Rommel were backed by Connie Mack. The White Sox sponsored Jocko Conlan. Conlan, Rommel, and I were in the same league, and all three of us went up to the majors in 1938.

Being in the minors as an umpire was upside down from what it was like as a player. It was just like the Nashville manager said: "There is no applause for an umpire." Oh, it was rough in the minor leagues in those days. Sometimes it wasn't too safe to be an umpire. The fans thought nothing of throwing bottles at us. The police were supposed to protect us, but they couldn't do too much for you.

One night Jocko Conlan and I were in Williamsport, Pennsylvania. We had a 1-0 ball game and congratulated ourselves on working a good game. But the home team had lost. As we left the ball park, I found out that a bunch of fans had put a pile of newspapers underneath my Chevy coupe and set it on fire.

Another time, in York, Pennsylvania, Francis Connolly and I gave a newspaperman and another fellow a ride out to the ball park. We told them we couldn't guarantee their safety, but they said nobody would bother us. Well, I had a controversial call on a home run. At that time the rule on home runs said the ball was fair or foul depending on where you last saw it, not where it left the ball park. This particular ball was probably ten feet fair when it went out, but it curved foul, so that's what I called it. They mobbed us after the game. We ran for the car and rolled up the windows. As we drove off, a guy threw a brick at us. It went through the window and hit the newspaperman in the back of the head. He was out cold until we got back to the hotel.

I spent two and a half years in the Eastern League. Mr. [Thomas H.] Richardson sold me to the American League in August 1938. I went up to replace Harry Geisel, who had broken his arm. I joined Bill McGowan and Joe Rue in Chicago on August 6. I worked third base the whole series between the White Sox and Washington, then laid over and joined Cal Hubbard and George Quinn. The first time I worked the plate was on the tenth. Eldon Auker and Thornton Lee were the starting pitchers, but neither had much that day. It was a hitter's game; Chicago beat Detroit, 8–7. When Geisel came back, I stayed on as the twelfth man. I'd go as part of a three-man crew to wherever they had an important series.

My first contract as an American League umpire was for $4,000. I also got $1,200 or $1,500 a year toward expenses. The league paid only for train fare. The most I ever made as an umpire was $10,000. I never did make as much as I did playing ball. That didn't bother me. I guess I was used to that because when I played, Ruth and Gehrig were getting the big money. I wasn't jealous. I was glad they did make good money because they were the great ballplayers.

I worked with Bill Summers for five consecutive years. He helped me an awful lot with learning how to umpire. When I went to spring training in 1939, Herb Pennock said to Summers, "Help George as much as you can." (Herb was a very good friend of mine; even though he was left-handed, he taught me to throw a curveball.) Bill told me that. As a ballplayer I knew the fundamentals of baseball and pretty much knew the basic umpire positions. But I didn't know the inside stuff. Bill told me how to get a better position behind the plate and on the bases, how to anticipate certain plays, things like that. Ballplayers don't really know how umpires work. And I found out that they don't know the rules either. Even some of the managers didn't know the rules. Guys like Bucky Harris and Jimmy Dykes did, though.

My experience as a player helped me most in dealing with the crowds and the big games. I was used to the major league crowds and the big stadiums, so I never had any worries about going behind the plate. I didn't get butterflies umpiring the World Series because I played in four Series. Being a player was a big help to me because I knew what to expect. I'd been through it all before.

I didn't have any special problems umpiring against guys I had played with. They didn't expect any favors, and they didn't give me any special treatment. I gave no breaks and got no breaks. They just treated me as an umpire, and that was it. I found out they could treat you pretty rough, too.

There was a difference in that between the American and National leagues. The National League would go after a rookie umpire right away, but the American League would go along with him for the first year. Nobody would say anything to him. Then, the second year, they'd start on you. The third year they'd either make or break you.

They really tested me my third year. I threw out seventeen men in Chicago in a game between the White Sox and the Browns. Mike Tresh, the Chicago catcher, started bickering too much on balls and strikes, so I had to throw him out. After Tresh was gone, the White Sox bench started bickering, so I started picking off the deadwood. You'd think it would have quieted down after I ran Tresh, but they kept jumping on me, so I kept bouncing them off the bench. Then the St. Louis club started after me, so I started picking off some of them. After the game Bill Summers said, "Well, I'll say one thing. You didn't show any partiality."

The next morning Mr. Harridge, the league president, called me. He said, "George, have you gone crazy?" I said, "No, Mr. Harridge, I haven't gone crazy. They are going to leave me alone out there, or I'm not going to be there." He said, "But don't you think you were a little rough on them?" I said, "No, sir. Not at all." He said, "But, George, *seventeen* men." I said, "All that yelling from the bench is unnecessary. I never read anywhere where it said you had to yell at the umpire in order to play baseball."

It's important for umpires to have the support of the front office. Harridge was pretty good at fining and suspending the players, but we thought that at times he could have been a little stronger.

I think I was tougher on the ballplayers than the fellows who never played ball. I was never rough on the umpires as a player; in all those years I was never put out of a ball game. That's why I thought umpiring would be okay. I could never quite get it straight in my mind why a ballplayer or a manager would go so far as to be thrown out of a ball game. So, when I started umpiring, I made up my mind to control that ball game even if I didn't last fifteen minutes. If a ballplayer got rough with me, I threw him out. I did it in the minor leagues, and I did the same thing in the major leagues.

Bill Summers was a great umpire, and he wouldn't take anything from ballplayers. They knew it, and they respected him. I figured if they respected Summers as strong as he was in putting them out and as tough a discipline as he held on the field, I wasn't wrong in my thinking on it. I remember before the 1944 World Series Ziggy Sears was complaining about umpires taking too much from the ballplayers. Bill McGowan pointed to me and said, "There is a fellow who will take nothing from them. We need more like that."

Umpires who took too much caused you trouble. When Summers and I went into a town, we always knew which umpires had been in there before us. As soon as ballplayers started giving us trouble, we'd bounce one or two of them out of there. Then they would settle down.

The secret of umpiring is discipline. The good umpire is the man who holds discipline on the ball field. If you run the ball game, the players will respect you and have confidence in you. You have to teach them to have confidence in you. I'd rather have a ballplayer say, "He is not a good fellow, but he is a good umpire" than to say, "He is a good fellow, but he is not a very good umpire."

I got a crew of my own in my sixth year. I had Ernie Stewart and Hal Weafer. Ernie had gotten in a jam with a senior umpire, so I took him. We got along all right. After he got straightened around and got a little confidence in himself, why, he was a very good umpire. He stayed with me the balance of the season and then moved on.

I don't know why or how he got fired. After he got fired, he called me from Cleveland, wanting to know if I could help him out. I was in Detroit at the time. I told him that I had saved his job once and couldn't do it again. Of course, I didn't know what it was all about. He didn't tell me. I never talked to anyone who did know. I worked with quite a few different umpires, and it was never mentioned. If anybody knew what happened, he didn't talk about it. I hear rumors, of course, but I don't believe in rumors. I only knew it had something to do with him trying to get more money for umpires. I raised that issue once myself; I was told to leave it alone. It couldn't have had anything to do with ability because he was a good umpire.

Everyone who stayed in the major leagues very long was a good umpire. You can't be too bad and stay around. If I was pitching, I'd want Bill McGowan to work my game. I never saw him miss one. Bill Summers was a great ball-and-strike man, too. So was Cal Hubbard. But Summers was not as good on the bases as McGowan. McGowan could do either one and do it very, very well. Some guys could work the bases better than the plate, but they all were good umpires.

I liked the plate better than the bases. Most guys didn't, but I would rather work the plate anytime. I don't know if being a pitcher had anything to do with it. It just seemed easier than the bases. I really liked those 1–0 or 2–1 games. They are the easiest to work because you had two good pitchers out there. The rough ones were those 18–17 games.

I was a hitter's umpire. Tommy Connolly used to say that Bill Dinneen and I were the only two former pitchers who were hitter's umpires. Eddie Rommel was not a hitter's umpire, but I was. I had a small strike zone. I made them come in pretty good with that ball. I was death on the high strike, and I made them come up to the knees on the low pitch.

I drew an imaginary box over the plate. If the ball went in the box, it had to be a strike. Of course, you still had to work your corners. Wildness never bothered me. For me the curveball on the outside corner was the toughest pitch to call. The guys who had that good curve, like Feller, Ted Lyons, and Tommy Bridges, were rough. Of course, there were really no easy ones to call back there.

I will never forget the night Bob Feller and Eldon Auker of the Browns got into it in Cleveland. The Cleveland ball park was down by the lake, and sometimes those insects—they called them Canadian soldiers—would come in off the lake. They looked like big white butterflies. That night it looked like the air was full of snowflakes. We went eleven innings, 1–0, with Feller and his good fastball and Auker with his underhand pitches. I never had such a headache in all my life as I did that night, straining to find that white ball through those butterflies. The Cleveland catcher, Rollie Hemsley, said, "Don't worry about it if you miss them, George. Nobody can see them tonight."

I saw so many great pitchers over the years it's hard to say who was the best. Waite Hoyt, Red Ruffing, Lefty Gomez, Lefty Grove, Bob Feller, Ted Lyons, Herb Pennock, Charlie Root—they were all great pitchers.

The fastest pitcher I ever saw? I saw Lefty Grove and Bob Feller in their prime. Those two were quick, I'll tell you. It's hard to believe anybody could have been faster than they were. I batted against Walter Johnson when I broke into the league. He had been around a long time and had slowed down quite a bit. I took two quick called strikes and stepped out of the batter's box. Muddy Ruel, the Washington catcher, was grinning at me. I said, "Muddy, I didn't see those pitches." He laughed. "Don't let it worry you. He's thrown some that Cobb and a lot of other guys are still looking for." If that was Johnson past his prime, then I'd say he was the fastest pitcher of all time.

Ted Williams was by far the best hitter I ever saw from behind the plate. He would take a ball just off the inside or outside corner and never even flinch. He had the best eyes I ever saw. I never saw him swing at a bad ball. It's like someone said: "If he don't swing, just call it a ball." And he was good to work with. Never said anything to you, never looked back at you to show you up. Jimmy Foxx was like that, too. He'd say, "You can miss the first two; just don't miss the third one." Foxx never said boo to anybody. Of course, the good fellows never give you any trouble. It's the mediocre ones, the ones on the fence. Those are the fellows who give you trouble.

Joe Gordon was another good guy. He was a fine boy, never gave the umpires any problem. But I ran him the only time he was ever put out of a ball game. It was in 1942. The Yankees and the Tigers were tied in the twelfth inning, when Gordon tried to score on a base hit. He slid into home, and I called him out. That was a big game, and he thought he beat the throw, so when he got up, he pushed me. I said, "Joe, you are through for the day." He just walked off. When the next inning started, he headed onto the field. I said, "Joe, you do not belong out there." He turned around and walked off without saying anything. I ran into him down in Lakeland after we were both out of baseball, and he asked if I remembered putting him out. I told him I did. He said, "Well, it was my fault. I never should have done what I did." He knew he'd done wrong. Touching an umpire is an automatic ejection.

Bucky Harris was a tremendous manager and a wonderful man, but Miller Huggins was my favorite manager because I came in under him. He had a lot of temperamental guys on that Yankee club, but he handled them. He was a little bitty guy, but he had an iron fist. He had plenty of intestinal fortitude, that fellow.

I saw Huggins go out on the ball field only once. He went after Bill Guthrie, the big guy who used those "dems" and "dose." One day Whitey Witt was on first base. Somebody hit a line drive to the shortstop, who threw the ball into the stands, trying to double Whitey off first. Guthrie motioned Whitey to go on to second base. Whitey said, "No. I get two bases. I'm entitled to go to third." Guthrie said, "I am giving you two bases. One dis away [pointing toward first] and one dat away [pointing to second]." Well, they had a big rhubarb about it. Huggins went out and said, "Bill, you are wrong. He goes to third base." Finally, Guthrie put Whitey out of the ball game. Then he said, "Mr. Witt, take da batboy wid ya." Oh, that made Huggins mad. Guthrie was gone the next year.

I don't believe in that rhubarb business. That stuff should go. Baseball is the only sport that permits that sort of thing. Football and basketball coaches can't go on the field. There is a rule in baseball that no player or manager shall approach an umpire on a judgment play and that only a captain or the manager can approach an umpire if an interpretation of a rule is involved. But they don't enforce it. I took that up with Tom Connolly, and he said, "Well, it has always been that way, George."

I said, "I know it has always been that way; but there is a rule in the book, and it doesn't have to be that way." I don't know why they don't enforce it. It would help baseball. You don't need rhubarbs to put life in that game. The Ruths and Gehrigs put life in the game.

Yes, I kicked some. We all missed some. Umpires are human the same as everybody else. When you kick one, you can't let it get to you. You know you kicked it, but you can't reverse it. It has to be final. If an umpire could reverse his partner, the ballplayers would crucify them. They'd be appealing on every judgment play. If you blow one, you just blow it, that's all. It hurts an umpire as much as the player when he blows one. But umpires make a lot fewer errors than ballplayers. I've told some players that. I said, "If you booted as many as I do, you'd be fielding way up in the nine nineties."

I admitted it when I kicked one. The good ballplayers and managers would understand. Bill Dickey was great about that. One time I missed a pitch. He said, "What was wrong with that ball?" I said, "Nothing, I just missed it." He never said another word.

I blew one on Pinky Higgins one day in Detroit. He caught a line drive, stepped on third, and threw to first for a triple play. I called the guy who slid back to third safe, so he didn't get his triple play. It was a very close play, but I knew I blew it. Pinky was good about it. He just said, "George, it was a close play, but I hit the bag before he did." That was all. He was a great guy anyway. Never quarreled with an umpire too much; very little, if any. I don't ever remember him getting chased.

Jimmy Dykes was like that, too. He had a reputation for being rough on umpires, but I never found him to be that way. One time, when he came charging out, I said, "I kicked it, Jimmy. That's all. Let's get on with the game." He just went on back to the dugout. See, most managers come out to protect their players. They can't see the close plays from in the dugout. They just go out there to show their player they will back them up and to keep them from getting the thumb. Umpires know that; we understood what they were doing.

I never did resent all the booing and yelling. You don't hear a lot of it. It is strange, but you concentrate so much on your ball game that you don't hear too much of it. But that all goes with the game and being an umpire. What I did resent was a ballplayer or manager coming out and cursing me and including my mother and father. That hurt. I think it hurts every umpire who gets that. You can't help but take it personally when they include your family. That's rough. Of course, they're not out there long when they do that. They are gone. But then, after you put them out, they really give it to you. They figure they're fined anyway, so they really unload.

I got it real good in Cleveland one day. Roy Cullenbine stepped out of the box, kicking on a strike I had called on him. Finally, I said, "There is only one place where you can hit, and that is up to the plate. You better get back up there." He said, "I'll get up there when I get good and ready." So I motioned for the pitcher to pitch. He threw it right down the middle, and I said, "Strike Three. You're out!" Well, we had a little argument. Lou Boudreau came out wanting to know if I had put Cullenbine out of the ball game. I told him, "No, as far as I am concerned, he can still play right field. But he is out on a third strike." That happened in the third inning, and those 60,000 fans didn't see the rest of the ball game. I guess I was the only thing they could see out there because they really gave it to me.

The next day a Cleveland sportswriter wrote a big story about it with the headline: MAJOR LEAGUE UMPIRE APPLIES MINOR LEAGUE RULES. I ran into him when I went to the ball park the next day. I said, "I want to ask you a question. Where do you buy the minor league rule books? If you find one, buy me one, and I'll reimburse you. As far as I know there is only one baseball rule book, and it applies to the minors and the majors." Just then the Cleveland business manager came by. He said, "You only made one mistake yesterday, George." I said, "What's that?" He said, "You didn't call strike three loud enough."

One night I thought we were going to have to forfeit a game in Cleveland. Bill Summers was working the plate, so he was in charge. The Tigers were in for a big series. Some guy threw a box or basket full of empty pop bottles from the top tier of the stands and hit the Detroit catcher, Birdie Tebbetts, in the back of the neck. I thought Tebbetts was dead. I thought they had killed him. They finally took him off to the clubhouse. That started it. The Cleveland fans started calling the Tigers crybabies, and of course, the players started hollering back at them. Then all kinds of stuff came flying out of the stands onto the field. We announced over the mike that we would forfeit the ball game if they didn't quit. Most of the time that would stop it, but they kept it up quite awhile.

I saw the guy who dropped the basket of bottles. I recognized him by the striped sweater he had on, so I pointed him out to the policemen. Well, the police made a mistake. They should have taken the guy to jail, but instead, they took him into the Tigers' clubhouse. Then they brought Tebbetts in. Birdie would fight at the drop of a hat, and I understand he gave the fellow a few pretty good licks. Would you believe the guy turned around and sued the Detroit ball club because Birdie Tebbetts hit him? After almost killing him? I guess the customer is always right.

One night in Chicago a fellow threw a bottle at Bill Summers and hit him in the groin. The usher saw it, so he told the police who did it and they took the guy downtown. The next morning Summers and I had to go to court. I'll never forget this. The guy admitted that he threw the bottle. So the judge said to Summers, "What would happen in the case of a ballplayer hitting an umpire?" Summers said, "He would be fined a thousand dollars and suspended for one year." The judge spun around in his chair about three times and then fined the guy $25. As we walked out, the judge kept looking at us; I looked back when we got to the door, and he was still looking at us. He knew that we were calling him every name in the book. It turned out that the guy who threw the bottle was the son of the city water commissioner. There's your politics.

I found that the big games were the easiest games to umpire. At least they were for me. I worked one World Series, one All-Star game, and two City Series between the Cubs and White Sox. They were easy to umpire because of the discipline. I remember when we met with Commissioner Landis before the World Series, he said, "I want this to be clean and damn clean." Landis was tough. If ballplayers cursed the umpires or in any way got rough with them, they lost their whole Series check. Landis wouldn't allow any of that stuff.

Rain and darkness were my two big headaches. Learning to judge those things was the hardest part of learning to umpire. When it starts raining pretty good or when it starts getting dark, one ball club wants you to call the game, the other ball club doesn't want you to call it. No matter which way you go, you are wrong. You just have to use your own judgment.

I called a game one time in Chicago because of high winds. It was a controversial decision. I thought it was too windy to play. In fact, I could hardly hold onto my protector. The wind was blowing guys around, so I called time and walked off the field. It was questioned at the time whether the game should have been called or not, so I waited maybe ten or fifteen minutes. Then it started raining. That rain saved the whole situation.

The toughest decision I ever had to make was whether to call a game on account of rain. It happened in 1945. Detroit and Washington were neck and neck for the pennant. Washington had already finished their season, so they had representatives in St. Louis to watch the final two-game series between the Tigers and the Browns. The game scheduled for Saturday got rained out, so there was a doubleheader on Sunday. The first game was delayed about an hour because of rain, and when we finally got started, it began to rain again. The rain never let up, and the field got real muddy. As the umpire in chief it was my decision whether to call the game or play it. It rained pretty hard at times, but I went through with it. Virgil Trucks, who had just got out of the Navy, threw bullets for five or six innings and then got tired; Hal Newhouser, the Tigers' ace pitcher, relieved him, and the Browns got a couple of runs. Detroit was behind, 3–2, in the ninth inning, when Hank Greenberg hit a grand-slam homer off Nels Potter. The Tigers won the game, 6–3, to win the pennant. That was a tough decision to make. We had to cancel the second game.

The most unusual call I ever had happened in Boston. A batter hit a ball that was rolling in foul territory. The Red Sox catcher threw his glove at the ball and hit it. I gave the batter three bases. A triple on a foul ball. Can you believe that? Of course, there was quite a rhubarb. But I called it right. The rule states that a ball is not fair or foul until it passes first or third base or settles in foul territory. The rules also state that if a fielder throws a glove at a batted ball and hits it, the batter is awarded three bases. Cal Hubbard made the same call one time. I think it has happened only twice in baseball.

I worked the first night game in the American League, May 17, 1939, in Philadelphia. I worked with Bill Summers and Red Ormsby. I had worked a couple of night games before in Scranton, in the Eastern League. They had portable lights there. They were terrible. Summers and Ormsby had never worked under the lights before, so they were a little worried about it. We talked about it in the clubhouse before the game. I told them about the lights I had worked under. I said, "Well, they've got good lights here; that's one good thing about it." Summers worked the plate. We got along fine. The lights were very good.

The biggest problem I ever had with night baseball was the balls hitting those big power poles the lights were on. The lighting was just fine, but there was some strain on your eyes. And it was sometimes pretty cold at night from the perspiration drying on your uniform.

Things were pretty tough during World War II. Our salaries were frozen, so we umpired a good long while without getting a raise. I didn't have a job in the off-season, so it was rough financially because prices kept going up. Transportation was very difficult. We traveled by train, and lots of times you couldn't get a seat. You couldn't get a Pullman; you had to ride the day coaches. They were full of soldiers and soldiers' wives. I sat on my suitcase many a thousand miles. Sometimes we'd travel from Boston to St. Louis. That was a night, a day, and a night to get there by train. It was rough.

There was talk about suspending baseball during the war, but President Roosevelt wanted it to go on. They did cut spring training way down as far as travel was concerned. They also started playing the national anthem before the ball games during the war. I guess that was to show we were patriotic.

The only umpire we lost to the armed forces during the war was Art Passarella. I recommended Passarella to the American League. I saw him when I was on tour with the Yankees through the Texas League. He worked the plate, and I worked the bases during an exhibition game. He looked awfully good. He would have been a great umpire, but he had off-the-field problems. I cautioned him about that. I even drove all the way to St. Augustine once to warn him. I told him if he didn't behave himself, it would be his last year. But he carried on just the same, and sure enough, he was released. He was a good umpire, that fellow. He held good discipline on the field.

During the winter of 1945–46 I had an operation for kidney stones. The doctor said the stones had kept the kidney from functioning for so long it was about to die. He told me that if he operated, I would be through on the ball field. At the time I didn't think he was right, but he was. I just couldn't come back after the operation, so I retired.

When I left umpiring, I missed the people, the crowds. I loved it on the ball field, the excitement. I did not miss the lonesomeness, I'll tell you. That was bad. Sometimes you'd go to dinner or a show with your partners, but sometimes you'd work with guys who would go their own way. That's when the nights were long. It was very lonesome being away from home all the time. My wife would travel with me only when I was in the East. It seemed I was always working in the western part of the league like Bill Summers. I went to a lot of movies to kill time. I was voted the champion lobby sitter. I just sat in the lobby and watched the people go by.

After I retired from umpiring, I was on my own resources. There was no pension in those days for players or umpires. I think it's wonderful that players and umpires get a good pension today. I got nothing from baseball.

After leaving the American League, I worked for three years as a supervisor of umpires for the National Association of Professional

Baseball Leagues. I traveled all around the Florida State League, the Georgia State League, the Southeastern League, the Alabama-Georgia League, the Georgia-Florida League—all Class D. I stayed in a town that was almost centrally located so that I could drive back and forth to various towns and see all the crews in the different leagues. I recommended several young umpires who made it to the major leagues. Lon Warneke, who used to pitch for the Cardinals, is the most famous. I saw him in the Florida State League.

After three years the association ran out of money, so I went to scouting for the Red Sox. It was a terrible job. I traveled thousands of miles over a summer—all over the southeastern part of the United States. Most of the time it was a wild-goose chase. You'd get a call to look at somebody, and when you'd get there, he couldn't throw the ball fifteen feet. I only signed one player, a left-handed pitcher who could throw the ball pretty good. He was seventeen years old and kind of temperamental. He quit. I quit, too, and took up playing golf.

Ernest Stewart in a publicity photograph taken in
November 1940, before his first season in the
American League. Courtesy National Baseball Library
& Archive, Cooperstown, N.Y.

Ernie Stewart

⊗⊗⊗

Ernest Draper Stewart
Born: Rocksprings, Texas, July 28, 1909
Height: 5' 9"
Weight: 160
Playing career: minor leagues, 1934
Umpiring career: Western Association (C), 1937; Three-I League
(B), April–August 1938; American Association
(AA), August 1938–1940; American League,
1941–August 1, 1945
No-hit games: none
All-Star games: 1942
World Series (games): 1944 (alternate)

The worst thing about umpiring is loneliness. It's a killer. Every city is a strange city; you don't have a home. Ballplayers are home 50 percent of the time, but umpires are not. I usually brought my family back to Philadelphia each summer, but that was home for only one team. I'd work a three-game series in Philadelphia and then be gone for six weeks. One year the family didn't go back with me because my wife was pregnant. I left home on February 24 for spring training, worked the season and the World Series, and got home October 20. It took me two weeks to get the kids to sit on my lap. Four months later I left again. I sat in a compartment on that train after leaving my family and bawled. I asked myself, "What am I doing here? What's the matter with me going off and leaving a wife and three kids for eight or nine months?"

There were two factors that caused me to go into umpiring. One was that I wanted to remain in baseball. I loved it with all my heart as a player, and so I wanted to be associated with it in some way. Second, there just weren't any good jobs around in 1934 to '36. I got odd jobs, but I didn't want to be a milkman or truck driver. Had I been able to get a good job, I might not have gone into umpiring. But because of a love of baseball and the lack of job opportunities, I went off to be an umpire. I am glad I did it, but I wouldn't umpire again for $100,000 a year.

I "resigned" as an American League umpire in 1945 after a short career of five years. There was pressure, but I did resign. It was a shock at the time, but it proved to be a blessing in disguise because it turned my life around. I have been asked to tell my story, but I have never before told it. Now it is time.

I was born July 28, 1909, in a little town in north Texas called Rocksprings. It was called Rocksprings because it had lots of rocks and lots of springs. My dad was a rancher, ran cattle and a few goats. We moved down to Sabinal in south Texas about the time World War I began. The Army used mules to pull cannon and ammunition wagons, so they got to be worth $500 a pair. Dad went across Texas and Oklahoma, buying every pair of mules he could get his hands on. He made big money, but when the war ended, he had 400 mules in the lot. The price went down to about $50 a pair, and we went broke. We had a pretty tough time for a year or so. I slept on a pallet on dirt floors.

In 1922 we moved to Southern California. I went to grammar school in Los Angeles, Long Beach Polytechnic High School, and the University of Southern California. I always liked athletics. I was a four-letter man at Long Beach Poly—football, baseball, basketball, and track. I went to USC on a track scholarship—I ran the 100 and 220—but later converted it to baseball. I played varsity baseball for three years and was captain of the 1934 team. We won two Pacific Coast championships. I made all-league a couple of years as a center fielder and led the league one year in hitting.

I was always extremely competitive. I not only believed in myself but was determined to excel in *anything*. Sam Berry, my coach at USC, loved me for it; I'd dive on my belly to catch a ball, go in head-first to score. It is my nature to be competitive; I have always had the

attitude that I could do anything within my abilities that I set my will
to do.

That's how I got through school. I liked school and determined that
I wanted to go to a university someplace. I did not have that influence
behind me at home because I lost my dad early. My older brother,
who ran the family, thought that I should be working as a roughneck
in the oilfields in Long Beach instead of planning to go to college. He
said, "You're an idiot. You'll never get through school. Go to work,
and earn some money." But that did not affect me at all. It just made
me more determined to go and to prove him wrong. I had no assistance from home. My mother couldn't afford it, so I went on my own.
Nothing was going to stop me from going to school.

The greatest four years of my life were at USC getting my B.A. degree. My success in business, baseball, and everything I have done
has been because of my association with USC. I have helped the
Trojans recruit athletes and have always stressed the importance of a
college education. You can't measure the value of your education in
dollars; you can spend a bonus or a big salary in a hurry, but you
can't spend that education.

The night I graduated from USC, June 15, 1934, I signed with the
Portland Beavers of the Pacific Coast League. Walter McCreedie was
the manager; Tom Turner, the owner. I could run and field real good,
but I was just an average thrower and a little pesty leadoff hitter. I hit
.225 that season. Boy, did I experience that old prejudice against
rookies. Half the ball club, the older players, never spoke to me all
year. They resented the fact that I was a college kid and had made the
team. They didn't say hi or good-bye or anything, and they never invited me to play cards. I was treated worse than an orphan.

During the winter the club decided to farm me out to Omaha in the
Class A Western League. I wrote back telling them that I didn't want
to go down. I was twenty-two years old, had played baseball night
and day all my life; I felt that if I couldn't stay in the Coast League
and go on to the majors, I wasn't interested in going down. They said
a year in the lower league would help me learn to hit better, but I declined the offer.

Even though it was during the Depression, I had some contacts that
got me jobs driving trucks and working in grocery stores for $16 or
$18 a week. But I had seams on my brain. I wanted to do something in
baseball. I said to myself, "Well, if I can't play, I'll try to umpire." So I
went around to the playgrounds on weekends and umpired makeup
games. I umpired with old catcher's gear—chest protector, shin

guards, and a mask. I got along pretty good, so I joined the Southern California Umpires Association. Now I got $5 a game and could improve my equipment a little; the first thing I bought was an old cheap blue suit.

I found that talking to older umpires was a great asset to me as a young umpire just starting out. They told me that I had to be tough, that I couldn't be friendly with ballplayers. I didn't believe that. I was raised in Los Angeles with Jerry Priddy, Peanuts Lowrey, Bob Lemon, and Vern Stephens. I played with them, ate with them; their wives were my wife's friends, and we were social friends. I thought I could handle them through friendship. It was a sad awakening when I found out that I could not. But I had been told. I think the worst name I have ever been called in my life was "a white-livered, California son of a bitch." It was one of my friends who called me that. Older umpires have years of knowledge, years of mistakes, and they can tell you things that will happen on that field before you have to go through it. Listen to them, and believe what they tell you. As a young umpire I had managers come up to me and say, "Where the hell did you learn that?" I said, "I've been told."

I worked as an amateur umpire for two years. The Chicago Cubs and the Los Angeles Angels had a farm club in Catalina called the Los Angeles Cubs. They played ninety games a season, five days a week, against semipro clubs from Los Angeles. Their manager, Doc Brooks, a former catcher and a Texas League umpire, helped me a great deal. I did well financially, too. I got $150 a month for umpiring and another $150 for taking care of the field; I mowed, watered, and lined the field and then called the game. They furnished us with a little cabin, and my wife was working as a beauty operator. You think I wasn't wheeling and dealing in 1935, '36 with that kind of job?

Bob Hughes, the old Pittsburgh scout, is the man most responsible for my umpiring career. He kind of raised me as a kid, as a player, and watched me umpire. I actually put my career in his hands. One day I said, "Bob, I'm going to ask you a question, and I want the truth because I'm going to direct my career with your answer. In baseball there's only one place to play, one place to manage, one place to umpire, and that's the major leagues. Do you think I have the possibility of being a major league umpire?" He said, "Yes, I do, Ernie." I took his advice, and off I went.

It was hard to get started in professional umpiring in those days. There were no umpire schools, no pot to draw from. You just worked every amateur game you could get your hands on and hoped that scouts, players, and managers would recommend you to the lower minor leagues. Sam Berry, my coach at USC, helped me get a job. He knew George Trautman, the president of the American Association, and told him to keep an eye on me. Bill Essick, the Yankee scout, was most instrumental in getting me started. He recommended me to Tom Fairweather, who was president of both the Western Association and the Three-I League. Mr. Fairweather sent me a contract for the 1937 season. He offered me $175 a month for the season and said he would give me five cents a mile for driving my car.

I accepted right away. That $175 was twice as much as I was making. I got in my old Model A, left my wife and first baby, and went off to the Class C Western Association. I was twenty-four years old. My family and friends thought it was okay for a college graduate to be going off umpiring because they thought I had major league ability. But my wife, Kay, didn't like it. She didn't like me being gone all summer; after that first year I brought the family back to wherever I was working, but she still didn't like the moving and me being gone so much of the time.

I had a good year and wound up working the All-Star game. (I had the distinction of working the All-Star game the first year in every league I was in in the minor leagues; I also worked the 1940 Little World Series between Louisville and Newark.) My partner was an old fellow named Eddie Goes, who had spent probably forty years umpiring. He was in his sixties—a big, tough German who had worked in the old Federal League. Eddie lived in Joplin and wanted to umpire so he could drink Budweiser all summer. But he was a lot of help to me.

Mr. Fairweather gave us the authority to fine ballplayers. We didn't have to report to the president so that he could make a decision like in the good leagues. We just fined them and sent the money to his office in Des Moines. Eddie Goes would keep his fines; he never sent in a nickel. We had some extra Buds with his fine money. The last day of the season I chased a pitcher in Hutchinson, Kansas, and fined him $5. Goes tried to get me to spend that $5 on Budweiser: "Ernie, don't turn that money in. Nobody will ever know about it." But I turned it in like I always did because I didn't want to get into trouble with Mr. Fairweather.

The next year I got a contract for the Three-I League. That was moving up to Class B. I got $195 a month plus a nickel mileage. I worked with Ed Harris. He and I slept together, ate together, fought together. That $195 was *all* we got. We didn't have expense money— had to pay for everything out of our pockets. To save money, we'd get a hotel room for $1 and share the bed, so it cost us only fifty cents apiece. Those were tough old days, but it was another good year for me.

I got a big break one night in Springfield, Illinois. After the game this fellow sitting in the boxes called me over. It was Frank Lane. He was scouting for Cincinnati and had just come from Columbus. Mr. Trautman had asked him to keep an eye out for a good umpire in his travels in the lower leagues. He told me that he had been watching me the last few nights and would recommend me to the American Association. A few days later Mr. Fairweather called: "Ernest, can you be in Columbus, Ohio, by noon tomorrow?" I said, "I sure can." He had sold me for $750 to the American Association.

I was teamed my first full season with Jocko Conlan. That was the beginning of one of the greatest relationships I had in baseball. We were a good umpiring team. We were good umpires, we hustled, and we had guts enough to run a ball game. One night in Louisville, in a game between the Colonels and Milwaukee, we chased nine players. They kept acting up, so we kept chasing them.

We had a ball—umpiring, running, fighting, laughing, doing everything in the world. We were both young. He had been in the league the previous year, so he was half a year ahead of me. Jock's strength was on and off the field. You can't really understand what that means unless you've experienced it as an umpire. A lot of umpires will be looking the other way when you need them. Never Jock. He always saw what you wanted him to see. I've been in a jam out there and said, "Jock, what did you see?" He'd let you know: he always saw it. He was super, just super. To this day we are close friends.

In my time the American Association had a top salary of about $650. You rode trains or buses and dressed in junky old hot dressing rooms that nobody cleaned or looked after. I've even dressed in the toolhouse. In Toledo we dressed underneath the grandstand and then had to crawl through the big two-by-four beams that hold up the bleachers to get to the field.

One time in Toledo Jocko and I were in a nightclub. A guy at the table next to us beat the hell out of a gal he was with. Jocko—we had had a couple of beers, and Jocko was quick to fight anyway—told the guy he shouldn't do that. The guy picked up a chair and hit Jocko right over the eye with it. Knocked him down. Jock got up, grabbed a beer bottle, and split that guy's head open. He was *out*. The police came and took the guy to jail and took Jock to the hospital. He had a slight concussion. The next night he had a headache and eight stitches over his eye. It was his turn to work the plate, so I said, "I'll work the plate." He said, "No, no, I can work it." Burt Shotton was managing the Columbus Red Birds, and Fred Haney was managing Toledo. We got up to the plate; Jock and I made up this story that Jock bumped his eye underneath that grandstand, dodging those two-by-fours.

Jock and I went up the majors the same year, but we went to the opposite league we thought we would. The American League took out an option on Jocko when he started out in the New York-Penn League. Baseball people knew Jock because he had played center field for the White Sox. The option meant that the American League could exercise the right to buy him at any time, even if the National League wanted him. I was not an optioned umpire. Jock felt that he was going to the American League, and during the year Pants Rowland and other scouts told me that the National League was going to buy my contract at the end of the year.

Mr. Connolly, who was the supervisor of the American League, followed the two of us a great deal that year. He'd stay a week at a time to watch us. He talked to Jock about me and talked to me about Jock. Well, to my surprise and Jock's disappointment, Mr. Connolly changed his opinion and bought me instead of Jock. Of course, I was happy to go up, but I was surprised that it was the American League. Mr. Connolly told me in later years that he bought me over Jocko because I had a little more size and was ten years younger. Jock was heartbroken. But then the National League needed an umpire, so they bought Jock. I was real thrilled at that. We just switched leagues. We umpired the 1942 All-Star game together and would have worked the 1945 World Series, but I had a problem come up and didn't make that assignment.

World War II almost got me, but I proudly say I got out of it. I took four or five physical examinations; that's how close I came to being called. I came close to volunteering several times, but I had a wife and two children, so I didn't want to go to war.

I beat the draft by meeting the various age and family categories of deferment set by the government. I worked for Lockheed during the off-season, so I had a 2-D deferment, which I had to give up each summer when I went umpiring. Bill DeWitt of the Cardinals put me in touch with a Colonel Christie, who was the head of the Missouri Selective Service Board. He transferred me to the St. Louis draft board for the summers. He did that for the Browns and Cardinals; somehow their players were never called, so those clubs kept their teams practically intact during the war. But the lady who was the head of the draft board in Eagle Rock, where I lived, was determined that I was going to war, and in 1945 I got the call that I was 1-A. Colonel Christie delayed the induction for thirty days. I passed the physical on a Friday in Philadelphia. The sergeant told us to report back Monday morning at 6:00 A.M. He said "Bring a toothbrush, razor, and a bag. You are in the Army." He told us we were going to Germany. The next morning I was at home sitting on the porch when the whistles began to blow. Germany had surrendered. When I reported Monday morning, they told us to go home. I beat the draft after all; the war ended between my induction physical and the day I was to report.

The American League assigned me to spring training in 1941 with the Washington Senators in Orlando, Florida. That was a blessing because I met Bucky Harris, one of the great managers of baseball, who helped me more than any other manager. Bucky took a liking to me. When we traveled by bus to exhibition games, he always reserved the seat beside him up front for me. I had had only four years of minor league experience and half the ball club was older than I was; if I sat back there with guys like Roger ["Doc"] Cramer or Ben Chapman, they'd eat me up.

I learned a lot from Bucky Harris. He taught me how to umpire knuckleball pitchers because he had a nestful of them— Mickey Haefner, Roger Wolff, Johnny Niggeling, and Dutch Leonard. Leonard was probably the best of the bunch, although Wolff won twenty games one year. Bucky said, "Ernie, to umpire these knuckleball pitchers, take your time. *Take your time.* Wait, wait, *wait* until that catcher catches the ball. Then there's plenty of time to call it." I followed his advice and got to be a good knuckleball umpire.

He taught me something else that I lived to experience successfully. He said, "Ernie, don't you be a homer." Now a "homer" is a kind of gutless umpire who gives the home club the best of a decison. We had one or two of those in our league. In my day the Yankees were the Yankees, the other teams put out extra-hard against them. Bucky told me that there were some umpires who gave the Yankees the best of it while in New York. That set in my mind, and I made it a point that I was never a homer any place. I never was called a homer. I never took anything away from the home club, but I never gave them anything; I've had a lot of ball clubs tell me that to my face. The visiting club likes that.

The last game of my first season was in Yankee Stadium. The Yankees' opponents were the Washington Senators. I worked behind the plate. At the end of the game Bucky Harris came over, put his arm around me, and we walked off together. He said, "Ernie, you've had a good year as a freshman umpire. You're going to make it. And you're not a homer."

I opened my first major league season in Cleveland, Ohio, in the old League Park with Bill Summers, Joe Rue, and Steve Basil. The White Sox beat Bob Feller, 4–3. The third day I worked behind the plate. It was a day game because only the stadium downtown had lights. Rollie Hemsley, a great guy to work back of because he'd stay way down and let you get a good view, was catching for the Indians. Al Smith, a little left-hander with the best curveball in the league, was the pitcher. As they were warming up to start the game, Hemsley said, "Now just relax. This guy throws a lot of curveballs, and he's got a good one, so take your time and don't call that ball too quick." That was great advice. I waited on it, and after the game Rollie said, "Super game, super game." That was a happy start, but the rest of the year was not so happy.

My first year in the league Mr. Harridge put me with Bill Summers. He felt that Bill Summers was probably the best and most qualified senior umpire in the American League to break in a young umpire. But I found that to the contrary, he was the worst. Bill Summers had a reputation for taking everything to the front office. He made it a tough year for me. He criticized me all the time and complained about me to Mr. Harridge. Bill was jealous of me. He always called me "a cocky college kid." He told Mr. Harridge that I was cocky and hard to handle. There is one thing I have never been in my life, and that's cocky. I have been confident that I could do the things I have done, but have been humble in everything. I don't care whether it was in umpiring or in business life today, I actually give credit to the Lord and not myself.

Mr. Harridge had a rule that the umpires should wear hats. We didn't wear them in California, so I didn't have a hat when I got back East. Bill Summers told me to buy a hat, so I bought a hat. The only time I ever wore it was when I was in Chicago. I'd always leave it on the train—I lost a dozen of them that summer. He'd tell Mr. Harridge, "That cocky college kid won't wear his hat." Mr. Harridge would call me in: "Ernest, are you wearing your hat?" I'd say, "Yes, sir, yes, sir." I'd have it in my hand then.

At the end of the year I went back home through Chicago, so I stopped in the office and asked Mr. Harridge to change my senior umpire. I told him I didn't get along with Bill. Bill Summers would not let me umpire. He kept me hooded all the time. I was an aggressive, hustling, loud type of umpire, and he just wouldn't turn me loose. He kept me harnessed. I felt I was caged in, and I wasn't doing as good a job as I knew I could do. Mr. Harridge asked me who I wanted. I told him Bill McGowan. "Why, Ernest," he said, "there isn't an umpire in the league who likes Bill McGowan. He can't get along with anybody. He'll ruin you."

I said, "I want a shot at him." I'd met him. He was like Jocko—a cocky, feisty Irishman. He was one of the great umpires of all time, and he told me himself, "You get a change and come with me, and I'll make an umpire out of you. Summers is going to ruin you." Well, Mr. Harridge reluctantly said okay.

I opened the 1942 season in Cleveland with McGowan and Art Passarella. Passarella and I were both in our second year. We got there a day ahead of time, and McGowan sat there I guess for twelve hours talking to Art and me about umpiring—do this, do that, do this, do that. I had the greatest year with him. He was just a super leader. When I'd get to Chicago, Mr. Harridge would ask, "How you getting along with Billy?" He'd say, "I just can't believe, it," when I'd tell him he was the greatest senior umpire. But I meant it from the bottom of my heart. Bill McGowan was super, absolutely great.

I pretty much was a pup out of McGowan. I didn't have any style when I worked with Summers because he wouldn't let me have a style. I liked McGowan's style, so I used it. I loved the way he called out his decisions. Some umpires would just say, "Strike." McGowan: "STRIKE!" I liked that. Same way on the bases: a great big "YOU'RE OUT!"

It's important for a young umpire to have a good senior umpire to work with. Bill McGowan was a terrific leader and teacher—he taught me how to run the ball game. Bill McGowan turned me loose, and I say humbly, not cockily, he made me a good umpire. I *was* a good umpire. I had the reputation of being a good umpire. Mr. Harridge said I was a good umpire, and McGowan said I was the best young umpire that he had seen come into the American League in the twenty-five years he had been there.

Bill McGowan was a great horseplayer. It was frowned on, but it didn't make any difference. He even bet when Mr. Landis was the commissioner of baseball. Mr. Landis called him in a couple of times, and of course, Bill denied it. Bill had a disease, a gambling disease. He had to bet horses every day. I didn't bet the horses. I wouldn't spend my money that way. I am very definitely Scotch; I don't sit on my hands, but I don't throw my money away either.

Being around Bill as close as I was, I came in contact with probably all the outstanding bookies in the United States. Being exposed to those people, I have been approached several times in my life to give them an advantage in a ball game. I have had them stuff a $500 bill in my coat pocket, and I'd pull it out and say, "God damn you, get out of here." A gambler wants you to take that first $100 bill. Now he's got you. He can say, "You took five hundred dollars last week; now I want a favor." I had that thing put up to me several times. I've had them say, "I can make it worth ten thousand dollars to you." I'd tell them, "Look, you think I'm going to be the first guy in the baseball history of umpiring to give you an advantage? I don't care if it's worth ten million, get out of here."

I was probably exposed to it more than the other umpires because I went with Bill every place. If we had a rained-out game, he'd say, "Come on, Ernie. Let's go down to the bookie joint." Sid Wyman rented a second story of a building just outside St. Louis. He had ten or fifteen operators hooked up to every track in the United States. Bill was in his glory out there. I didn't want to go with him, but I'd go. I'd just sit around and listen to them. Sid and I were very good friends. You know, he never took a nickel off Bill McGowan in his life. He let Bill bet every race in the United States and just called it even at the end of the day. I've seen Bill lose $2,500 in a day. Sid would say, "Why, Ernie, I wouldn't take a nickel from him. He's got a disease. He's sick; the man's sick."

Bill had that weakness, but it never affected his umpiring a bit. When he walked out on the field, his mind was just on that game. Then the minute the game was over, he'd say, "Hurry, got to get downtown, see what my horses did." Bill McGowan was a super umpire and a super guy.

The greatest umpire and individual that I ever worked with was Jocko Conlan. He just had all the attributes of an umpire—a little old feisty Irishman with the guts of a burglar. He had good judgment, feared nothing from the office down, and would give his life for you on the field and off the field. We ate together, slept together, fought together, and everything else. You don't find many people, particularly umpires, that you become this attached to. I only had two, Jocko and Bill McGowan. I enjoyed Jocko more than I did Bill because he was more of my age and did things I wanted to do, whereas I kind of followed McGowan around like a pup.

Cal Hubbard was also an excellent umpire and a super guy to be with. We enjoyed each other. We were both college graduates. We sat in our rooms or someplace and talked for hours about college football, rules, whatever. And he was very strong on the field, very strong. He was not as good an umpire as McGowan or as Conlan, but he was big and forceful. He could keep them at a distance. Don't think he couldn't. He chased them quickly! He didn't listen to any guff at all. Hubbard had the best knowledge of the rule book of any umpire I knew. In his later years he shot his eye out hunting one year in Missouri; a pellet ricocheted off a rock and hit him in the eye. He came back and tried to umpire in the spring, but he couldn't, so the league made him supervisor of umpires for twelve or thirteen years. He was well equipped for that because he was such a good rules man.

Now, you say, "What makes an umpire?" First of all, you must have judgment. You can be the most educated person in the world, have the finest eyesight in the world, and you can't umpire a lick if you can't distinguish what you saw. For a person to see what he sees and to put it into his muscle reactions, to be able to call a bang-bang play or determine balls and strikes, it's judgment. It isn't something that you develop; it's something that is God-given. You are born with that kind of judgment. And I had it.

Not all umpires have that kind of judgment. I remember a Sunday doubleheader in Detroit with the Washington Senators. I was working with Johnny Quinn, one of my umpiring friends. He was a sweet little Irishman, but he couldn't umpire a lick on earth. He had sold banners and popcorn around the stadium in Philadelphia, and when he got to be an umpire, Mr. Mack helped him get into the big leagues. Bucky Harris, the Washington manager, did not like Quinn because he knew he could trample all over him. Well, one of the Senators tripled. Quinnie, who was umpiring third base, called him safe, but he was out five feet. Now you might think since that was a Senator, Bucky Harris didn't mind having the decision. Oh, yes, he did. He resented it that his guy was called safe because Quinn missed the play. Bucky Harris came over to me in back of the plate and said, "Ernie, if that guy misses a play on one of my guys where he's safe and he calls him out, I'm going to undress him. He called one of my guys safe at third, and you know he's out ten feet." Now Quinnie is in trouble by missing a play.

Quinnie was at first in the second game. Bucky had told him, "You miss a play, and I'm coming after you." I'll be damned if he didn't miss the first play. A Senator was safe at first by a step or two on a routine grounder, but Quinnie called him out. Harris came out of that dugout like a shot and ran over Quinnie, just *ran* over him. If you're constantly missing plays and getting into trouble, you will never really have respect and control of the ballplayers, and they will sure as hell holler at you. That's all there is to it. They're not going to sit there and take a bad decision. So, if you are not necessarily a bad umpire, but if you're not what I call a real good umpire, it's like anything in life: It isn't any fun.

The most asinine question that has ever been asked an umpire in the history of the game is: "When you miss a play out there, don't you kinda even it up?" If I've missed one, I got twenty-six guys hollering at me. The next inning, if I even it up, I've got the other twenty-six hollering at me. Two wrongs don't make it right. You just forget what you did and let it go at that. There isn't ever a *thought* in an umpire's mind of missing a play to make it even. I don't care if I missed the ball and I called it a strike when it wasn't a strike; if the next one's a strike, baby, it's a strike. I'm going to call it. And if the guy says, "You didn't call the last one like it," I say, "Maybe I didn't, but I damn sure called *that* one." You never think: Well, hell, I missed one on him last time; I'm going to give him a close one this time. You just couldn't umpire that way. You'd be so worried about evening up that you could never get through the game.

To be an umpire you have to be bulldoggish. That's developed a great deal by being associated wth the ballplayers. When I was a small kid in Rocksprings, we'd catch wild burros and ride them. When they wouldn't pitch, we'd kick them in the side with our spurs until we created a sore. Then you'd hit that sore with the spur, and he'd throw you about thirty feet in the air. Now that's an umpire. You start out and you're not too mean, but they spur you until you get to where you're strict and stern. You have to be that way; otherwise, ballplayers take advantage of you.

The umpire that upset you was the wishy-washy guy, the sweet talker who tried to grin his way out of everything. I've seen guys in the American League stand out there and take abuse. I've seen them let the bench holler at them and grin back. I've seen guys pushed from home plate up against the backstop screen and not put anybody out. They're not a pleasure to work with or to be with. Ballplayers and managers did not respect that type of umpire. Like I said, if they can put any fear in you at all, then you shouldn't umpire.

One time, when I was visiting Mr. [William C.] Tuttle, the president of the Pacific Coast League, in his office in Wrigley Field after the season, he was telling about his most successful umpire. He said, "Bill Durran is the best, Ernie." I asked what made him the best. "Well," he said, "he can stand out there and grin at those guys calling him every name in the world. He never says a word, just grins." I said, "Well, Mr. Tuttle, somehow or another, when a guy calls me a white-livered son of a bitch, it's not funny. I got to put them out."

Ollie Anderson, who umpired in the minor leagues probably fifty years, gave me one of the best pieces of advice. I used to take Ollie with me when I first started out in Los Angeles. He said, "Ernie, don't let those ballplayers *mar your game*. When you let them holler at you from the bench, you've got to be hearing, and they'll mar your game. Go over to that bench, and shut them up or chase them out." Boy, that was so true. Bill McGowan could not stand for you to holler one word at him. He'd go to pieces. But you'd know you were not allowed to holler a word; he wouldn't let you. He was so sensitive when he worked the plate, he'd whip off that mask right away if that bench hollered at him. If he didn't do something about it, he was liable to call the next pitch a strike. I learned that before I ever started, so I never had bench jockeying. In my day they could come out and protest a ball or strike call, but I never let them do it. I never let them umpire from the bench, never. No one can umpire back of that plate and concentrate on that game with a bunch of guys hollering from the bench, calling you names, calling you impotent, calling you *everything*. You lose your concentration. They'll mar your game if you put up with that. They don't always have to swear at you. If they holler, "Goddamn it," or "Bear down," *shut them up*. The word "homer" is an automatic: I'd rather be called an SOB than a homer. You can't stand around and think about it. You just knock them off real quick, and they'll guard their words. Like Ollie said, "Don't let them mar your game."

To be a good umpire, you must have also good character and honesty. I'll never forget one time in the American Association. Jock and I were in Minneapolis, which was playing Indianapolis. I was on the bases. It was kind of a wet night. Don Lang, my Long Beach friend, was running on second base. Never in the history of my semipro, minor, or major league career—maybe twelve or fourteen years—was I ever hit by a batted ball. I was young, quick, and could get out of the way. The score was tied, 4–4, in the latter part of the game. A batter hit a line drive that hit in front of me. I jumped away from that ball, but it ticked my pants. I felt it. We wore bell-bottom pants in those days, and that damned ball just ticked me. I didn't know whether anyone saw that or not, but I couldn't chance it. I immediately hollered, "Time!"

The ball is dead, the batter gets first base, no runners can advance, and you can't score unless the bases are loaded and it's a force play. Lang had scored, but I sent him back to second base. The manager came out. I explained what happened. He said, "Ah, nobody saw it." I told him that I felt it, so I had to call it. Well, he got mad. "God damn you, I wish that ball would have hit you right between your eyes and gone through your head." Well, I said, "God damn you. You're through." He said, "Why are you putting me out? I never swore at you." I said, "You're not going to make a remark to me like that. You want me killed. Get out of here."

The first guy I put out in the big leagues was Ben Chapman, the Washington left fielder. He had played with the Yankees but got into trouble with some fans, so was traded to the Senators. He was a great big Tennesseean, built like a giant. He was a great ballplayer, but an ornery bastard. I spent a lot of time with him in spring training that first year. We'd take grounders at third base and bet on who'd make the most errors. I thought he was my friend. The first series I had him in the regular season was in Philadelphia. Roger Wolff, who was later traded to Washington, was pitching for the A's. He threw Big Ben a knuckler. Strike one. Nothing said. Another knuckler. Strike two. A third beauty. Strike three. Ben never moved his bat. He just turned around and said, "You pretty boy son of a bitch." I said, "Ben, you are through for the day." "You're not putting me out!" I said, "No, I've already put you out. Get out!" Bucky Harris came over. "What's the matter, Ernie?" I told him. "Good boy," he said, and went back to the bench. Ben never called me that again. He might have wanted to, but he never did it.

I was short-fused, very definitely so. At times I was possibly a little too quick. But at the same time you're better short-fused than you are to let them stand around you and argue all the time and mar your game. One day we were in Detroit. The Tigers had Paul "Dizzy" Trout, a big Indiana farmer, who weighed about 210 pounds and was built like Joe Palooka. He could pitch, but he had a wild man's temper. Hal Newhouser and Trout won 56 games between them that year [1944]. Well, Trout was running on first base. Someone hit a ball down to second base, and Trout went for second. The little Philadelphia second baseman, Irv Hall, was fielding the ball—in the runner's path, but the runner has to give the ground, not the fielder—when Trout, who was aggressive and mean anyway, ran over him. The ball came loose, and Trout ran over and put his foot on second base. I said, "You're out." "What am I out for?" I said, "For running over that second baseman. You can't run over him." Well, he ran over and grabbed me. I said, "Now you're out twice—at second and out of the game." I told the manager, Steve O'Neill, that the game wouldn't resume until Trout was off the bench and in the clubhouse; I wanted him off the bench because I thought he might come back out there after me.

Oh, that Trout was a *wild* man. One day in Detroit a fan was heckling him real good. As Trout came off the mound when the inning was over, instead of going to the bench he went over and grabbed the guy and jerked him clear over the low rail behind third base. The dugouts emptied, and finally, the police had to take the guy away from Trout. I was behind the plate and saw the whole thing. I told Steve O'Neill that Trout was out of the game. Steve asked, "What for?" I said, "He can't do that. For Christ's sake, if it wasn't for you guys, he'd have killed him. He can't grab a guy out of the stands." I put him out of the game right then because he was marring the game. The next day the Tigers fined him $250 and suspended him for five days.

I have cussed ballplayers. I tried not to do it, but I did it a few times. I did it with Bob Muncrief, a pitcher for St. Louis, and with Mule Haas, the third-base coach of the White Sox. One day Mule gave it to me, and I let him have it. Jimmy Dykes, the manager, came out and said I couldn't do that. I told him I called Mule the same thing he called me. When I got back to the hotel, Mr. Harridge called. "I understand you cussed Mule today." I said, "Yep, I sure as hell did." He told me I couldn't do that. I knew that; but sometimes your feelings get pent-up, and you feel like calling him something better than he called you. Sometimes I'd get more satisfaction out of doing that than I would putting them out of the game.

We were twice as hard on the crybabies who kicked all the time. We tried to give the guys who were always crying something to cry about. Roy Weatherly, the Cleveland center fielder, was one of the worst crybabies I ever saw. I made it a point never to miss a strike on him. In other words, I never let him get away with one. If it was close enough to call a strike, it was a strike. You don't take away anything, but you sure don't give anything either. Now with a Joe DiMaggio or a Ted Williams, if the pitch was marginal, it's a ball. It's not that you think that it's DiMaggio or Williams up there; it's just that you tend to see it that way. It's just that you get geared against one guy a little bit but not against another guy.

One year we cost Weatherly a bonus. Cleveland was making a run for the pennant. Roy was a good ballplayer. They needed him in the lineup, but he kept getting thrown out. In fact, Cleveland had a bunch of rebels—Jeff Heath, Hal Trosky. Anyway, the owner, Mr. Bradley, told Roy that he would get a $500 bonus if he didn't get put out of a game the rest of the year. Somehow or another the umpires picked that up. Well, Roy was going to have a pretty tough time getting that bonus.

Roy had a bad habit. If he got real mad, he'd swing at the next ball; he didn't give a damn where it was. Of course, the pitchers knew this, so if Roy got into a pretty good little argument about a strike, you could be sure the next pitch would be a curveball in the dirt and he'd run up and take a swing at it.

One day we were in Cleveland. Cal Hubbard was working the plate; I was at first base. We were just dying to be the first ones to get that $500 bonus away from Roy. During the game Hub called a strike on him, and Roy, in his high-pitched Texan voice, said, "Hub, I can't hit that kind of pitch! That ball almost hit me." Hub said, "Right down the middle." Sure enough, the next pitch was a big old curveball in the dirt, and Roy ran up and took a big swing at it and missed. Hub said, "Roy, you can't hit that kind either, can you?" Whew! Up went the smoke. Roy got all over him, and Hub said, "Roy, you're out. Get out of the game." Now Roy realized what happened, and he toned right down. He said, "Hub, Hub. Now wait a minute. I didn't mean that. Don't put me out. If you put me out, I lose a five-hundred-dollar bonus, and I could live all winter in Texas on that five hundred dollars." Hub said, "Roy, you are out!" I don't know whether Mr. Bradley gave him the $500 or not, but we felt pretty good that we might have had some bearing on the 500 bucks.

I remember one time when I wasn't short-fused up in Boston. Bobby Doerr, who played second base for the Red Sox, was a thick-legged athlete who pulled his hamstrings quite often. One time, when he was hobbled for a few weeks, they brought up a utility infielder, Ben Steiner, from Louisville. He was a little pop-off guy. He always squawked, was never out, and all this, that, and the other. So as umpires we talked about him. We said, "Well, let's knock him off really quick when he says anything and put him in his place." So that day he tried to steal second, and he was out two or three feet—that's out a mile to an umpire. Wasn't even close, but he jumped up with a handful of dirt and hollered, "No, no, I'm not out." So I said, "Well, you're out twice now. You're out because I called you out, and you're out because I'm putting you out." He went back to the bench and told Joe Cronin that I'd put him out of the game. So Joe came out. "Goddammit, Stewart, you're too cocky, you're too quick." I didn't answer him because he was such a sweet guy. He was my friend. We used to drink beer together in spring training. But if he had used any profanity, I would have run him.

The next day I was working back of the plate. Steiner was on second as a runner. Cronin was in the batter's circle. The Boston hitter singled to center field, and here came Steiner for the plate. It was a little closer that time, but they got him. "You're out!" He jumped up at me again, but Cronin ran in and told Steiner to get out of there. Joe could really put on a show when he wanted. He turned his cap off to the side of his head, got right up in my face, and said "Goddamm it, Ernie, let me tell you something. You know what I did when I went fishing yesterday? I caught a fish that long, and if you don't believe it, I'll take you with me and prove it to you." Then he turned around and walked away from me. The fans yelled, "Kill him, Joe, kill him." They thought he was eating me up. That was one of the few funny incidents in my life. I stood there real deadpan and listened to him and thought, Boy, if this isn't pretty good. He walked away from me just a-storming and a-kicking, but he knew that kid was out.

Cronin later became president of the American League, and one regret I have about getting out of umpiring is not being able to work for him. I know I could've gotten along with him. He would have been a pleasure to work for.

Mr. Harridge was not a joy to the umpires. He was not a good boss to the umpires. He was not stern enough with the ballplayers; he did not know baseball; he didn't even attend games. He'd come to the office as secretary to Mr. Ban Johnson, and when Mr. Johnson died suddenly, then Mr. Mack fronted for Mr. Harridge and got him (he called him his "boy") to be president of the American League. Mr. Harridge was afraid to go to a ball game. He was afraid to be exposed to it. He feared the White Sox, and he feared Jimmy Dykes. Jimmy Dykes knew it. He used to tell some of those weak-kneed umpires, "You go tell Harridge that's what I said." Mr. Harridge was an old lady; he was not a pleasure to work for. He didn't back you strongly enough, he was critical of you, and he listened to stories. He just wasn't a man; he was a weak kind of guy. His wife had to drive him to the office. You know in athletics you have to have real men to work for or be an official under or it's just not pleasant.

Mr. Connolly, our supervisor, was a nice old gentleman. He had a tremendous knowledge of the rules. There wasn't anything in the book that he didn't know. Even at his advanced age—he was in his seventies when I was there—he had a good clear mind, and he knew the rules. He didn't say much to you about what you were doing, but he was severe with you on misinterpretation of the rules. The only advice that he ever gave me directly was in my first year of spring training in 1941. I had worked with the Washington Senators and then went over to Lakeland, Florida, with Detroit for the last half of the exhibition season. Mr. Connolly told me in the hotel room after watching me work a game, "I want you to be a little more enthusiastic and call your strikes a little louder with more definition." He had followed me for a year in the American Association and never said anything, but maybe because I was breaking in as a rookie umpire in the big leagues in my first spring, I might have been a little quieter or a little softer than I had been. You know what I did? For the next few days I went down into the lakelands around the city, where there was nothing but pelicans and crows, and I practiced calling balls and strikes louder and more definite. Before the week was over, Mr. Connolly said, "You got it, my boy. You got it."

I used spring training for physical conditioning. The first year Bucky Harris gave me a uniform, and I worked out every day at third base or in center field. I pitched some batting practice, and I even played in some intrasquad games. It soon became known around the league that you issued Ernie a uniform in spring training.

Of course, I worked the exhibition games, but a major league umpire doesn't really need that to prepare for the season. All you need is a day or two to get used to the speed of the ball. I proved that to Mr. Connolly one year. I pleaded with Mr. Harridge to let me skip spring training. I told him I could get ready by working some college games at home. I opened the season in Philadelphia behind the plate. Mr. Connolly was in the stands; I guess he wanted to see how bad old Ern was without spring training. I say with all humility that I never missed a pitch. He came into the clubhouse after the game and said, "Ernie, you really are in good shape, aren't you?" I probably could have umpired that game without seeing a pitch all winter because your eyes get trained to make the calls.

I was a good pitcher's umpire because I gave him every strike that I could. I didn't give him high balls and low balls, but I'd give him marginal balls on the corner. If he could get that ball over that black edging around the plate, it was a strike to me. I guess you could say I had a wide strike zone. I never worked in a league where the pitchers didn't like me. A lot of them told me they were glad I was back of the plate. I'd call that good curveball right on a corner, even if it was outside by the time it got back to the hitter. A guy who'd take a ball an inch or two off the plate is taking it too close.

I put out Hank Greenberg in Washington on a close call like that just after he got back to the Tigers after the war. Greenberg was my friend, did a lot of nice things for me. Mickey Haefner, the little knuckleballing left-hander, was pitching for the Senators. He got two strikes and then threw Hank a little squeegee curveball inside a little bit. I called it strike three. Greenberg turned and said, "The goddamn ball was two inches inside." I told him it was a matter of opinion; two inches were pretty marginal. When he got back to the bench, he yelled, "Goddamm it, Stewart, open your eyes." I called, "Time," turned toward him, and said, "Hank, good-bye." Steve O'Neill, the Tiger manager, came out asking why I had put him out. When I told him that Hank was bitching about the ball being two inches inside, Steve said, "The hell with it, he's not that good, Ernie," and went back to the bench.

Boston had a little crybaby, [Lamar] Skeeter Newsome, who played shortstop for two or three years and hit about .240. He was up to bat one day in New York, I remember just as plain as day, with two strikes and two balls. The pitcher threw a curveball. So help me, it was right there—oh, a rocking-chair pitch. "Strike three!" He turned around. "Strike three? You wouldn't call that ball on DiMaggio." I said, "No, Skeeter, you're right. See that center-field sign out there? It says four hundred forty feet. That's where DiMaggio would have hit that one. No, I wouldn't have called it on him because he wouldn't have taken it."

Ted Williams would never count how many strikes you called on him. You just never wanted to call a bad third strike on him. He used to say, "Ernie, I only want *one*." He wouldn't get up there and take big, wild swings. He wouldn't miss the ball; he'd get a piece of it every time. He may as well just have walked up there with two strikes on him.

His philosophy of hitting was to look at all times for the fastball. He said, "I'm going to get it one time or the other. I look for it on every pitch. If it isn't a fastball, I'll take it." He took a lot of fastballs, too, because he wasn't ready to snap that bat.

Now as an umpire I worked the opposite way. Every ball to me was a curveball. I anticipated the curve because it was the hardest ball to call. If I got the fastball, all right, I don't have to anticipate the fastball. But when I got the curveball, I was ready for it. I never told that little secret to another umpire; he might have disagreed with that. It was my philosophy, and it worked for me.

I didn't pay any attention to abuse from the fans. I just had a deaf ear for it. But it was the opposite with a ballplayer—I had my ears open for *him*. After you're in the league a few years, you can distinguish every voice. I've chased a guy off the bench, and he'd say, "It wasn't me." I'd say, "I *heard* you." After you've lived with them, played with them, associated with them, you just know them; that's all there is to it. But I had no reaction to the fans. You naturally don't appreciate them hollering, but at the same time they don't really have any influence on your attitudes or actions. The public image of umpires is not directed to a given umpire; it's just something that has grown with the game. People holler that umpires are blind, but they know umpires are not blind. Some umpires have bad judgment; they miss what they *see*.

I never got upset about the game. Not that I wasn't nervous when I walked on the field, particularly the day you worked the plate or an All-Star or World Series game. Any athlete who tells you he isn't nervous before the game is either numb or lying. The same thing with an umpire; an umpire is an athlete. In the 1944 World Series a National League umpire was trying to tell Bill McGowan and me that he wasn't nervous. I noticed when we started down the steps to the field that he didn't have his cap on. No, he wasn't nervous. He just wasn't fully dressed.

To know the rules, you must constantly study that rule book. I carried one in my suitcase, and I read it on the trains, in my room, everywhere. The way to study the rule book is to read a rule and then put it in play in your mind, visualize it, make application of that rule to the play. In your mind you see that play in the field, and then, when it shows up, it's like it's been there before. I've had guys say, "You don't have to memorize the page or the rule; you just have to know it when it comes up."

A team of umpires should never, I mean *never*, under any conditions lose a protest where a rule is involved. It just should be an unforgivable sin for umpires not to know a rule. The only way you can lose a protest as an umpire is by misinterpreting the rule, and an umpire should never lose one. I never lost one. And I've been in a spot two or three times when, being either the senior umpire of the group or the umpire in chief back of the plate, I have overruled another umpire.

That happened one night in Philadelphia. Bobo Newsom liked to use a trick pickoff play where he'd straddle the rubber and then throw to a base. The St. Louis center fielder hit a triple. He made a belly-flop slide into third base and called, "Time." Art Passarella, who was umpiring third, called, "Time." Bobo straddled the rubber and then threw to George Kell, who had sneaked behind the runner. Passarella called him out. Luke Sewell and the Browns argued that the ball was not in play, and I had to agree with them. When time is called, the ball is not in play until the pitcher comes in contact with the rubber. Bobo was straddling it, so the ball was not in play. I had to overrule Passarella. Mr. Mack was furious. He couldn't come out on the field because he had on street clothes, but he sent his son Earl (the Little Weasel we called him). He said, "We're going to protest this game." I said, "Great, Earl. Let Dad protest this game, but he ain't going to win it." Connie Mack did protest the game, but it was disallowed, because I had made the correct decision. Mr. Connolly was disturbed that Art missed the rule but was glad I changed it. Naturally I changed it. That's what senior umpires are for, and if I hadn't changed it, I could have gotten fired. Mr. Connolly was very severe on misinterpretations of the rules. In fact, he almost let Art go for missing that one.

You see, umpires are responsible for each other where rules are involved. Not on judgment plays—safe or out, ball or strike—but on rules or where trapped or dropped balls are involved. If one umpire makes a mistake on a rule and the others let it go, they would be severely criticized by Mr. Harridge and Mr. Connolly. It isn't good when the league has to allow a protest on the rules. Changing another umpire's decision is not oneupmanship; it is just that the entire crew is responsible for everything that happens. If there is disagreement about, say, a trapped ball, the entire crew would discuss it, and the majority would rule. You have to umpire as a team.

A very difficult call in the old Yankee Stadium was the fly ball into the corners. You had to be really on your toes when they'd pull that ball in around those big white foul poles. It was very difficult to see if the ball was inside or outside that line. One day I was working third base in New York. Bobo Newsom was pitching for the Athletics. Every Yankee could pull. In batting practice they would work on pulling the ball because of the short fences down the foul lines. Frankie Crosetti was up with the game tied in the fifth or sixth inning. He hit a line drive down that third-base line. I squatted down to get the view of it and could see that ball go curving—fair ball! It must have been about thirty feet foul when some fan caught it, but it was fair when it went over that fence. Out came the Athletics. Their dugout was on the first-base side, so they had a good shot at that left-field foul line. But not like old Ern, because I was *down* there. Earl was stomping around, and Mr. Mack was standing up in the dugout, waving his lineup card. (He wasn't allowed on the field because he never wore a uniform, but, boy, he'd shake that card at you.) Big Bobo—he got the name Bobo because he called everybody Bobo—came over. "Bobo," he said, "you haven't called one right all year." I said, "Bobo, you just got that backwards. You mean I haven't *missed* one all year." "Well," he said, "you might be right at that."

After the inning George Kell, a sweetheart of a guy, who was playing third base for the Athletics, went in on the bench. I saw Mr. Mack talking to him. Then the bench quieted down. Al Simmons, who was coaching third base for the A's, stayed to listen to what George Kell said. When Al came out to third base, he said, "Ernie, you ought to know what George Kell said about that home run of Crosetti's. He told Mr. Mack that you called it right, it was a fair ball." I said, "I appreciate that, Al, but it was a fair ball even if he said it was foul."

Experience is the great teacher, the only teacher. I guess umpire schools serve some benefit; but in my time we didn't have them, and if I had it to do over again, I'd do it my way because I got so many more games of experience. I worked several hundred games before I ever took my first Class C contract. I learned on the field better than any thirty guys in a group with half a dozen instructors. I really got some fine points. I was better equipped in my first professional baseball assignment—I'm going to say it because I believe it—that any young umpire that can come out of any umpiring school today. I don't give a damn how hard he works in it. He can't substitute my three years of experience. They go to these schools, learn positions and this and that, then work a few weeks of games and go out into a small league. With no more experience than that they can get into a lot of trouble. The first "son of a bitch" you're called is a little shocking. Professional baseball can be very cold and very tough. In the small leagues there's always a retired ballplayer who's managing, and he knows all the tricks. There's no substitute for experience.

There are lots of little things that help an umpire. Because I played, I could anticipate what might happen so I wouldn't be caught off guard. It helps to know how players think, what might happen in certain situations, and so on. You'd study signs to know when they were throwing curveballs or fastballs, when they were stealing or hitting and running, things like that. Of course, the players gave you their signs for pickoffs, who'd be covering a base, and so on. You kept those secrets; you never told anybody. Lou Boudreau and Bob Feller had a great pickoff play; they'd pick off fifteen to twenty guys a year with it. Nobody in baseball knew it except Cleveland and the umpires. It's like the old boys said: You could be on second base patting the bag with one foot and they'd throw you out between pats. Boudreau would flash the sign with his glove to Hemsley; Hemsley would flash it to Feller; then Feller would count to two and throw you out without ever looking at you. That's the play that fooled Bill Stewart, the National League umpire, in the 1946 World Series.

Why do umpires all look like undertakers? Well, I can tell you one reason why. I was umpiring in Muskogee, Oklahoma, my first Sunday in the Western Association. There was a great big farmer—he must have been six feet seven inches, 290 pounds—who could out-cuss any individual I ever heard in my life. He was so bad and loud that the management had put him out of the grandstand and made him sit in the bleachers. He sat right down by first base, and he needled the umpires all the time. Joplin, which was a Yankee farm, was playing Muskogee. The Joplin ball club had a lot of kids on it I knew from Los Angeles—Jerry Priddy, Phil Rizzuto, Johnny Lindell. Well, Muskogee was at bat with the bases loaded and two men out. A guy hit a line drive to Jerry Priddy, the second baseman, who made a leaping catch for the game-ending out. Well, I thought it was a pretty good play, so I walked off the field with a great big grin on my face. That big farmer called me over. He reached over the little board fence, grabbed me by my coat, and said, "What are you laughing about? Are you glad Muskogee got beat?" I said, "No, sir, no, sir." "Well," he said, "if I catch a grin on your face the rest of the season, I'll take you down to the river bottom and hang you from a mesquite tree."

That was a great lesson to me. I never manifested any sorrow or joy on the field the rest of my life. I was an alternate in the 1941 All-Star game in Detroit, when Ted Williams hit the home run to win the game, he went around those bases, jumping and clapping. I could have gone with him, but I remembered Muskogee. I walked off the field like I had been struck by something. An umpire can't manifest anything. If he has any expressions on the field, the ballplayers will actually jump him. They'll say, "What in the hell are you laughing about? It's not funny." I had learned that lesson, and of course, I learned a few more.

I enjoyed the time on the field. When you get to the point where you are competent and confident in your work, you can relax and enjoy the game. I enjoyed it as much on the field umpiring as I did if I was sitting in the stands, watching the game. I appreciated the good plays, the diving catches, the belly-flop slides, the triples and the home runs, and the good pitching performance. That was one of the highlights of umpiring—to see the game every day. You can concentrate and still enjoy the plays.

The hours off the field are long and lonely. Boy, those old four walls really get to be something in those hotels. Had I been like some guys who'd sit around the lobby or in their rooms, I'd have gone crazy. I had a few friends in the league, and they'd invite me home to dinner. On Sunday, in every city in the league, I'd go to church. I'm a member of the Church of Christ, and they pick you up real quick. The preachers would invite me over for dinner. Being an athletic bug all my life, I managed by spending most of my days in gyms. I had a guest membership to athletic clubs in every city in the American League. I'd shoot baskets, swim, lift weights, work out in the boxing room, play handball or volleyball. I worked out every day except when I had the plate. I loved training and was in tiptop shape.

Of course, an umpire's duties involve more than just working the game. We had to be at the ball park two hours prior to game time. One umpire, generally the one scheduled to work third base, stayed out on the field to supervise batting practice, fielding practice, the dress code, fraternizing, and so on. About an hour before the game the plate umpire got the balls ready. To start the game, you had to have forty-eight new balls rubbed down with a little mud and water to remove the shine and slipperiness. About ten minutes before the game we'd go to the dugout and then be at home plate five minutes before game time to get the lineups and discuss ground rules or special problems. The umpire who works the plate is responsible for the timing of the game; you check your watch and memorize the time the game began and ended. After the game the plate umpire counts the unused balls and puts them under lock and key and orders additional balls for tomorrow's game. The umpires hold the key to the ball bag and make sure that new balls are in boxes with unbroken seals. Then you make out a slip to send to the league office, telling the time of the game, who won, and so on. If there were any incidents such as a protest or chasing a player, the umpire involved makes out a written report. It's a long day, but the excitement and enjoyment of being involved in the game make it worthwhile.

I was fortunate enough to be with the New York Yankees a lot during DiMaggio's hitting streak in 1941. I was with him in Washington when he got his hit in the forty-second game to break the American League record [George Sisler]. Then I was with him in Boston when he got his forty-fifth-game hit to break the National League record [Willie Keeler]. I'd seen DiMaggio in that hitting streak squeak out a marginal base hit in the ninth inning, but when they stopped him, he was at the height of his hitting. He had gotten three hits in Shibe Park one afternoon, and the next night I was behind the plate in League Park in Cleveland, with Bob Feller pitching in Joe DiMaggio's fifty-sixth game. He got three hits—two doubles and a single. He could always hit Feller good. He was a great fastball hitter, and Feller was a great fastball pitcher.

The next day, July 17, we moved to Municipal Stadium because they had lights there, so I was at third base when DiMaggio was stopped. But he hit three of the damnedest shots you ever saw. Honestly, he should have had three hits. He literally turned Kenny

Keltner around twice on line drives that hit in front of him. Keltner had to backhand them. He did it *twice* in the game, and no other third baseman could have done it because he was the best in the league. DiMaggio came to bat in the eighth inning with three on and one out. He hit a ball down to Boudreau at shortstop. The ball took a bad hop, but it hit on the heel of his glove and they got DiMaggio out on a bang-bang doubleplay. That stopped it.

Oh, I can tell some stories about how those Yankees rose to the occasion to get DiMaggio to the plate one more time. One time they came up in the ninth inning down 4–1. DiMaggio had made the next to the last out in the eighth inning, so he was eight hitters away. It seemed there was no way to get him up there. But they got him back up. With two runs in, the bases loaded, and two outs he got back to that plate, and he got a hit. They never charged or hollered; you could just feel that ball club. They knew what they had to do, and I've seen them get him back lots of times in the ninth inning with two out, and they just fight and get him back up there, and he would keep it going.

I feel that there are two records that will never be broken: Cy Young's 511 victories and Joe DiMaggio's fifty-six-game hitting streak. The rest of them they will get to some way, as they got to Ruth. But not that fifty-six. Where have all the great hitters gone? Under the lights.

I enjoyed great hitting feats. I saw Harlond Clift of the Browns hit four home runs in a doubleheader in Chicago. He hit three in the first game and one the first time up in the second; they walked him the next three times up. I wish they would have pitched to him to see if he could have hit more. I saw Rudy York, a nice, big, happy-go-lucky half-Indian, hit a bunch of home runs. Boy, he could whack that ball. He had a drinking problem, or he would have stayed a lot longer. Just like Paul Waner. (He drank heavily, played with a little buzz on like some others.) Beans Reardon and I saw Waner drink a half pint of bourbon before an exhibition game one year; he told us he'd finish the rest of it about the fifth inning. He was a master of the bat; great bat control. But he played under a little influence of alcohol. I guess it gave him courage.

Of course, to watch Ted Williams was always a thrill. Whenever Boston was playing, I used to sit there in the stands and watch him take batting practice. I've seen him pop that ball up on the deck three or four shots in a row; he'd leave the batting cage, and the crowd would stand and applaud just like he had hit a home run with the bases loaded. If you're a baseball fan and you don't enjoy that, you don't enjoy the game.

One time we were in Boston for a series with the Athletics. The A's pitchers pitched to Williams only five times in the three-game series; he had five home runs. They walked him every other time. In the ninth inning of the third game the Athletics had a one-run lead. Williams came to bat with two out and a man on first base. Mr. Mack walked him intentionally, moving the tying run to second base and putting the winning run on first base. Jimmy Foxx then hit a long drive into center field that Mike Krevich caught to end the game. When the game was over, I asked Mr. Mack why he put the winning run on first base and the tying run at second base. Mr. Mack said, "Ernie, he beat me two ball games, and I'm not going to let him beat me three."

People always ask me, "Who was the best ballplayer in the league?" Joe DiMaggio was the best. He could do more things better than anybody in the league. Ted Williams was the best hitter, but DiMaggio could field better, throw better, run better, and hit great. He just didn't make mistakes. If he went for an extra base, he made it every time. He was the kind of ballplayer who never ran you out of an inning or took you out of an inning. And he was so sweet to work with. He was a real quiet guy.

Bill Dickey was another class guy. He never turned around and asked for a pitch in his life. He knew he was big and hard to work behind. Sometimes on those old hot afternoons about the fifth or sixth inning he'd start coming up on you. I'd have to say, "Look, Bill, you're standing up on me now. I don't want to see the plate. I want to see the pitcher. Let me see him, will ya?" Then he'd get back down. If I'd miss a low ball off his pitcher once in a while, he'd just throw the ball back and say, "Stew, did I block you?" He was a great catcher and a great guy.

Bill did disappoint me one time. The Yankees had brought up a rookie pitcher from Kansas City—a big kid who threw hard and had good breaking stuff. Dickey was the type of catcher who would do anything to block a ball. Well, with men on base, this rookie threw a breaking ball into the dirt. Dickey gave it the sweep, and back to the backstop it went. When he came back to the plate, I said, "Bill, I'm ashamed of you." He knew what I was talking about. He said, "That goddamn rookie, to hell with him!" I said, "Bill, for Ruffing or Gomez you'd stick your head in the way of that ball, and then you make that young pitcher look like a billy goat." He did it. I have seen older players come up to bat against a rookie pitcher with nobody on base, two out, or something, and the catcher would say to the hitter, "All fastballs." Well, he'd get all fastballs and shoot, he'd hang a rope out for you because he'd rip. I guess it's human nature. Being a rookie in any sport is no fun.

But Dickey was a class guy, and he proved it one time in Yankee Stadium. The Senators, who were three games out of first place, were there for a doubleheader [June 20, 1943]. The place was packed to the rafters. Washington had a real good ball club that year—Jake Early, Stan Spence, George Case, Mickey Vernon, and those knuckleballers. In the sixth inning the Yankees were leading, 1-0. The first Washington hitter, Stan Spence, got a hit and then Vernon hit a home run. The Yankee pitcher, a rookie by the name of Charley Wensloff, who usually had great control, suddenly got wild. He walked Bob Johnson and Jerry Priddy and then threw three straight balls to Ellis Clary. After the third one to Clary, a curveball inside, he slammed his glove on the ground. That's automatic: He's gone.

Joe McCarthy came charging out of the dugout. He said, "God damn you. You didn't put my pitcher out, did you?" "Oh, yes, I did." He said, "If you put that pitcher out, I will turn this crowd loose on you. They'll mob you." I said, "Oh, no, you won't, Joe, because I'll give you thirty seconds to get out of here, and if you don't, I'll forfeit the game." (You have to have a little experience to bite them back.) He turned to Dickey. "Bill, was it a strike?" Dickey said, "It was not a strike, Joe." McCarthy turned and walked away.

I said to Dickey, "If I could, I'd give you a great big kiss." He said, "Well, Ernie, that old son of a bitch should know enough to ask me a question like that because I'll tell the truth." Now not all ballplayers were like that. Mike Tresh over in Chicago wouldn't tell the truth. If McCarthy had asked him, he would have said, "Yes, boss, perfect strike."

Now after I chased Wensloff, the Yankees brought in Ernie Bonham. I had umpired Bonham in the American Association. He was a beautiful person, a big, strapping guy—six feet two inches, 215 pounds—who could throw hard. He was a starting pitcher, but they brought him in in relief because they wanted to win that game. Bonham was a control pitcher. He threw hard but could usually spot the ball. Well, he walked Clary and the next two guys before retiring the side. He walked in two runs. The Yankees lost that game, 5-3. I thought: They've put that one down on my ledger.

In the second game I worked third base. A runner got to first, so I moved over to second base. Joe Gordon, the Yankee second baseman and a good friend of mine, said, "Ernie, do you want to know what the old man thinks about your decision?" I said, "Sure, I'd like to know what he thinks." Joe said, "He thinks you made a great decision. He told Charley in the clubhouse, 'I don't know what you did to minor league umpires in throwing your glove or anything like that, but you are in the major leagues now and you can't do that now. You cost us that ball game, and the next time you do that it is gonna cost you five hundred dollars for getting thrown out in a crucial spot.' " That made me feel good.

Now there was another incident that didn't make me feel so good. In the clubhouse Bill Grieve said, "Ernie, I wish you hadn't put Wensloff out." I could have hit him in the mouth. I said, "What the hell are you talking about? You mean I'm going to let that guy throw his glove and make me look like a jackass and not put him out?" He said, "Well, you cost the Yankees a ball game." I said, "I didn't cost the Yankees anything. They cost themselves a ball game." And that's the way the *New York Times* wrote it up: "Stewart's an old-time umpire." Grieve would never have put him out. He was a little wishy-washy smily umpire who was pushed all over the American League. But I proved myself right there.

One of my favorites of all time was Ted Williams. Contrary to all newspaper and magazine articles that have been written about Ted Williams calling him bad, temperamental, hard to get along with, he was the sweetest, easiest-going, nicest person that I've ever been associated with. He never squawked on anything. He was nice to the ballplayers. He'd sit and talk to rookies, show them how to hit, what to do.

He loved to play, and he loved to hit. He would have had so many batting records if he hadn't spent five long years in the service. They took him out, at his peak, for three years. He was hitting over .400. He came back and had great years and was hitting over .400 again when the Reserves got called up in that damn Korean War, and he had to go again for two years. They took those years away from him, so his greatness never was completely fulfilled. (The same thing with Bob Feller. Feller lost four years in that Navy. The year he left he won 25, and the year he came back he won 26. He would have won another 100 ball games had he not lost those years.)

I have a story to show what kind of guy Ted Williams was. It happened in Detroit right after the 1941 All-Star game where Williams had hit the home run in the ninth inning to win the game. Bobo Newsom was pitching for the Tigers. He had a big old "Annie Oakley" curveball that was nothing on earth but a crowd rouser. He never tried to make it a strike, and he never threw it unless he had a five-run lead or there were two out or two strikes. He threw it when he didn't want you to hit the ball. Williams was hitting. Cronin, who was playing shortstop and managing at that time, was in the on-deck circle. Newsom had two strikes on Williams and threw that big old slow curveball up there. I called it too quick. Strike three. Honestly, it was the only bad pitch I ever called in my life where it was *really* a bad pitch. There are always marginal balls, but this was a *bad* pitch. I wish it would have been strike two; then Williams would have another chance. But I took the bat out of his hands. (I couldn't change it, couldn't call it back. I could have crawled into a hole. I was sick.) Well, Cronin got on me right now. But Ted said, "Wait a minute, Joe. Do you make an error at shortstop once in a while? I play left field, and I make an error once in a while. Ernie umpires, and he makes an error once in a while. Let's go!" He trotted out to left field. Cronin said, "Ernie, what in the hell can I say now?" I said, "Nothing Joe, it's all over now." The guy was just great.

The only club I didn't care for was the Philadelphia Athletics. The team was good, but the management wasn't. Mr. Mack was a nice gentleman, but he was not the saint that everybody has painted him to be. The umpires didn't like Mr. Mack or his son, Earl, the messenger boy we called the Little Weasel. Mr. Mack was instrumental in getting Mr. Harridge his job, so he had a lot of influence on the president. Mr. Mack would call the front office anytime he felt he didn't get the best of something. He was very tight with his players and ran a skimpy organization. I trained with the A's one year in Southern California and then traveled east with them. One day on the train Mr. Mack told me that he could make more money ending up last than first. "What I like to do," he said, "is keep my ball club in contention from first to fourth place until the first of July. By that time we have made enough money that we can tail off, and with a last-place ball club you don't have to raise anybody's salary. With a first-place ball club everybody wants a raise, so I can make more money ending up last than I can first." He actually told me that.

Most clubs provided beer, soft drinks, and sandwiches for the umpires and between games of doubleheaders; the concessionaires would bring in lunch. They catered to us pretty good because they knew an extra three or four minutes between games could bring them a lot of additional sales. We always ate slow, gave them thirty minutes instead of twenty-five. If they were nice to us, we were nice to them. But in Philadelphia we wouldn't give them an extra minute. Mr. Mack never sent a hot dog into an umpire's dressing room in his life. So, baby, we'd ring the bell right on twenty-five minutes in Philadelphia.

One thing I detest about the umpires today is that they call time too often. They'll call time twenty times in a ball game. By their calling time the ball is put out of play. You cannot put that ball back in play until the pitcher puts it back in play. Mr. Connolly told us not to call time unless there was an injury or something of that nature, so I wouldn't call it for every little thing. What am I going to kill the game for? It happened so many times where some little something would happen after the play was apparently stopped. Like Mr. Connolly said: "Keep the ball in play."

One time up in Boston, Alex Kampouris of the Senators hit a triple. After he slid into third base in a cloud of dust, he hollered, "Time!" I said, "No, no time!" He yelled, "Goddammit. Time." I said, "No, the ball's in play." "All right," he said, "then I'll pull off my shoe." After he took his shoe off, I said, "Now put your shoe on and get your ass out of here." Ossie Bluege came running out wanting to know why I chased Kampouris. I said, "He wanted time, I didn't give him time, so he pulled his shoe off on me." Ossie said, "Fair enough," and walked away.

The status of umpires is better today than it was in my day, but it's far from perfect. In my day they didn't have too much respect for you. They loved you if you were a good umpire, but when it came to conditions, money, dressing rooms, pensions, we didn't have much. It was like nobody cared. Today the umpires have organized so they are a little better paid. They have their pensions, and they get their medical expenses. Things have improved, but it's far from adequate. Baseball is still miserly when it comes to umpires.

It was a concern for the status of umpires that ended my career. It began one rainy night in Washington in July 1945. Detroit was in town. I was sitting by myself in the corner of the Washington dugout, waiting for the rain to stop. Art Passarella came over to me and said, "Ernie, the commissioner is in the dressing room. I think you should hear what he has to say." So I went upstairs. Art, Hal Weafer, and Commissioner Chandler were there. Art and Hal asked Commissioner Chandler to tell me what he had said to them. He said he wanted to improve the lot of the umpires. He said he thought we should be getting $5,000 a year to start instead of $3,500, that we should have better dressing rooms, better expense money, and so on. He said to me, "Why don't you come over to my office tomorrow? I'll make up a list of ideas that I have and you can present it to the umpires and see what they think about it."

I'll never forget the room: 215 Senate Building. I went over the next afternoon. This was Chandler's first year as commissioner, and he had good intentions. He said, "Ernie, I want you to do me a favor.

You write each of the umpires the things that I've outlined here, and let's see what they think. Let's start the ball rolling for better conditions." Now the commissioner of baseball was talking to me. I did not have the idea. I did not go to him; he came to me.

Well, I wrote to the umpires, and I got a reply from two or three of them. But one of them—and I've been told who it was but I do not know that it was him—showed Mr. Harridge my letter. (I'm sure it wasn't Bill Summers. Many umpires told me that Summers was the stool pigeon. I confronted him once in St. Louis, and he just sat in the car and said, "Ernie, I didn't do it. I know I got the reputation, but I didn't do it.") That letter really upset Mr. Harridge. He didn't want anybody monkeying with his umpires and he didn't want an umpire to make anything or have anything if he could stop it. So he sat down with his lawyers and decided to ask me to resign.

Mr. Harridge sent me a telegram in Boston where I was working the Yankee–Red Sox series and asked me to retire immediately because I had been disloyal to the umpires. Well, that upset me because I had never been disloyal to anybody and certainly not to umpires. I called him and told him that Mr. Chandler had asked me to do it. I said that Mr. Chandler was my superior and that I felt it was all right to do what he asked me because he was the commissioner of baseball. Harridge said, "Well, when he learns to keep his nose out of my business, he is going to be better off." (Harridge, Frick, and Chandler were very definitely bitter enemies because Harridge had wanted Frick to be the commissioner, but Larry MacPhail got Chandler in.) Finally, he said, "You just sit tight for a while, and we'll see. But I don't want you umpiring for a few days." I was suspended on August 1.

Bill McGowan was terribly upset when he heard about it. He called Mr. Harridge and told him not to let me go. He said that I had another twenty-five years in the league and that I was not only a top umpire but the best young umpire he'd ever seen come into the American League. Mr. Harridge said, "We'll see."

Then Mr. Chandler called. He wanted to know if I had heard from Mr. Harridge. I lied. I said, "No." He said, "If you hear from him and he tries anything, son, you call me. I want in on this." I said I would.

Mr. Connolly, the supervisor of umpires, came in from his home in Natick. Oh, he scolded me. I told him the story. I was pleading for my life because I wanted to stay in baseball. He said, "You got yourself in it, and you'll have to get yourself out of it." I said, "Mr. Connolly, you can pick up that telephone, call Mr. Harridge, and save my job." He picked up his old felt hat and started for the door. I said, "Mr. Connolly, if you walk out that door, you're walking out with my job." He said, "You got your foot in it; get yourself out." He walked out, and I never saw him again. And I never liked him since.

A few days after that Mr. Harridge called again. I was still on the payroll. He said, "Ernie, I still want you to retire." I told him that if he insisted on it, I was going to insist on a hearing in front of the commissioner. He said it wouldn't do me any good, but I told him I would insist on it anyway. Then I called Mr. Chandler to tell him that Mr. Harridge wanted me to retire. He said, "Don't do it. Call for the meeting." I said, "I'm calling it. You notify Mr. Harridge."

In the meantime, I had written letters to each of the other eleven umpires asking, "Have I ever been disloyal to you in any respect?" I got eleven replies. They all said that I had *never* been disloyal. I still have those letters.

I was burning when I walked into that meeting in Washington on August 15. Mr. Chandler, Mr. Harridge, and three lawyers were there. I said to Mr. Harridge, "Christ Almighty, you can't even face me? I'm just an umpire. You have to have three of your lawyers?" He told me again that he wanted me to retire. I told him again that I didn't want to retire. Then Mr. Chandler took it up. He said to Mr. Harridge, "Ernest is a good boy. He's well educated. I know his record. He is a fine umpire, and I don't want you to misuse him this way." Mr. Harridge said, "I have the authority to handle my umpires as I see fit. I admit that Ernie is a good umpire, but I don't want him on the umpire staff. I want him to resign."

They passed a sheet of paper to me. It read: "I do hereby resign as an American League umpire this day. . . ." I looked at it and let Mr. Chandler look at it. I said, "Mr. Chandler, what should I do?" He said, "Well, son, I guess you'll have to sign it." I was disappointed in him. I said, "Mr. Chandler, if Judge Landis was sitting in that chair where you are today, he would take that goddamn letter and tear it in bits and throw it into the street and tell Mr. Harridge and his three lawyers to get their asses out of here." (That's what Mr. Landis would have done. He was tough. And he had a foul mouth: he'd call you anything on earth.) "But you don't have the power that Mr. Landis had, so okay." I signed it, and I threw it across the room.

When we left the room, Mr. Harridge came over and put his hand out. I didn't shake it. He said, "I'm sorry." I said, "No, you're not sorry. You just made me resign. I've got to change my life. You're not sorry. I won't shake hands with you."

So I had resigned. It hit the headlines. I went on home. I was bitter about my fate. Not against baseball, players, or owners. But I was bitter against Mr. Harridge. I saw him several times after that, but I have never spoken to him.

Shortly after my dismissal, Bob Considine of the International News Service invited me to lunch. He said he could sell my story to the *Saturday Evening Post* for $5,000. That was about equal to my year's salary, but I knew it wouldn't last a lifetime. I said, "Bob, I don't want the five thousand dollars. I don't have an enemy in baseball, and I don't want an enemy in baseball. I love the game. I love the people in it. Let's just leave it there." In those days I would have said a lot more than I have today. Guys still come up to me and say, "Ernie, how in the hell have you kept your mouth shut this many years?" I don't know. Several years after I quit, I was at a baseball party. Joe Gordon came over, gave me a big kiss, and said, "Either baseball is paying you off or you have to be the greatest guy in the world." I said, "Take your pick, Joe." I never got a nickel out of baseball. What good would it do to pop off? None.

I had an opportunity to go back. That winter I got a phone call from Mr. Roy Hamey, the president of the American Association. He said, "Ernie, I just got back from the major leagues meeting. I can get you back in the American League if you will work for one year in the American Association. I will pay you your major league salary and will guarantee that you will be back in the major leagues next year." I said, "Mr. Hamey, I don't want back in the American League." Then Mr. Trautman, who had graduated to commissioner of the minor leagues, called. "Ernest," he said, "you are making a mistake. You can have your job back after working one year in the American Association. The American League has guaranteed your full salary. I'd like to see you come back." I said, "Mr. Trautman, I don't want to come back." Mr. Essick, who had helped raise me as a kid and was then chief scout in California for the Yankees, called. "Ernie, you are making a mistake. You're young; you're an excellent umpire; you got your life in front of you. Go back." I told him it wasn't going back to the American Association and eating crow for a year that bothered me. It's just that I was out of baseball and wanted to stay out. I wanted to try something else.

I wanted out of baseball because I knew I could do better things in life than umpire. As it turned out, it was a blessing in disguise. I would not have my family today had I stayed an umpire. My wife would have taken my three children and quit. She said, "I'm going to give you another year or two, and if you don't get out, so help me I'm not going to live with you." Since that day I have learned to know my family. I have enjoyed life ten times more than when I was umpiring. My neighbor and I bought a hardware store. The first year I was out of baseball I made $13,000; the most I ever made in baseball was $9,200, including $2,500 in World Series money. After four or five years I went into business for myself. I have been extremely successful in the floor-covering business. I make more money than the president of the American League.

I have lived happily out of the game. Sure I missed it. Sure I had nightmares. Sure I worked the World Series in my sleep. Sure I was back in the league many times in my nightmares. But at the same time I say truthfully from my heart, I have enjoyed my life and family much more since I have been out of baseball. And the dollars and cents—there is no comparison. I say this in all humanity. Bill Summers called me a "cocky college kid." I'm not cocky. I'm grateful—for my life and my being. The Good Lord has blessed me.

Joe Paparella, American League umpire from 1946 to
1965, before a spring training game. Courtesy National
Baseball Library & Archive, Cooperstown, N.Y.

Joe Paparella

⊜⊜⊜

Joseph James Paparella
Born: Eynon, Pennsylvania, March 9, 1909
Height: 5' 10"
Weight: 165
Playing career: none
Umpiring career: Canadian-American League (C), 1938–39; East-
ern League (A), 1940–43; American Association
(AAA), 1944–45; American League, 1946–65
No-hit games: Hoyt Wilhelm, September 20, 1958
All-Star games: 1948, 1954, 1959 (first game), 1964
World Series (games): 1948 (6), 1951 (6), 1957 (7), 1963 (4)

The other day I picked up the Baltimore ball game on the radio. Chuck Thompson, the Orioles' announcer, was talking about a young player who was born and raised in Scranton. He said, "Wait a minute. Scranton, Pennsylvania. That's where Joe Paparella came from. Boy, what a great umpire he was." It made me feel real good to hear that. I'd love to have people remember Joe Paparella as a pretty good umpire. I hope I satisfied everybody and did the kind of a job that I was hired to do. I would like to be remembered that way and even someday be considered for the Hall of Fame.

I was born in 1909 in Eynon, Pennsylvania, a little coal mining town of about 900 people near Scranton. My family was from Italy. We weren't poor, but there was just enough money to feed and clothe us. My dad was killed in the mines when he was a young man, forty-two years old. I was just a baby when he died. I was raised by two brothers, who were a little older, and a widow mother, who had seven children. I played baseball like most kids, hoping that someday I would be a big league player. But I was the worst curveball hitter you ever saw. After high school I had a tryout with the Cleveland Indians' farm team at Wilkes-Barre. They offered me $80 a month, but I didn't think that was enough money, so I started working in the coal mines. You see, I had gotten married at an early age. My wife was sixteen, and I was seventeen; we've been married ever since.

The chance to do some umpiring came one morning when I was standing around watching an amateur ball game and was asked to take the place of an umpire who didn't show up. I got a $1.50. Well, that $1.50 seemed like $150 today. The president of the league called and asked me to take another game on Sunday morning. I said I would as long as I got another $1.50. It was more or less a necessity for me to umpire that game for $1.50 because the mines were on strike at the time.

From then on I forgot about playing baseball and concentrated on umpiring high school and amateur league games. I was eighteen years old, fresh out of high school. There was nobody around who had enough knowledge of the game to tell me anything about umpiring, so I just had to pick it up as I went along. One year a fellow by the name of Walsh and I were chosen the best amateur umpires in the area, so we got to work an exhibition game of barnstorming major league All-Stars in Scranton. It was a real thrill because Babe Ruth was on the major league team. (As it turned out, I later played the part of the umpire in *The Babe Ruth Story*.)

My real break came in 1937. I was working an amateur league championship game over in Dunmore. A Catholic priest named Gallagher came over to me after the game. He said he liked my style and asked if I had ever thought about turning professional. I told him that was my dream. He said he would recommend me to a friend of his who was the president of the Canadian-American League, a Class C league that took in towns in northern New York like Amsterdam, Rome, and Gloversville plus a couple of Canadian towns in Quebec. Three days later I got a call to report to Ogdensburg, New York, for an interview. I drove up and came back with a contract for the next season. I got $180 a month, which wasn't much money when you figure that I had to send money home to support my family and also pay all my expenses on the road. I made the play-offs that first year, and guess what my salary was the second year? A hundred eighty a month. I never even got a five-cent raise.

I was in the Canadian-American League for two years, and then Tommy Richardson, the president of the Class A Eastern League, bought me in 1940. I was so happy because the Eastern League was home for me with towns like Scranton, Williamsport, and Wilkes-Barre in Pennsylvania and Binghamton and Elmira in New York. In the middle of the 1943 season I was asked to report to the American Association. But my wife got sick, and I wouldn't go anywhere with her in the hospital. That fall the Association invited me to attend the Little World Series and talk about joining the league. I drove up to Syracuse, and as luck would have it, George Trautman offered me a job while I was sitting in the boxes, watching the ball game. But I really had my heart set on going to the International League because the towns were closer to my home. It wasn't fifteen minutes after I had shaken hands on going to the Association that Mr. Frank Shaughnessy of the International League came over and asked me to go to spring training with them. I said, "Mr. Shaughnessy, if you would have said that twenty minutes ago, I would have jumped sky high. But I just agreed to go to the American Association."

While in the American Association, I got called out of St. Paul to take my physical for the Army. The sergeant asked if I knew anything about dead-reckoning equipment. I didn't know what he was talking about, but I said yes. Then he explained that, at the age of thirty-four I could get a deferment if I was doing something that was in the best interest of the country. A Navy man came over and said the Gyro Corporation in Binghamton needed help with the plotting boards and dead-reckoning equipment. I took a shot at it because I figured that was better than going into the service. I stayed with Gyro for the rest of the year. Now I had to decide whether to stay with Gyro or go back to baseball and take a chance on being drafted. My wife and I talked about it all winter long. When the time came, I just could not say no to baseball.

There were hardships in the minor leagues during World War II. The biggest problem was transportation. I remember one time Milt Steengrafe and I worked a game in Milwaukee on a Saturday afternoon, then rode a coach all night long to get to Minneapolis in time for a Sunday afternoon doubleheader. I don't believe we got more than a few minutes' sleep on the train; the trains were all packed, and with people standing in the aisles you couldn't do more than catnap. We always rode coach; there had to be an emergency for you to get a sleeper. Very few minor league parks had good dressing rooms. I've had to dress in the sheds where grounds keepers kept the lawn mowers, and sand, and the like. We couldn't afford anything better than the cheapest hotels. It would practically take a day's wages to take a cab to the park, so we walked or rode streetcars. Of course, the quality of the game deteriorated, too. The best minor league players went up to the majors to replace the big leaguers who went into the service, so we got a lot of high school kids and amateur players.

To earn more money, I worked in the off-season for Harry Sugarman, who has one of the largest department stores in northeastern Pennsylvania. In fact, I started by building shelves for Harry when he had a little drugstore and I was umpiring amateur ball. He expanded as the years went by, and I stayed with him during my major league career—running the personnel office, buying appliances, and even working the floors at night.

I had a lot of support from my family in those days. It wasn't easy traveling all the time, being away from home six months a year, and making very little money. But my wife urged me to continue with umpiring because she knew I loved it and because she didn't want me to have to go back into the mines. I remember the times I'd call her long distance. I'd be down a bit, missing my family and wondering if I should do something else for a living. She'd say, "Don't quit. You are so close, don't quit now. You love it. You have talent for it. Don't worry about us. We'll get along just fine." She was an inspiration to me.

There is no question that I was determined to be successful in the umpiring business because I had nothing to fall back on. Today the fellows are well educated, and they can always do something else if they don't make it. I couldn't say that. Beans Reardon couldn't say that. Al Barlick couldn't say that. Reardon didn't want to go back to the shipyards, Barlick didn't want to go back to the coal mines, and Joe Paparella didn't want to go back to the mines. A lot of us in those days had to work just that much harder to be successful. I think that our background was the drive that made us work so hard.

Then, in 1945, the American League bought my contract. Bill Veeck had just come home from the Marines, and there was a big Welcome Home Day for him in Milwaukee. Fortunately for me, I was working the plate that night. I had one of those tremendous pitchers' duels that always make an umpire look good; my grandson could have called that game. It just so happened that Mr. Trautman, the president of the league, was sitting with Mr. Harridge, the president of the American League. They made an agreement right then and there, and

I went off to spring training with the American League in 1946. I stayed for twenty years.

When I learned that I had been picked, I was the most surprised guy in the world. I believe I was the first umpire hired by the American League in eleven years. With only eight clubs, three umpires to a game, and no retirement age, there were few opportunities to move up. In all honesty I must say I thought that there were a couple of fellows in the American Association who would go long before me. I thought they were better umpires; I admired their work, and I knew they had much more experience than I did because I had only been in the league two years.

How well I remember my first game in the majors. It was opening day, April 16, 1946 in Washington, D.C. The Boston Red Sox and the Senators. Ted Williams hit a 430-foot homer into the center-field bleachers, the longest home run ever hit in Washington. Bill Summers, Bill Grieve, and Hal Weafer were my partners. Believe me, when the game started, we should have made a ground rule that the ball was in play if it hit an umpire because I was so petrified I'd never have gotten out of the way. It wasn't that I was scared. It was just that my dream had come true. I looked straight up into the sky, stared for gosh knows how long, and said to myself, "Here you are. Now stay here." I'll never forget that moment as long as I live. I've had a thousand things happen that I could say was my biggest thrill in baseball. But the biggest moment of my life was the day I walked out on that field for the first time.

The World Series was another dream come true. As a kid I would listen to the Series games, read about them. In fact, I used to chisel my way to New York when I was a youngster to see them. As an adult I waited in line with a buddy all night to see the New York Giants and the New York Yankees play the opening game of the 1936 Series. We wound up sitting in Commissioner Landis's box. It rained all through that game. Carl Hubbell pitched the entire game, and after that they called him Rain-in-the-Face Hubbell. We got soaking wet, but we stayed through it, sitting right back of Mr. Landis. We sat there because no one else was sitting there, I'll bet there weren't a hundred people in the stands. I never said a word to Mr. Landis; in fact, to be truthful, we didn't even know at the time it was Commissioner Landis.

The first World Series I worked was 1948, the Cleveland Indians and the Boston Braves. Yes, I saw that disputed call on the Phil Masi pickoff at second base. I knew the pickoff was coming. Lou Boudreau and Joe Gordon had a time signal for the pickoff, especially with Bob

Feller pitching. We talked about that in the dressing room prior to the start of the series. Bill Stewart of the National League said, "I haven't seen one of those guys pick me yet." Poor Bill, he got caught flat-footed on the play.

The World Series game I was most charged up for was the opener in 1963. The reason was that I had read too many newspaper articles prior to the start of the Series. That year the Dodgers and the Yankees were shoo-ins, and I had my assignment about three weeks before the end of the season. The newspapers were full of stories about the pitching match-up of the century: Whitey Ford and Sandy Koufax. The more I read about it, the more I worried about it. Even when I walked out onto the field, I had those articles on my mind, how two of the greatest pitchers in baseball history would be going at each other with the whole world listening and watching. As luck would have it, I had a great game. Koufax struck out fifteen for a World Series record. Nobody paid much attention, but Ford struck out four and the other Yankee pitchers six, so there were twenty-five strike-outs in the ball game. Everything worked out just beautifully for me, no problems at all. I went back to the hotel that night so relieved, and I thought: Why in the world did you cross your bridge before you got to it? I made up my mind from then on that I would never worry about a ball game again. But I think I had more pressure on me in that game than any other time in my career. And I was a veteran!

In those days the World Series assignment came quite fast, every third year, because there were only thirteen umpires in our league. Mr. Harridge would not put two young umpires in the World Series to save his life. He always picked a veteran and a new fellow. Now you have to wait six or seven years to work the Series because there are more umpires. I think the rotation system used today is good. In all fairness to a guy, if he has been in the league for five years, he should be ready to work the Series. Otherwise, he shouldn't be in the league.

I worked with some outstanding umpires. Of course, I didn't have an opportunity to see much of the fellows in the National League, but I did work a few games with Al Barlick in spring training and the World Series. Every time I worked with Barlick he turned in an outstanding game. In my league Bill McGowan was a great umpire. I only worked with him at the end of his career, though. The best umpire I really got to know was Cal Hubbard. I worked with him seven or eight years. What made him a great umpire? He carried the respect of the ballplayers, carried the respect of the management, and he knew how to handle the ball game. He was rough, tough, and fair.

When he walked out in back of the plate, brother, you could hear a pin drop. He took charge from the minute he put that mask on. Nobody but nobody would get out of line. And he was a good ball-and-strike umpire, I mean *real* good.

There is no question that Hubbard was the man most responsible for my career. He was the supervisor of our staff for years after he had that hunting accident and lost his eye. When I got to the big leagues, he took me under his wing; if anybody ever treated a person like his own son, Cal Hubbard treated me that way. I was told it would take five years before I could establish myself as an umpire; it might have taken ten if it wasn't for that man. He taught me more about umpiring in one year than I had ever dreamed there was to learn. If I wasn't in the right position, he'd move me over, and if I was calling pitches a little too quick, he'd flash a sign. We would go out nights after dinner and walk maybe a mile, and all we would talk about would be baseball, baseball, baseball—umpiring, not the game. We'd sit in the lobby of the hotel and go through the rule book; we'd tear that rule book apart. My success in the major leagues was due to Hubbard. I don't know if I would have made it if it wasn't for him.

I broke in quite a few umpires. Johnny Rice, Ed Runge—I could name a lot of them. I tried to teach them the same things that Cal Hubbard taught me, to work with them the same way he worked with me. Hubbard did so much for me that I wanted to pass it on to the guys who really wanted to be good umpires. If a fellow really wanted to learn how to umpire in the big leagues, I'd stay with him day and night. And I'd try to keep the players and managers off him. I talked to a lot of managers about that: "Give him a chance. Let's see what he can do." That's how I broke them in. But if a guy thought he knew it all or said, "See you tomorrow," after the game was over, I didn't bother with him.

When I first started umpiring, I used to jump around a lot. I'd yell out strikes, and on the third strike I'd really get up in the air. When I got to the big leagues, Hubbard called me down for that. When I started to jump around, he'd say, "Your dago is showing." And when I'd scream out strikes in my high-pitched voice, he'd say, "You sound like a girl." After he needled me about it, I developed a normal strike call. Everybody on the field could hear, but I'll guarantee you couldn't hear me in the second deck, probably not even the first deck. I always had a real quick strike call. I didn't hesitate. As soon as I saw a strike, that right hand went up quick.

It's true the National League umpires put more color in their umpiring than we did. That also goes back to Cal Hubbard. He hated what he called showboating. Mr. Connolly, a refined old gentleman, didn't pay much attention, but when Cal took over as supervisor, he toned us down quite a bit. "I don't want you sacrificing judgment for color"—those were his famous words. He kept after us, and after a while we became very subdued. Personally I think a little color is good for the game. If I were supervisor of the American League, one of the first things I would do is try to put a little more zip into our umpires, a little more jumping around. As crew chief I tried to rouse my men a little bit. I'd say, "Let them know you are out there; don't stand like a pole. If those club owners see us standing around, they might think they can get by with three umpires."

There are other differences in umpiring between the two leagues that go back to the days of Tom Connolly and Bill Klem. Who's to say what's best? Personally, I think we had a much better look at the ball behind the plate by being over the top of the catcher than the National League guys did crouched to one side. I just think you can see better on a straight line than from an angle, but it's hard to say. I do think, however, that the American League rule about umpires at first and third base standing in foul territory is asinine. The National League umpires are much better off straddling the foul line. If you are in foul territory, you have a chance of missing a shot down the line, but if you are looking right at it, there is no chance of missing it. But I strongly disagree with the National League about putting the second-base umpire on the infield with a runner on first base. He should be in the outfield like in the American League for one reason and one reason only: If he gets hit with the ball, that kills the play. It doesn't happen often, but it happens. And you can get the same shot at a tag at second base from the outfield position if you hustle, maybe better because you watch the flight of the ball all the way instead of losing it when you turn.

I don't believe the talk about the American League giving the high strike and the National League giving the low strike. I've been in quite a few World Series, All-Star, and exhibition games against National League players, and I never changed my strike zone. Neither did the other fellows, and we never had any trouble on balls and strikes. Most of that talk comes from reporters and announcers who sit way up high in the press box and call the pitches. They can't call pitches from up there; they're just guessing.

Calling pitches is the toughest job in the game, but I loved it because you're really in the game back of the plate. On the bases you start daydreaming when there isn't much action, and the next thing you know you're in trouble. But behind the plate, brother, you are in the game every second. You never take your eye off the ball. You follow that son of a gun all over the ball park.

I was one of those fellows who worked right over the top of the catcher. I didn't shift to the inside on right- or left-hand hitters because I always believed that if you looked at a pitch at an angle, you couldn't honestly see it. I set myself right behind the catcher and then formed a strike zone in my mind for each hitter. If the ball passed through the rectangle, it was a strike. I drew a different rectangle for each hitter. For me, the strike zone was not the way a man stood at the plate; it was his normal stride when he swung. Sometimes they would get cute, like Lou Boudreau, who'd straighten up on you. But I found if you kept that rectangle in mind, the pitches would call themselves.

No question that the high and low pitches give you the most trouble, but the most difficult call for me was the half swing. There is no way in God's world that the poor fellow back of the plate can see it because on most half swings the catcher jumps up and blocks you out. All you see is part of the bat go around, and now you're guessing again. I think the rule about appealing to the umpire at third or first base is great; it should have been part of the rules of baseball from the day the game was invented.

An umpire is not right all of the time. You miss one once in a while. But when I made a call, down deep in my heart I thought I called it right. If you kick a call, and I don't mean those real close plays, it happens only because you're asleep.

In order to be a good umpire, you have to have the desire to learn something every day. Every umpire feels that he is the best umpire there is. But the best umpire is the guy who feels that way and then learns something the next day. I tried to learn something each game from the first day I stepped out on that ball field to the last day I walked off that ball field. When a fellow goes off the field feeling down deep in his heart that he hasn't done that good a job and then takes inventory of himself to find out why, that's what makes a good umpire.

As far as rules are concerned, you got to be like the priest in church: You have to know that rule book like he knows that Bible. Anybody can learn the rules, but not everybody can understand them. A lot of things that happen on the field aren't covered by rules, and sometimes one rule will supersede another rule. When you are out there, you can't go into the book; you've got to have the answer right in your head, and you've got to have it the minute something happens.

Cal Hubbard had the best answer as to what makes a good umpire. He used to tell us: "What you have to have in this game is to be rough, be tough, but have an even disposition." I've worked with fellows who lost complete control of themselves in tough situations; they were good umpires when everything was going smooth, but the minute that clutch thing came about they would go to pieces. I also worked with guys who were great umpires in any situation, but they had short fuses; they couldn't control their tempers, and when they'd explode, they went to pieces. It's just like Hubbard said: "If you can't control yourself, you can't control the ball game."

As an umpire I would not tolerate being abused or embarrassed. You call a lot of questionable pitches behind the plate. I would tolerate a pitcher asking me where the ball was, but I would not tolerate him charging in from the mound. If he'd start for the plate, I'd say, "Take one more step, brother, and keep on going." The same thing with the catcher. Take Yogi Berra. He'd say, "Dag"—he always called me Dag—"where was that one?" "Yog, I didn't like it." "What do you mean you didn't like it?" Finally, I'd say, "Look, Yog, it's nothing until I call it, and when I call it, that's it, so stop your crying. Keep quiet if you want to stay around." That's okay, but if Yogi had jumped up at me and screamed in my face, he'd be gone. The same thing on the bases. If the manager came out in a sensible way and said, "Pap, you missed that play," or "You were out of position," or, "It looked like he was in there," I'd say, "That's your judgment from in the dugout. I'm on top of it, but maybe I should go in there to get a better view." But if he came out screaming and calling me a lousy so-and-so, he'd be dead. I didn't like guys abusing me, and I didn't like them trying to show me up.

I'll never forget something that happened in my first year in Yankee Stadium. I called a Yankee out at second, and out came Joe McCarthy, the manager. It was a Sunday afternoon, and there were probably 50,000 fans there. He said, "You know, young man, I've been telling the fellows what a hell of a chance you got of staying up here. You're going to be one of the greatest umpires. For God's sake, I don't know how you could miss that play." Then he walked away. That's all he said, but the fans were really yelling and screaming at me. McCarthy didn't say anything, but he did put on a show to get them worked up. With his arms flapping and all, it looked like he was eating me alive. He got away with it, but if he had done that later in my career, I would have done something about it.

Of course, I never tolerated profanity directed at me, and I never used profanity with a player. I'm no saint. I've said things when I get mad that I've regretted. But I tried hard to control it when talking to players or managers because if you cuss them, you've opened the door for them to cuss you.

That old saying "Familiarity breeds contempt" applies to the ball field. You can't be too nice to ballplayers, or they will take advantage of you. They know how far they can go with each umpire. "You can go this far with this guy, but don't go any further because he'll crack his whip on you"—I've heard that a thousand times. You can be a nice guy and be an umpire, but you can't be a nice guy and be a good umpire. There wasn't a nicer guy in the world than Cal Hubbard, and he was just as tough as anyone who ever walked on the ball field. He'd crack his own brother if he got out of line out there.

I worked with many outstanding players, but two of them stand out as being particularly good with umpires. Ted Williams stands ceiling-high. He very rarely looked back at an umpire at the plate. And he would try to help you even to the point of getting players off your back. If you finished the season with Boston, he'd come to the dressing room, shake your hand, wish you and your family a happy winter, and thank you for being associated with the game. He was the only one ever to do that. The other great one was Joe DiMaggio, another perfect gentleman. But without question the most outstanding was Mr. Williams.

I wasn't bothered by the abuse from the fans. I just wouldn't listen to it. I knew that I was going into a profession where I wouldn't have a friend when I walked out onto that field. Let's face it, the public regards the umpire as a necessary evil. Your own family will holler at you if they're rooting for a particular ball club. I trained myself in amateur ball not to hear it. Sure, I could hear a lot of rumbling coming out of the stands, but it would never affect me. I did have rabbit ears for the ballplayers, but not the fans.

Sure I feel bad about the way umpires are treated. We go out there and do the best we can; we're human, so we make a few mistakes. I don't mind the average fan who chirps and yells and roots while enjoying the game. But I hate the guy who abuses you. In the first place, those loudmouths couldn't do our job, and in the second place, they wouldn't have enough nerve to go out there. But up in the stands he's one big brave guy. I resent the guy who boos a player because he made an error or an umpire because he thinks he missed a play.

I never feared violence, but I worried about it at times. Especially back in the old days when the fans were much more radical. You'd wonder about it when you'd made a call on a close play that ended the game. Some parks were tough, like Comiskey Park in South Chicago. Your life might depend on whether you can get a cab and get away, especially after a night game. You can get yourself killed in spots like that. I thought of those things many a time.

I've been hurt numerous times, but I never left a game because of an injury. I had my right elbow fractured one opening game in New York when somebody fouled one off of Whitey Ford, but it didn't take me out of the game. I never missed a ball game until I got sick one time in Boston. I was sweating bad when I got to the ball park, so my partner called the Red Sox physician, Doc McCarthy. He said I was in no condition to go on the field. I told him that I had never missed a ball game to that point, and I wanted to get out there. He said, "You're not doing no such thing. You're going right to the hospital." So I went to Sancta Maria's Hospital. They examined me and found out the crab I had eaten the night before was bad. It took three days to get over that.

Maybe if I had had an ounce of brains, I'd have walked out when I got hurt. But you couldn't hardly do that in those days because you would leave your partner all by himself. Today, with four-man crews, an umpire is foolish if he doesn't get out of there when he gets sick or hurt. Three men can work the game; we used to work it with two.

I'll never forget the time Boston came into Chicago for a crucial series in July 1951. All four games were one-run decisions, and a couple of them set records. It was the toughest series I ever worked.

Boston won a twi-night doubleheader on July 12 to take over first place. They won the first game, 3–2, and after a twenty-minute break the second game started. It went seventeen innings, 4:01, at the time the longest night game in American League history. Saul Rogovin pitched the entire seventeen innings for the White Sox but got beat, 5–4. We started at five o'clock and didn't get out of the ball park until a quarter after two the next morning; by the time we got downtown to the hotel it was nearly four.

The next night I was behind the plate. Wouldn't you know we went nineteen innings? It lasted four hours and forty-seven minutes. That was the longest American League night game by innings in history and tied the major league record for the longest night game. We also set a major league record for the most innings in two consecutive games, thirty-six. Just like the night before we had a marathon pitching performance: Mickey McDermott went seventeen innings for the Red Sox. But the White Sox won it, 5–4.

We almost had another extra-inning game the next day. Clyde Vollmer got a clutch hit in the ninth to give Boston a 3–2 win.

Those marathon games were tough. Most fans don't realize what a physical beating umpires take. For nineteen innings I was constantly bending up and down on every pitch. You don't sit down for half an inning like the players. Nobody asks if you want a drink of water, or whether you want a cigarette, or whether you have to use the john, or whether you're feeling well. After working eighteen perfect innings, you can miss a pitch in the nineteenth, and they will scream at you. It's like I always said: An umpire is a necessary evil.

Mr. Harridge had a policy, and Joe Cronin continued it, of assigning special crews to important series, especially during the end of September, when there was a pennant race going on. He would pick those he thought were the best umpires and send them in. When I was the dean of the staff, Mr. Harridge would tell me to go someplace and pick a crew. I'd say, "Mr Harridge, you are the president, so you decide who will work with me." I wasn't going to pick anyone because then I'd be in trouble with the rest of the fellows. After we worked the series, we'd split up and go back to our regular crews.

That happened many, many times in my career, so I was involved in a lot of important series. The one I remember most was the Detroit-Yankee series in 1961. Being the oldest umpire in the league, the dean of the staff, I worked back of the plate in the first game in Yankee Stadium. Detroit was leading the league by three games going into the series. Time and again during the night before the opening game I thought about how much the series meant to both clubs, but especially to Detroit because they hadn't won a pennant in a long time. I kept saying to myself, "Don't do anything out there where they can put the monkey on your back and say it was the umpire who beat us. Let them beat themselves. Whoever is going to get beat, let them beat themselves." I felt the pressure of that game. As luck would have it, it was just a perfect ball game. Nothing happened to put any of us in any kind of trouble. The next night, when we went out on the field, Bob Scheffing, the Tigers' manager, came over and said, "Well, we got beat last night, but by gosh we weren't beat by the umpiring. The umpiring was just outstanding." I thought that was great.

It might sound strange, but I always felt it was easier to umpire in the major leagues than in the minors. The major leaguers played the game better—they ran faster, hit a little better, and pitched much better. Also, they were easier to work with. I'd call a play in the majors, and nobody would say a word; but if I made the same call in the minors, the benches would clear.

I concentrated so hard on doing my job that I really didn't appreciate a ball game. I resolved at the beginning of my career that I would forget about what would happen on the field. The next day someone would tell me about some play, and I'd ask when it happened. They'd say, "In the fourth inning. Where were you? Downtown?" I was an umpire, not a spectator. I wasn't concerned with how good a play someone made. If you concentrate on your work and don't anticipate plays, you will be a good umpire, but if you're out there admiring the action, you'll soon be in trouble.

Now a no-hitter is always a great thrill for an umpire, and anybody who says they don't know when one is on is not telling the truth. I had quite a few no-hitters. The most memorable for me—I was working the plate—was when Hoyt Wilhelm beat Don Larsen and the Yankees in the rain in 1958, September 20.

The game was played in Baltimore on a Saturday afternoon. It had rained all Friday night and was drizzling that morning, so I thought sure there would be no ball game. In fact, I didn't even think we would report to the park. Well, we got no notice of a postponement, so we went out. When I got to the dressing room, the phone rang. It was Paul Richards, the Baltimore manager and general manager, asking me to come up to his office. I told him I didn't make a practice of going to the front office, but he said he wanted to talk about today's game, so I went. He said, "Joe, let's try and get this ball game in. I don't mean go out there and get in five innings and then call the thing. Call it if you have to call it, but go as far as you possibly can because we'll be on national television and we're guaranteed thirty thousand dollars."

I knew Baltimore could use the money because they weren't drawing well that year. I said, "All right, if Casey Stengel agrees, I'll start the game. You just remember one thing: I don't want to hear one word from you or your players about the rain or accusing me of trying to drown you." (That's what players always yell at umpires when it starts to rain: "You trying to drown us?") "I'll start the game if you give me the lineup cards and go with it as long as I can."

We were late getting started. It was still drizzling. The field was a mess—it had really taken a beating from the heavy rains the night before. The mud was several inches deep, and there were puddles everywhere. The players were slipping and splashing all over the place. Larsen and Wilhelm both had shutouts going through the eighth inning. There was nothing that even looked like a base hit since the Orioles got one in the first inning. With two outs in the bottom of the seventh, Gus Triandos hit a fastball into the left-center-field bleachers off reliever Bobby Shantz to give Baltimore a 1–0 lead. I had been seriously thinking about not going into the eighth inning because the field was really in bad shape, but now I couldn't call the game because the Yankees would say I had waited until the Orioles scored. So I stayed with it.

We went right into the ninth inning. Hank Bauer, the last Yankee up, said, "Pap, do you know that guy Stengel wants me to lay one down?" I said, "Well, Hank, if that's what he wants, you better do it." He bunted one three or four inches fair but slipped and fell as he tried to get out of the box. The ball finally lost its momentum spinning in the mud and just went foul. Bauer never got out of the batter's box. On the next pitch he popped up to the second baseman. The game ended with Wilhelm pitching a no-hitter and Larsen a one-hitter for six innings. It was one of the greatest pitching performances I ever saw, and it happened when the game probably shouldn't have been played.

I think the pitching in my day was much better than it is today. Then each club had four outstanding starters; you never heard of relief pitchers in the sixth or seventh inning. Those guys rarely got knocked out, and if you didn't knock them out early, you could bet nine-to-one they'd pitch the entire game. Nowadays they're struggling to go five innings so they can go into the record and maybe win one.

Talk about great pitchers. The first game I ever worked behind the plate in the major leagues was against the guy who invented the slider and had the best slider ever seen—Red Ruffing. Knuckleballs? Washington had four knucklers, one lefty and three right-handed. Nobody ever threw a better sinker ball than Bob Lemon. Who was ever faster than Bob Feller? Hal Newhouser over in Detroit had a curveball that would drop off the table. Ted Lyons over in Chicago and Eddie Lopat, Allie Reynolds, and Vic Raschi in New York—their stuff was as good as, if not better than, the best pitchers today. One year [1952] Cleveland had three guys—Early Wynn [23], Mike Garcia [22] and Lemon [22]—who won twenty or more games each, sixty-seven among them.

Some ball parks were better to work in because of the background. You read where the background has so much to do with hitters; well, the same thing applies to umpiring. If you have a park with a low center-field fence so that the ball comes out of the white shirts in the bleachers, you have a problem picking up the ball. I thought that two of the finest parks for a plate umpire were Detroit and Boston because the bleachers were closed off in center field. Baltimore was the worst in the league by far. All those painted houses back of the center-field fence made it pretty tough. They also had the scoreboard in the wrong place, so at night the ball would come out of the lights. But now that they have moved the scoreboard and planted trees in the center, it's much better. Of course, all the new parks today are fine.

Minnesota was number one in my book when it came to taking care of umpires. Calvin Griffith always had a boy in the dressing room to take care of your every need. The minute you reported to the park he'd come in and ask if you wanted anything to eat or drink. And the minute the game ended, bingo, he'd be back again to serve you. They would even bring dinner to the dressing room if you wanted. In all fairness, there wasn't a place in the league that wasn't satisfactory. But when you talk about first class, it was Minnesota.

I worked under two presidents who had very different personalities, Joe Cronin and Will Harridge. Cronin was a ballplayer, a manager, and a general manager before he became president of the league. They say, "Once a ballplayer, always a ballplayer." I'm not criticizing Joe because I think he was a great boss. But I think that Mr. Harridge was more of a fatherly type of president as far as the umpires were concerned. When we were in Chicago, we had to report to his office every morning. He just loved to see the umpires. He was always concerned about you and your family, and he tried to help with any personal problems you might have. He felt that a happy home made for a happy umpire and that a happy umpire made for a good umpire. I never had a father, but if I had known my father, I believe I would have admired Mr. Harridge as much as my dad, he was that kind of person to me. I have nothing to say against Joe Cronin. He treated me fine. It's just that he was of a different school, a ballplayer and manager, and I think that rubbed off on him a little bit.

The front office was always concerned about our behavior. There were certain places in each town that were off limits because they didn't want us patronizing bars where undesirable characters hang out. Baseball has been very sensitive to gambling since the Black Sox Scandal, and we'd get bulletins from the commissioner telling us to stay away from certain places and people to avoid all suspicion of wrongdoing. I'd get a prank call once in a while, but no one ever approached me about doing business with them. If anyone had, I'd have probably fractured his skull because I would never even think about something like that.

I've seen a lot of changes in the game during my time. Going from the two- to the four-man system has made umpiring a lot easier. You get so much better coverage on the field. It helped an awful lot with spectator interference, trapped balls, and balls hit down the line. With two or even three men you often had to guess on those close plays, but now they are on top of the plays.

There has been a big change in the behavior of fans over the years. Before World War II fans were really radical. You got tremendous abuse, especially in the small minor league towns. Things changed after the war. Fans became much better educated about the game because of the coverage in newspapers, radio, and especially television. I think that as the fans became more knowledgeable, they became less radical and abusive particularly because they understood much more the position of the umpire.

There is no question that television has had a great impact on the way people regard umpires. We first started using instant replays in the American League. CBS had been televising the games and then wanted permission to use the replays. Mr. Harridge, Cal Hubbard, and I talked about it. CBS showed us some slides of what they would use. They said they were not going to try to embarrass an umpire but just show a close play and let the viewers decide. I'm tickled to death that we approved it for the simple reason that it has shown that umpires are right 99 percent of the time. It has been a shot in the arm to umpires because the public now realizes what a good job umpires do. Those people who used to say we were blind or crazy or that we didn't know what we're doing out there now appreciate what a good job we did.

Of course, sometimes it shows the umpire made a mistake, but I don't agree with those people who say that replays should be used to make close calls. A spectator pays for two things. One is to see his team win, and the other is to holler at somebody, either the umpire or the visiting ball club. They've got to boo somebody; that's what they go to the ball games for. How many people go to a game and never say a word? You can't holler at a camera. Besides, the camera doesn't always give you an accurate picture of what happened. I am convinced without a reasonable doubt that you can't call pitches on television. I know fellows who are outstanding umpires, and they couldn't be missing all those calls it looks like they're missing on television. You don't always get a true picture because of the camera angle. Television replays are fine as far as they go.

I was in the game when the first colored player, Larry Doby, entered the American League. There were rumors around that we were going to have a colored player, and then we had word that Bill Veeck had signed Doby and was going to play him in Chicago. Mr. Harridge said that it was happening, that we were going to accept it, and that we were not to let anybody abuse him because he's colored. That was his statement: No concessions; just treat him like a human being. Period.

One of the nicest things that ever happened to Larry Doby happened in his second game. Rudy York, a big, strong guy—and what a nice person—was playing first base. Doby got a single, and while Chicago was making a pitching change, York made a speech to him as if he were his own son. He welcomed him into the league and then said, "Forget you're colored. You're a ballplayer. If you want to make good, go out there and hustle. No one is going to get on your back because of your color, but they might if you don't hustle or are a fresh guy. Just play the game, mind your own business, and do the things that you came into this league to do and you'll be all right." I pretty near fell over. Here was a guy from down South [Alabama] welcoming a colored player into the big leagues. Larry Doby never forgot that. I don't know how many people could come into the leagues with all that responsibility Larry Doby had on his shoulders and carry it through like he did. He was a perfect gentleman. Everybody loved the guy up to the end of his playing career. He was just the opposite of Jackie Robinson.

There weren't many problems with integration in the early days. There was some resentment here and there, grumbling like: "They're going to take our jobs," or "He's only playing because he's a nigger." I told them, no way. They're going to take your jobs only if they're better ballplayers. The Negroes worked real hard to make good in baseball, in all sports, in fact, in order to get ahead. Just like I did.

There was a long time between when Doby came in and Emmett Ashford started as the first colored umpire. Mr. Cronin sent Charlie Berry and me down to San Diego to scout him when he was in the Pacific Coast League. Ashford was very, very colorful, but he would sometimes sacrifice judgment for color. In spite of that, he could umpire. The thing that hurt Emmett Ashford was his age. He came into the league at an age when most umpires were already thinking of retirement. There wasn't really any resentment of Ashford by the umpires. There were some remarks like "Look at that hotdog," but that was pretty normal for anyone to say.

I have a vivid memory of how I left baseball. I remember it so well because I have often wondered if I did the right thing. I was in Detroit one day. I had been on a six- or seven-week road trip going from one city to another, one hotel to another, never even unpacking my bags. It hit me all of a sudden. I just couldn't go any further.

Sure, an umpire's hours are great if you only count the ones you spent on the field. We used to get most games over in an hour and thirty-five minutes; an hour and forty-five minutes was a long game, and if you went much beyond that, you'd have to report to the president on why the game went so long. It's the hours off the field that get to you. You spent a lot of time traveling in those days because you went by train instead of planes like today. Then there was so much to do to get ready for the game. I'd get up in the morning and be on edge, waiting for the time to get to the park. After the game you'd go back to the hotel, have dinner, walk around, or sit in the lobby. Those were long, long days.

It's a lonely life. Unless, of course, you were the kind of guy who liked to be on the go all the time. But if you were a family man, it was a very lonely job. I had to gear myself to the point where it wouldn't get me down. I was determined not to let it get to me because it would affect my performance on the field. I tried not to worry about my family or think about how much I missed them. I stayed pretty much to myself. I was the kind of guy who could entertain himself. I was a great one for browsing. I'd spend hours walking around the big department stores and never buy a thing. I didn't care for the movies like some guys, but if we had a night game, I'd listen to the broadcast of a day game. And I passed the time doing a lot of reading. I was a fanatic on rules because of Hubbard, so I'd tear that rule book apart. Anything to occupy my mind so I wouldn't get lonely. Of course, I contacted my family quite often; I called home two or three times a week.

Right up to the day I made up my mind to quit, I never really thought seriously about retiring. There were so many things involved. It wasn't that I got tired of the traveling, or the game itself, or the people I was working for, or the people I was working with. It just hit me: How many more years did I have left? How long have I been away from my family? How much more could I gain financially, compared to spending more time with my family? When I figured the whole thing out, I decided it wasn't worth it.

I called my wife and told her to take the first flight to Boston the day after tomorrow. I met her at the airport and told her that I had decided to retire. She said, "Well, I knew it was going to happen someday. Maybe it's about time." That was the first time she agreed with me about retiring, and she sounded very happy about the idea, so I thought it must be the right thing to do. We had breakfast and then went to Joe Cronin's office. I said, "Joe, I'm in here for one reason and one reason only. I want you to set up my pension plan. I'm giving you notice. I'm retiring after this year." He said, "You're crazy." I said, "No, I'm not. I mean it." He said I'd change my mind when contract time came around. I told him, "Don't send me a contract because I'll send it right back. I am not going to work next year. I'm through." He still didn't believe me.

From there I went to Chicago for the last series of the year. Friday, Saturday, Sunday, and the season was over. I worked the plate Friday night, but for the first time my heart just wasn't in the game. After the game I called Ed Runge up to my room. Runge and I were like brothers and still are. He was a tremendous umpire. I think he was the best young umpire who ever came into the American League, and I think he was the best young umpire when he left the league. Anyway, I said, "Ed, will you pack my work bag tomorrow? I'm going home." He tried to talk me out of it, but my mind was made up. I tried to get Cronin on the phone but couldn't reach him at that time of the night. I was going crazy thinking about it, so I took the first flight to New York, rented a car, and drove home. I had quit two days before the season ended.

Cronin still wouldn't believe I was retiring. He sent me a contract, and I sent it back. He called. "What's the matter, not satisfied with the numbers?" I said, "No, that's not it. I told you I retired. I'm through." Finally, I said, "Joe, you announce my retirement within the next seventy-two hours or I'm going to give it to the papers." That was it. He announced it on January 1, 1966.

I was told that I would never make it, that I would miss it too much, that I'd go out of my mind. Nothing was further from the truth. I spent six or seven weeks in Florida during spring training, and I did have that urge to be out there. And when I came home the opening day of the season, I felt it a little bit. But as the season progressed a few weeks, I lost it completely. I don't miss the demands of the game or the traveling. I do think time and again about the people I worked with. I do miss that part of it.

Baseball don't owe me a darn thing. I owe baseball everything. To come out of the coal mines with only a high school education and get to where I got in the great game of baseball, brother, that's a story in itself. If it wasn't for baseball, I wouldn't be living on a lake in Pennsylvania in the summer months and in Florida during the winter. Sure, I've given baseball my whole life. I have put every ounce of strength that I've ever had in my body into the game of baseball for the best interest of the game and to do the right job for the people I worked for. But I got a good return out of it and still am getting a good return out of it. From the bottom of my heart I'm thankful to God that there is such a thing as the National Pastime because it's done so much for me.

Bill McKinley in a photograph that accompanied new stories of his contested call that Yankee Joe Pepitone had been hit by a pitch in a 1964 World Series game against the Cardinals. Courtesy National Baseball Library & Archive, Cooperstown, N.Y.

Bill McKinley

ⓔⓔⓔ

William Francis McKinley
Born: Kinsman, Ohio, May 13, 1910
Height: 5' 11"
Weight: 170
Playing career: none
Umpiring career: Ohio State League (D), 1939; North Carolina
            State League (D), 1940; Michigan State League
            (C), 1941; American Association (AA), 1942,
            April–August 1946; American League, August
            1946–1965
No-hit games: Bill Monbouquette, August 1, 1962
All-Star games: 1953, 1958, 1962 (second game)
World Series (games): 1950 (4), 1952 (7), 1957 (7), 1964 (7)

I always enjoyed baseball, but I didn't get much support from home. My dad was a very religious man, a Presbyterian. On Sundays we went to church three times. On the Sabbath there was no newspaper, no radio, and, of course, no baseball. I finally just had to sneak away on Sunday afternoons and go to the ball park. But I made sure I got home before chore time!

Not one member of the family encouraged me to go into baseball. When I went off to the St. Louis tryout camp, Dad thought it was the silliest thing I ever did. Even when I got the job in Class D ball as an umpire, he told people around home, "He'll get through with that foolishness pretty soon and come back and cut meat." My brother took him to see me in a major league game one time in Cleveland. It was the only ball game my dad ever saw. I don't remember what he had to say about my success.

I was born in Kinsman, Ohio, May 13, 1910, the year my parents moved to Ohio from Pennsylvania. I was the youngest of four children, two sisters and one brother. I lived on the farm until I was eighteen years old. I didn't have an opportunity to go to college after graduating from high school, so I went to work cutting meat in my brother's meat market. I was a butcher for three or four years, during which time I played semipro baseball on Wednesday, Saturday, and Sunday, like they used to do in those days.

In 1932 I went to work for the Pennsylvania Power Company in Sharon, Pennsylvania, about twenty miles from my home. The power company sponsored a team in a softball league. They needed a catcher, so I went down there to give it a try. While I was catching for the power company team, I got the desire to play ball seriously.

Then, in 1935, I saw an ad in the *Sporting News* from Branch Rickey inviting young men to try out at his baseball camp in Hot Springs, Arkansas, under the supervision of the Cardinals' coaches and instructors like Rogers Hornsby, Johnny Mostil, Max Carey, Dizzy and Paul Dean, and Lon Warneke. They charged $60, $10 a week for six weeks plus board and room of $12 a week. That ad fascinated me, so I borrowed some money from an insurance policy, and away I went to Hot Springs in March.

When I got there, I discovered that there were 385 other kids who had the same idea. They divided us up into eight teams. There were four diamonds down there, so we played every day, sometimes doubleheaders. Branch Rickey and his scouts watched the games, and whenever they saw somebody they thought might be a professional ballplayer, they signed him to a contract.

It took me until the next to the last day in camp to impress anybody. Finally, a scout asked me if I would be interested in going into the St. Louis farm system. I said, "Where do I sign?" I didn't even read the contract. I later found out that the contract was for a trial with Norfolk, a Class D team in the Nebraska State League.

I went back home for the month of April, then set out at my own expense to Norfolk. In those days a Class D team consisted of fourteen players. That meant a lot of fellows had to play when they didn't want to play, and pitchers had to play other positions after they had pitched. Even the coaches and managers played. I was in camp just one week, seven days, when a fellow approached me. He said, "I understand that you are trying out as the catcher on this club." I said, "That's right." He said, "Well, I have been watching you, and you are not going to hit good enough to make it. Besides, I am the manager *and* the catcher." Somehow some of the desire I had to be a ball-player left me.

For the next three years I went back to cutting meat for my brother and playing semipro ball. Then I got the urge again to get into baseball somehow.

At the time the Cardinals were holding that tryout camp in Hot Springs, George Barr, a National League umpire, was running the first umpire school. He only had about six fellows there. Before I left the camp, Barr said to me, "Young man, if you don't make it in professional ball, come back to my school and give umpiring a try." That was the least of my thoughts or desires then, but it sounded pretty good in 1939, so away I went to Hot Springs again, this time to try out as an umpire.

I had never umpired a ball game in my life until I went to that school. But I found that my experience as a catcher was very valuable as far as working behind the plate is concerned. It eliminated the fear of being behind the bat that a lot of fellows had. Also, I didn't have any problem getting used to working while wearing all that equipment.

By 1939 the school had begun to take hold. They had better than 100 fellows there. We worked the Cardinals' tryout games, which made it pretty nice because we got a lot of work in real action. At the end of the six weeks Mr. Barr called me into his office and asked if I'd like to give professional umpiring a try. I told him I would, so he said, "I got a job for you in the Ohio State League. A hundred dollars a month and pay your own expenses." I wasn't in a position to hold out, so away I went to the Ohio State League. That was Class D, six teams, two umpires to a game.

Having to pay your expenses out of $100 a month meant that you were really on the ground floor at the end of the season. You had to go to work right away at something else because you had saved absolutely nothing. But you don't go out into professional ball for the money. You do it to fulfill your desire to be a ballplayer or an umpire. Some fellows refused to work for that kind of money, and of course, they wound up without jobs. Mr. Barr always said, "Don't worry about the money in minor league ball. Who are you? You're nothing. You've got to have experience. Nobody is going to look at you until you get to AA ball as far as big league umpiring is concerned." I kept that in mind, so I didn't worry about money my first four years.

In 1939 I attended the Centennial Convention of Baseball in Cincinnati. That's where I met Bill McGowan, the American League umpire who had just opened an umpire school. He invited me to attend his school to learn the American League style of umpiring. I had already learned the National League style of working with the inside protector from Barr, so I thought it would be a good thing to do because in those days your style of umpiring made a difference. So in the spring of 1940 I attended McGowan's school in Jackson, Mississippi. (Later, as a major league umpire, I was an instructor at his school in Cocoa Beach, Florida.)

There wasn't too much difference between the two schools other than that Barr taught you to use the inside protector and McGowan taught you to use the outside protector. There really isn't anything to teach other than the basic principles of the game, mechanics, and how to handle situations.

McGowan got me a job for the 1940 season in the North Carolina State League. That was also Class D, but they paid a little better, $125, and they played only six days a week because the blue laws in North Carolina prohibited Sunday games.

The next year, 1941, McGowan got me a job in the Michigan State League. That was Class C, a little faster ball, $160 a month and $1 a day expenses. Mr. Tom Halligan, the president of the league, was a good fellow to work for. In the minor leagues I worked for a varied group of presidents. I don't know how most of them got to be the president of a league because they didn't know much about baseball, that was for sure. Most of them didn't back their umpires, so you were out on your own on the field. But Mr. Halligan backed his umpires. He watched us work and made sure everything was going all right. We appreciated that very much.

The president of the league is very important in determining the breaks you get in moving up the ladder because he is the man you are working for. If he likes you, he is going to try to advance you. Fortunately Mr. Halligan thought I could do the job in AA ball because about a month before the season was over he sold my contract to the American Association. I went up with Earl Halstead, who now edits and publishes the baseball *Blue Book*. We replaced an older fellow who had gotten sick and another fellow who had gotten fired because of booze. That was my first big break. Now I knew I was going to be scouted by the major leagues.

Umpiring in the minor leagues was no picnic. Some of the facilities were horrible. In the Ohio State League we had to dress at the hotel because there wasn't any place to dress at the ball park unless you used the shed where the grounds keeper kept his tools. Fortunately the league was spread out geographically, so you could commute each day. You worked only a one-game stand in a town and then moved on to the next place. The North Carolina State League was a little better. It had some pretty good dressing rooms. So did the Michigan State League. In the American Association some were good and some were bad. I could talk now about how bad things were, but I really didn't think it was that bad at the time. I was getting a chance to go into professional ball, so I just forgot about those things.

It was harder to forget about some of the incidents on the field. They were a little hard to take some times. Lots of times we didn't get any backing from the president of the league. That was the problem. You'd chase somebody and send in a report, and time after time nothing was done about it. Oh, maybe sometimes they'd fine a guy $5 or something like that. But you knew a ballplayer didn't care much about that because often the club would pay it. In some respects the discipline was horrible. You realized after a while that you weren't going to get any backing, so you had to take the responsibility yourself—maybe take a little more on the field or just throw them out and make them sit on the bench.

Sometimes the behavior of the fans was pretty bad, too. We got lots of threats. Several times in the Ohio State League and the Carolina State League the ballplayers had to help us off the field. They would form a line with bats in their hands, and we would walk through it, get into our cars, and leave. That sort of thing discourages a fellow. There was supposed to be police protection in organized baseball, but we found out that in Class D the policeman was there until maybe the seventh inning, when he'd get tired and go home. Seems like the riots always came in the eighth and ninth innings, when there was nobody there to help, so we had to fight through it ourselves. That's why a lot of fellows only worked about a month or two and away they went home.

The American Association teams went to spring training just like the major league clubs, so in the spring of 1942 I went to Florida with Kansas City. In midseason I got drafted into the Army. I didn't pass the physical because of a defective eardrum, so they sent me back to baseball. During the winter things got a little tougher in the war. The draft board told me I could hear good enough out of one ear, so away I went into the Army.

I was in the Army for three years. We were twenty-seven months in the European theater under the First Army. I was in what was called a salvage repair outfit. When the battles were over, we would gather up the clothing and shoes, then launder them and fix them up for reissue. We got involved in the Battle of the Bulge, but fortunately our outfit was far enough behind the lines so that nobody got hurt.

I was a mess sergeant. They found out from my record that I was a meat cutter, so I got a job in the kitchen right away. Apparently one of the mess sergeants was not doing a very good job because the company commander fired him and gave me the job. I had it for the rest of my Army career. At least I ate well.

I came home from the service in October 1945. There was a rule that servicemen could go back to their jobs if they were able to handle it, so I went right back to the American Association. In late August 1946 I got my big break. I was working in Kansas City when I got a call from Mr. George Trautman, the league president. He said, "You have been sold to the American League. Report to Chicago tomorrow. Game time is one-thirty." Just like that.

I couldn't believe it. I had had no warning during the season that it might happen. I was working with some good umpires in the Association, fellows I thought would go before I did. They had more experience and more stature physically than I did. They were bigger, heavier than I was. One of my partners, Pat Padden, just about fainted when I told him because he thought he would go ahead of me. I thought he would, too. But that's the breaks of the game. You either get them or you don't. George Pipgras had gotten sick, so they needed a replacement, and I was the one.

The next morning I took a plane to Chicago, where I joined Eddie Rommel and Jim Boyer for a series between the White Sox and the Cleveland Indians. Rommel was the crew chief. He had had a great career as a pitcher with the Philadelphia Athletics and was a veteran umpire. He didn't help me as much as some umpires did later on with the finer parts of the game, but he was a good guy to break in with because he knew his way around.

They put me at third base my first game to break me in sort of easy. Everything went along beautifully; nobody said a word. The next day I went to first base, and the game went along fine. The following day I was supposed to go behind the plate, but Tommy Connolly, Harridge's supervisor of umpires (Harridge didn't know anything about umpiring), came into the dressing room and said, "Young man, I want you to go back to first base again today. This is the rubber game of the series. I don't want you to get in trouble. You take your turn behind the plate tomorrow night, when the Tigers come to town." I said, "You're the boss."

Everything went along beautifully until the ninth inning. Joe Kuhel, the Chicago first baseman, stepped up to the plate in the last of the ninth with the White Sox behind, 1–0, and hit a line shot down the foul line into the right-field bleachers. At that time in Comiskey Park the foul line was an illuminated line about two inches wide that went from the field boxes clear to the roof of the stands. All I had to do was turn around, set myself, and call it. If it was fair, all I had to do was point "fair" with my left arm; if it was foul, all I had to do was point "foul" with my right arm. That ball just missed the foul pole on the fair side, but I was thinking with my right arm, so I thought "fair" and pointed "foul." I caught myself immediately, pointed "fair," and waved it a home run.

Well, that brought *every* ballplayer on *both* clubs to first base. Five years of experience went right down the drain. I was speechless. I didn't know what to say. They were all over me yelling, "What was it?" "What did you call it?" Finally, Rommel got within hollering distance and yelled, "Hey, what did you call it?" I said, "It's a home run, Eddie."

That got rid of Chicago. They were happy. But Lou Boudreau and his Cleveland gang were still there screaming. Rommel finally took over, which is sometimes the senior man's job when he has a young man in trouble. Eddie cleaned house. He told Boudreau to get them out of there or he'd run a half dozen into the clubhouse.

I had the decision right, but it was the way I called it that caused the problem. They hold you to your motions, especially in a case like that. Oh, I was embarrassed. I wanted to crawl under the foul line and right out into the street and go home. But you have got to stay there and take it. That's part of the experience you go through, the way you learn things in umpiring. That never happened again. The home run tied the score. Danged if Chicago didn't win the game in the tenth inning. That always happens in a situation like that.

The next day, when we went up to Mr. Harridge's office before going to the ball park, he called me in. He said, "Young man, do you have any physical defects?" I told him, "No, not that I can think of offhand." "Well," he said, "what kind of decision was that you made last night?" I said, "Well, sir, I had too many arms in motion, and it brought out the whole house." He said, "I'll say it did." (He had been there watching.) I said, "That will never happen again; don't worry about that." That seemed to satisfy him. That's all there was to it.

The next day I worked the plate for the first time in the major leagues. I had Hal Newhouser of Detroit and Joe Haynes for Chicago. I had never seen a curveball like the one Newhouser threw that day. Fortunately Newhouser was the kind of pitcher who had good control, so most of his pitches were strikes. The Detroit catcher, Bob Swift, said, "Kid, just take it easy, and don't call them too quick, and you'll be all right." That was nice of him; I sort of expected him to turn around and give me a blast. Other than griping on balls and strikes here and there, nothing serious happened. I got by pretty good.

I encountered some resentment at first because I was the first graduate of an umpire school to make it to the major leagues. The players read about it in the papers, and they'd yell things like: "Why don't you go back to school and learn what it's all about?" A few, very few, of the umpires also resented me a little. I'd make a call, and they would say things like: "Where did you learn that? In school?" But it soon blew over. McGowan was a highly respected umpire, and he had been my teacher. He got it around to the guys that the schools would make better umpires, and most of them accepted that.

Having been trained in both the American and National League styles, I don't think it makes much difference whether you work second base on the infield or in the outfield; it's fifty-fifty because slides into the bag open up one way as much as the other. I found that in the minor leagues or where there are only two umpires, the inside protector is better because you have to do a lot of running. But in the majors or where there are three or more umpires, then the outside protector is definitely better because it protects you more. Behind the plate the fellows with the inside protector have a little better look at the low pitch and the inside corner, but they're guessing at the high pitch and the outside corner.

Actually, when it comes to calling balls and strikes, you have to have your own system. There are two things that are essential. The first thing is to be able to see the pitch. I've had several clinics, and I told the kids the same thing: "I don't care if you stand on one leg; just get to where you can see the pitch." The second thing is to be comfortable. Get rid of that tension after each pitch. If you're not comfortable back there, it will drive you crazy in four innings.

I always got worked up for games behind the plate. The bases were important, but I didn't get butterflies like before plate games. It didn't happen in only a big game; it happened almost every day I went behind the plate. Of course, after the first pitch or two, or after the catcher turned around and said, "WHAT?" I was back in the groove.

I found that I had to adjust my strike zone according to each hitter. For me the important thing was the batter's height. The stance had nothing to do with it. Gene Woodling was the worst guy I ever saw at the plate. He was all hunched over and would uncoil when he swung. If you put the strike zone between his knees and letters, there would almost be no strike zone at all. Now on guys like big Frank Howard or that little Nellie Fox, who stood way back in the batter's box, you had to call the pitch where it crossed the plate instead of where they were standing. On fellows like that a pitch would be a strike coming over the plate, but by the time it got to where they were standing it would almost be in the dirt. You just have to adjust to each individual man. That's what makes calling balls and strikes so difficult.

One of the easiest games I ever worked in my life was the only no-hitter I had. Bill Monbouquette of the Red Sox beat Early Wynn in Chicago, 1–0. That was in 1962. There was nothing to it with those guys throwing the ball right over the plate and making them hit it all the time. I didn't know Monbouquette had a no-hitter until the eighth inning. I said something to the Boston catcher, Jim Pagliaroni, and he didn't answer. I said, "What's the matter with you?" He whispered, "Shhh. Don't say anything. The guy is pitching a no-hitter." Then I felt the tension; I felt myself bearing down a little harder.

My most difficult game was working the plate in the longest game, time-wise, in American League history. It happened in Detroit, June 24, 1962. The game started at one-thirty and ended at eight-thirty, exactly seven hours later. We went twenty-two innings before the Yankees finally won, 9–7. I never left the field, although a kid did bring me a little cup of water once. My back and legs got to aching something terrible. Toward the end of the game Yogi Berra asked me to brush off the plate. I said, "Brush it off yourself, you dago. I know where it is." I wasn't about to bend over at that point. I should have gotten extra pay for going twenty-two innings behind Berra.

I never considered myself either a pitcher's or a hitter's umpire. Some guys were more toward one or the other. Ed Runge was a pitcher's type of umpire. Now I didn't take anything away from a pitcher if it was close enough. Cal Hubbard used to tell batters when they complained about a call, "Don't trust me. I'm liable to miss one. The strike zone is between those two white lines" (meaning the inside lines of the batter's boxes). Cal used to say, "If you can save getting in a fight with the catcher and pitcher, that's what's important. The hitter doesn't really know where it is." I found that to be true.

I wasn't very colorful. Art Passarella was quite a showman, but I couldn't umpire like that. When I first came up, I heard the veteran umpires complaining about fellows who were loud and boisterous, so I took that as good advice. Bill McGowan once said, "If you are going to put on a big show, you better be right *all* the time." I never forgot that. I never put it on unless it was a called third strike; we were taught to really put it on then.

I wasn't what you would call a great rule man. I couldn't quote a lot of the rules, but when a situation came up, I could rule on it. You can't just know the rule and be a good umpire. There are three essential things you can't get out of the book—good eyesight, common sense, and good judgment. Good eyesight is being able to see exactly what is going on all the time; good judgment is handling the rules the way they should be handled; common sense is dealing with various situations properly. You can instruct someone to be a better umpire, but if he doesn't have those three things, he isn't going to be an umpire.

The biggest asset I had going for me was hustle. If I missed a play, it wasn't because I didn't hustle. That helped me a lot. Apparently word got around that I was hustling and trying to do a good job, so guys should leave me alone. I heard McGowan tell somebody that one day, so I kept on hustling. I found it helpful to pretend that the ball was going to be hit in my direction on every pitch. I was able to concentrate by getting into the game that way.

My philosophy was to leave the game at the ball park. I tried to get the game out of my system and not worry about anything until the next day. And I never carried grudges. I figured every day was a new ball game. If a guy had given me lots of trouble, the next day it was forgotten. If you brood about past games and carry grudges, you will never be able to relax and will always be in trouble.

The booing bothered me to a certain extent. You can't help resenting it. I've even been booed before the game started. After I began to watch professional football, I said to myself, "I am in the wrong business." But I just made up my mind that I wasn't going to let it bother me. You would have ulcers as big as a football if you let it worry you. Some fellows never made it because they couldn't take it.

That happened to [Nicholas] Red Jones. Red was a good umpire, but he had what we called ear syphilis. He heard *everything*. It took his concentration off the game. It bothered him so much that they finally had to fire him after six years. He worked with Steamboat Johnson down in the Southern League for several years and was a hardened veteran, but he just couldn't take what he heard.

Umpiring is an individual thing. You cannot copy anyone, although other umpires can help you in improving your work. Of course, Bill McGowan and George Barr taught me a great deal in their schools, and Eddie Rommel helped me in handling various situations on the field. Cal Hubbard probably helped me the most. He took over as the supervisor of American League umpires after Tommy Connolly. Hubbard would do everything he could to help you on the field. Connolly never helped you as far as the basics were concerned, but he was a great rule man. Connolly was more of a front-office man. He would always say, "Now don't get excited. We don't want to make the club owners mad." That would tear our hair out sometimes.

You can get into trouble if you try to copy other fellows. That happened to Augie Guglielmo. When Augie came up, he went with Larry Goetz. Goetz had a short fuse; he ran a lot of guys. Goetz was the kind of guy who would tell a new man, "Don't take it. Run them." Guglielmo tried to run them like Goetz, and he ran himself right out of the league.

I worked with some very good umpires. I worked with the whole staff my first year because I was the swing man. Bill Summers was a good umpire, and McGowan, of course, was great. They were both in the twilight of their careers when I came up; they were probably kept longer than they would be now. I didn't see McGowan in his prime, but everybody, even umpires, said he was great. Ed Hurley was a very good umpire who knew the rules inside out and ran the ball game in an ironclad fashion; he didn't take anything from anybody, and everyone knew it. Art Passarella was a good umpire; his trouble was off the field, not on it. Nestor Chylak came up in 1954. He was the best young prospect I ever saw; he was with me for seven years, and he turned out to be a great umpire. I didn't get to see much of the National League umpires, but Jocko Conlan, Beans Reardon, and Larry Goetz were good ones. Augie Donatelli was a very good umpire, one of the better ones I ever worked with.

I noticed a great change in umpires and ballplayers during my career. There was quite a bit of rivalry between the two leagues, even among umpires. You could tell that they sort of hated each other. Bill McGowan would run Bill Stewart right down the sewer when he saw him. There was quite a bit of that among the old-timers. That early group I joined was a pretty rough-and-tough bunch.

The same thing with the ballplayers. It seemed the modern players were better educated and more interested in life in general and the future instead of just the day-to-day ball games. The old ballplayers didn't seem to care about much other than playing ball. They whooped and hollered, swore and spit tobacco, and got drunk at night. I could see that withering away.

Players and umpires used to curse each other, and rhubarbs would be one big cursing match. No more. The ballplayers don't want to be cursed. I had never heard such language before when I went to the big leagues. I couldn't believe what I was hearing. I really learned it at the umpire school. I had come from a religious family, and it was quite a shock. Not that I was lily-white or anything like that, but the language was so vicious. My goodness, the language in the dressing rooms was awful. I never could understand why they had to use that kind of language all the time.

I saw so many great plays over the years that it's hard to remember them all. I appreciated all those good plays; we used to talk about them after the game. The most amazing thing I ever saw was the time Mickey Mantle almost hit one out of Yankee Stadium. I was behind the plate. I think Virgil Trucks had a count of one-and-one on him when he hit that shot. It hit the bottom of the flag holder on the top of the right-field stands. That was the longest hit I ever saw. After Mantle hit it, Bob Swift, the Tigers' catcher, turned around and said, "I must have called for the wrong pitch."

I worked three All-Star games. You don't have the pressure in them like in the Series, so they are a lot of fun. I worked the one in Baltimore in 1958, when nobody got an extra-base hit. That was the first All-Star game in history where all the hits [13] were singles. Jocko Conlan and I switched behind the plate in the 1953 game in Cincinnati. The National League was the home team, so Jocko worked the first four and one-half innings behind the plate, and I worked the last half of the game. Umpires used to switch behind the plate in those days. The leagues insisted on doing things half and half; besides, they didn't think one fellow should have to do all the work back there because we didn't get paid for the All-Star game other than expenses. After I retired, they had the host-league umpire work the entire game behind the plate.

I worked four World Series. That's always a big thrill for an umpire. My first one was 1950, the Yankees and the Philadelphia Phillies, the "Whiz Kids." I worked the foul lines with Al Barlick. That was the first time they put the alternate umpires on the field working the lines.

My first plate game was the fourth game of the 1952 Series. Allie Reynolds and Joe Black pitched. They were both great; they each gave up only four hits. Reynolds struck out ten, and the Yankees won, 2–0. That was the Series when Billy Martin made that fantastic catch of Jackie Robinson's pop fly with the bases loaded to save the final game.

That was also the Series when Art Passarella blew the call on Johnny Sain at first base in the tenth inning of the fifth game. I had the worst look at it of anybody in the park from over at third base. Art called Sain out, but the pictures showed that he had the throw beat. Bill Dickey, who was coaching at first base, argued a little bit, but there wasn't much of a beef. That was an important call because the score was tied and the Dodgers went on to win it in the eleventh inning, 6 to 5. Nobody said much about it in the dressing room after the game, but when the newspaper carried those pictures the next day, well, Passarella got pretty upset.

I had a big rhubarb in the 1964 Series. Joe Pepitone caused it. Bob Gibson, the St. Louis pitcher, threw a curveball that broke inside and hit Pepitone's pants. In those days uniforms were much looser than they are now, and that ball just brushed his pants. I saw it, so I told Pepitone to go to first base. He didn't go. He just stood there. Tim McCarver, the catcher, said, "What are you talking about? The ball hit the bat." I told him, "No. It hit him in the pants." Johnny Keane, the Cardinals' manager, came out and screamed and hollered awhile. It wasn't too bad, but they carried it a little further than I thought they would because the ball definitely did not hit the bat. A photographer took a picture of it that proves the ball didn't hit the bat.

I think the biggest ball game I ever had was when I worked the plate in Yankee Stadium in the seventh game of the 1957 World Series between the Yankees and the Milwaukee Braves. I worked the plate in the third game, but I really felt the pressure in the dressing room before the game, when I was rubbing up those 120 baseballs. I said to myself, "You can forget about the other six. This is it." I knew I was the guy who had to run the game that meant the championship of the world. I knew that I was going to be picked off by television cameras and a whole battery of newspaper men from all over the world. I kept thinking that any little mistake I made would be blown up in the papers tomorrow.

Another thing on my mind was Lew Burdette. I had seen the Yankee pitcher, Don Larsen, many times, so I knew him. But I had never umpired Burdette before. All I had in my mind was all that talk about him throwing a spitball. One of the National League umpires, Augie Donatelli, said, "Forget it. He doesn't spit on the ball, but he goes through all those motions before every pitch, so it looks like he does." He told me the Yankees would be asking to see the ball.

That's exactly what happened. Burdette would go to his cap, go to his hair, and all this and that. Then the Yankees would say, "Time. Look at the ball." The first time I asked for the ball, Burdette rolled it in on the ground to the catcher. He could have dumped it in a bucket of water, and it would have been dry by the time I got it. So the next time I stepped out in front of the plate and said, "Hey, *throw* the ball to me." He did. I never found anything on it. After a while the Yankees forgot about it and went on with the game. Burdette shut them out, 5–0, for his third win in the Series.

In all my career I caught only one pitcher throwing a spitball that was really soaked up. That was Dean Chance when he was pitching for the California Angels.

Now you had to watch some of those pitchers because they'd give you the business with the ball. The worst was Pedro Ramos of the Washington Senators. We had to watch him like a clock. He would go to his mouth with his hand and then pass it down over his shirt before he pitched. His fingers never touched his shirt, but you couldn't tell that from behind the plate. The first thing you knew, that ball was all brown and sticky.

I had a big rhubarb in Washington one day over him. The Orioles were there, and Paul Richards, their manager, didn't miss a thing. Paul kept needling me about watching him, kept asking me to look at the ball, all that sort of thing. Finally, he got mad and said, "Let's go out and see where he's got it." So I went out and looked him over— hat, shirt, pants, glove, everywhere. You can't find it. You can never find anything on those fellows.

Ramos finally gave me an opening because he wasn't going to his shirt after going to his mouth. I told the catcher, Earl Battey, to tell him to stop it or I was going to call the pitch a Ball. Well, he did it again. The pitch came right down the middle, and I said, "Ball." Ramos came halfway to the plate, hollering and screaming, and Battey started yelling, too. I said, "I told you. If you do it again, I'm going to throw you out of here." Ramos did it again, and I threw him out. Oh, there was a big hullabaloo about it. For a while after that, every time they announced my name before a game in Washington a roar broke from the stands.

I later found out he had the stuff in his cheek. Lots of ballplayers chew stuff, but Ramos was chewing something that was sticky and gave him a good grip on the ball.

The most important player an umpire has to work with is the catcher. The greatest one I ever saw to work behind was Jim Hegan of the Cleveland Indians. He couldn't hit over .250, but he was the greatest mechanical catcher I ever saw. It's just too bad that he couldn't hit better. And he was the best I ever saw at handling a pitching staff. He had rough-and-tough ones like Early Wynn, Bob Lemon, Bob Feller, and Mike Garcia who would do anything to win a ball game. They would chew up an umpire if they could, but Hegan kept them off the umpires. He wouldn't let them come up hollering and screaming. His point was that if you keep the fellow from getting mad, you keep him in the ball game.

Hegan could tell you off pretty good. But he never turned around to show you up. He always said it over his shoulder while he was down in his crouch. That's what an umpire likes: a catcher who controls his pitcher and doesn't try to show you up.

I saw so many outstanding players, but it isn't too hard to pick an All-Star team of fellows who played in American League during my time. Jim Hegan would be my catcher. Brooks Robinson was the most fantastic third baseman, no doubt about that. George Kell was great, too. The best shortstop was Luis Aparicio. I would put Joe Gordon at second base; he was late in his career when I got there, but he was still great. Bobby Richardson was also a fine player, and he never said a word to umpires. Nellie Fox was a tough little bugger; he would do more things to beat a ball club than anybody I ever saw. Then at first base I'd have Mickey Vernon. The outfield, of course, would be Ted Williams, Joe DiMaggio, and Mickey Mantle. The right-handed pitcher would be Early Wynn. There were several outstanding left-handers. Billy Pierce was a good one, but Whitey Ford was probably the best.

I'd say Wynn was the greatest pitcher I saw. He could stay out there and pitch nine innings, extra innings if he had to. Wynn was the type of guy who could remember a hitter. He didn't just throw out there; he pitched to the guy's weakness. He consistently ran the count to three-and-two. Not because he was wild like Tommy Byrne, who couldn't throw a ball over a card table. Wynn did it on purpose because he never wanted to give the batter a good pitch to hit. We hated him for it. Wynn was smart, and he was tough. If his mother was up to bat, he would hit her between the eyes if it had anything to do with winning a ball game. If a manager came into the dressing room and said, "This game means the pennant. Who wants the ball?" Wynn would be the first to grab it.

Bob Lemon would probably have been better than Wynn if he hadn't been so wild. Bob Feller threw harder than anybody I ever saw, but he was too wild to be great. You wouldn't want Feller to pitch a game you really had to win.

Of the hitters, Ted Williams was the greatest. He never said a word to the umpires, not one word. If he got mad, he took it to the dugout. Never said anything to me other than "Bear down, Mac, you're better than that." He'd say that while he was looking right out at the pitcher, so nobody knew he was talking. He never tried to show you up.

He got a little unhappy with me once. Ted was 6′ 3″, so they liked to pitch him down around the knees. One day in Chicago Billy Pierce threw one down there, and I said, "Strike." Williams never turned around, but he said, "That wouldn't have been a strike on Tom Thumb."

Bucky Harris was a great manager and a good fellow. I didn't see anything wrong with Joe McCarthy when he managed Boston, but he wasn't there very long. Casey Stengel wasn't too bad. He would come out and show off, but he wouldn't show you up or curse you. He would just come out with that double talk and all that lingo, which meant nothing, and then turn around and walk away. Of course, he was winning all the time, which might have helped. Al Lopez wasn't too bad. He wouldn't abuse you with the language, but he would talk you to death. We always had to warn him on the time limit, or he'd be out there all day. Freddie Hutchinson was no bargain. Neither was Paul Richards. Jimmy Dykes was a needler; he could needle you to death. Pinky Higgins in Boston was a very nice fellow; no problems with him. Steve O'Neill was at Detroit when I first went up, but by then he was too fat and had the gout too bad to bother coming out hollering.

Most of the clubs were pretty good to work with. The Red Sox were a real good outfit when Pinky Higgins had them. The Cleveland Indians were pretty good when they had their championship teams, but not later on, when Frank Lane got a hold of them. The St. Louis Browns, even though they were always down, were a good bunch. Detroit was pretty good; so was Washington under Bucky Harris. But the Philadelphia Athletics were a little different. They didn't seem to have much discipline; the old man, Connie Mack, was too nice to them. The Yankees were okay because they were winning so much, but they had three guys who were tough to umpire for.

Yogi Berra wasn't a bad guy, but he was a pest. He would get the crowd and the bench on you with his actions. He was always turning around, saying something. That's the worst thing a catcher can do because it gets everybody on you. You could never change him. I think he did it not knowing what he was doing.

The problem with Roger Maris was his personality. He just had none. He was a surly type of guy. I would rather have a fellow come right out and speak to me than give that surly kind of look.

Mickey Mantle was okay when he was going good, but when you took the bat out of his hands on a called third strike, he was very bad. At first he was all right, but when the publicity began to pour in and he got big in New York, he changed. He got real surly, and he drank quite a bit. I think he came up too quick, especially in a town like New York. The press was just more than he could handle.

The Yankees dominated the league—all baseball, really—during my career. Every place I went people would say, "We hate the Yankees. They win all the time. They have all the money." They did win all the time, but they didn't have all the money. Tom Yawkey could have bought out the Yankees lock, stock, and barrel. It wasn't the money. It was the organization upstairs and the way they handled ballplayers coming up and going out.

George Weiss was probably the best general manager in baseball. At least he got greater results than anybody else. It seemed he could tell when somebody was on the way down, so he would trade him for a bundle, in either money or players. He could get guys from other teams that were supposed to be washed up and fortify them. Fellows like Johnny Mize and Enos Slaughter would get a second wind and star for them. They had fellows on the bench who could take the regulars' place any day, and those guys out there knew it, so they kept scratching every day with no letdown. I think their success came mainly from that winning habit. That was the secret of their success.

Detroit was my favorite town. It is a perfect park for an umpire to work in. There are no ground rules—no wires or yellow lines, no trouble around the dugouts, no problems back of home plate. The ball is in play all the time there. That is beautiful for an umpire. Keep the ball in play. Let the players chase it. And you always see real good there because of the dark-green seats and fences. No big white signs or scoreboards in your way. Ted Williams would say the same thing. It was a great park to hit in, which means it was also a great park to umpire in. Also, they treated you well—the dressing rooms were fine, and the concessions people treated you well.

You make a lot of memorable decisions in twenty years, but I had an interference call one time that I felt especially proud of. It happened in New York. Phil Rizzuto was on first base and tried to go to second on a hit-and-run. Just as Jerry Priddy, the Detroit second baseman, got ready to field the ball, Rizzuto stopped, then jumped over the ball in front of him. Priddy flinched, and the ball trickled off his glove. Immediately I said, "You are out."

Bill Dickey, who was coaching at first base, came running over. "Did Rizzuto hit him?" I told him no. "Well," he said, "then it couldn't be interference." Stengel came out, and Dickey said, "He admitted Rizzuto didn't hit him." I told Stengel the same thing: "You don't have to hit him, Casey. Rizzuto jumped right in front of him. It was interference. That's all there is to it." Before the next pitch the

Yankees protested the ball game. They finally lost it, 4–3.

When we got into the dressing room, Bill Summers, the senior man, said, "Why did you tell them Rizzuto didn't hit Priddy?" "Because," I said, "he didn't hit him." Summers said, "It couldn't be interference then." I said, "Why not? Why isn't it interference? Here is a guy ready to field the ball, and Rizzuto jumps right up in front of his eyes. Isn't that interference?" "Well," Summers said, "I would have made him make contact." I said, "Holy cow. I must be crazy. The rule doesn't read like that."

Pretty soon Frankie Crosetti brought the extra balls into the dressing room like he always did, and he asked me, "Do you think you were wrong on the decision, Mac?" I said, "No, I don't. You played shortstop. How would you like to have a guy come along and jump right in front of you just as you were getting ready to field the ball?" He said, "You're right. Forget it. They're not going to protest the ball game."

I felt pretty good about that. My senior man was wrong. It was out-and-out interference, and I was proud I made the call.

I also never let them get away with that phantom tag on double plays. Nellie Fox did that a lot. Foxy was a little guy, so he didn't like getting knocked into left field by those big guys running down from first base to break up a play. I remember one time Chico Carrasquel fed him the ball. Foxy took the throw two steps across the bag and threw it to first. I called the runner safe. Paul Richards, the White Sox manager, usually came out on everything, but that time he didn't say anything because it was so obvious.

An inning or two later Foxy ran across the bag again when Ted Williams came sliding into second. Again I said, "You're safe." This time Foxy said, "What are you trying to do, make new rules?" I told him, "No, just catch the ball on the bag. That's all you have to do. That's what it says in the book, you know." Now Richards came out. "What are you doing, picking on him?" "Nope," I said, "I just want him to catch the ball on the bag." After that he did it.

I felt good about those calls. Why should I be good to the White Sox and give Boston the shaft? I wasn't doing anything new. It's been in the rule book for years; only some umpires haven't got guts enough to call it.

It's the same thing with runners going out of the baselines to knock out the pivot man. You give them a body length sliding either side of the bag, but when they go out of the lines to hit that guy, you should call two outs. The fans can see when the rules are not being applied. It's not good for the game. You've got to call them the way the book says.

It just is not possible to umpire a ball game with two men and do it right. I know because I tried it after I retired. After I left the American League, I worked college games at Ohio State and Kent State for two or three years and even worked the American Amateur Baseball Congress World Series down at Farmington, New Mexico. After I moved to Florida, I worked a few college games. But I soon quit. I couldn't see working games with two umpires. You can't see all the plays; you have to guess so much of the time because you can't possibly be on top of all the plays. As a result, you always get a lot of yelling and screaming.

I did it for a little pin money. My last year I got $15,000—that was after twenty years. I didn't retire with the fabulous pension umpires are getting today. I get a pension, but it's meager. I thought umpiring college games would supplement my income a little bit, but I didn't need the money that bad.

The American League umpires didn't organize as soon as the fellows in the National League because we didn't handle it right. They got hold of a lawyer and got permission from the National League club owners for him to come to their annual meeting and state the case for the umpires. We should have done that, but we didn't.

I was involved in trying to get something organized in 1965. We knew the National League umpires were organizing, and Ed Hurley in particular kept hounding for more money. So the five senior men, the crew chiefs, went to the league president's office to carry the ball. We had a secretary outline the things we wanted. I don't think Joe Cronin liked what we were doing. He said he would take our program to the club owners' meeting that winter. Cronin took it upon himself to present our requests rather than giving us a chance to see the club owners. The result of the meeting was that I got a letter saying that I had been retired. There was an option of retiring at fifty-five if we wanted, but they made it mandatory. Ed Runge, Joe Paparella, and I were let go. I don't think they wanted to give us what we wanted and were trying to head off an organization.

I wasn't very happy about it because it came as such a surprise. There was no warning. Just a letter, an eight-cent letter, saying I was through. It came about December 28. After twenty years in the league I thought I should have had a little more warning than that.

Five years in the minor leagues and twenty years in the major leagues are proof enough that I could do the job as a professional umpire. I think I did the job very well. The salvation I got out of the whole thing was doing something I wanted to do—make a living in professional baseball. That's something a lot of people never get to do.

Jim Honochick (left center) restrains Cleveland's Vic
Power during a home game with the Orioles in 1959.
Also pictured are umpire Charlie Berry, manager Joe
Gordon (35) and George Strickland of the Indians.
Courtesy National Baseball Library & Archive,
Cooperstown, N.Y.

Jim Honochick

⊖⊖⊖

George James Honochick
Born: Oneida, Pennsylvania, August 19, 1917
Height: 6' 1"
Weight: 230
Playing career: minor leagues, 1941–43, 1946
Umpiring career: Eastern Shore League (D), 1946; International League (AAA), 1947–48; American League, 1949–73
No-hit games: Virgil Trucks, May 15, 1952; Jack Kralick, August 6, 1962; Sonny Siebert, June 10, 1966; Tom Phoebus, April 27, 1968
All-Star games: 1951, 1954, 1960 (both games), 1966
World Series (games): 1952 (7), 1955 (7), 1960 (7), 1962 (7), 1968 (7), 1972 (7)
Championship series: 1970

One morning while I was shaving in June 1946, when I was playing for Baltimore in the International League, something out of the clear blue sky came into my mind about being an umpire. I didn't know anything about umpires, but that night, when I was out in left field, I concentrated more on watching the umpires than on my playing. I was fascinated by what they were doing. I made it a point to walk off with them after the game and asked if I could talk with them about umpiring. They invited me into their dressing room, even though I had heard it was taboo for players. There was Artie Gore, Roy Van Graflan, and Max Felerski. I told them about the feeling I had about wanting to be an umpire, and they encouraged me because I had a good temper and had never bothered umpires. I must have stayed there a good half hour talking with them.

The next morning it was still with me, so I went over to see Tommy Thomas, who was the general manager as well as the manager of the club. I said, "Tommy, I have a funny feeling. Something inside tells me I want to be an umpire." He laughed. "I'll be a SOB. You're the dumbest SOB I've ever seen come out of college. You want to be an umpire? Do you know what an umpire's life is like?" I told him that I knew nothing about umpires but that I had become fascinated by what they do and that there was something in me that wanted to be an umpire. Well, he started telling me all the pitfalls—how everybody hates you, that you have no friends, and all that stuff. So I told him I'd think about it some more.

But during the game that night I watched them again. It just stayed with me, so a few days later I went to see him again. "It's been almost a week now," I said. "I get up in the morning as an umpire; I go to bed at night as an umpire; it's with me all the time. I don't know anything about the umpiring profession; maybe you can help me." Tommy didn't want me to leave, but he called a friend, Tom Kibler, the president of the Eastern Shore League. He said, "Hey, I've got a dumb bastard here who says he's a college graduate, but he can't be because he wants to be an umpire. Nobody can go to college and want to be an umpire."

I got on the phone and asked Kibler for a job. He said he had just gotten rid of two umpires and needed replacements real bad but couldn't use me because I didn't have any experience. Finally, he said, "Look, I'm going to do Tommy Thomas a favor. Would you be willing to come down here and work for expenses only? No salary, no contract. If I like what I see after a week, I'll give you a contract; if not, you go back to Baltimore."

That was fine with me, so I started to round up the necessary equipment. Everything was hard to get in 1946. I bought a blue serge suit from Brooks Brothers, found one umpire's cap in a sporting goods store, and got shin guards and a mask from the ball club. I called Kibler and told him I was having trouble getting all the equipment. He said I could borrow a chest protector from my partner and could wear my baseball shoes. (I never thought about working the plate.) I was to report to Hans [Hanson] Horsey, the supervisor of umpires, in Denton, Maryland, who was going to be my partner and put me up during my trial.

Horsey was an elderly man who had played major league baseball with Cincinnati back in 1912. We had a long session where he told me about position, technique, the league, and so on. The next day, Sunday, July 15, we drove over to Milford, Delaware, for my first game.

When we walked up to home plate, who should be there as manager of the Cambridge, Maryland, club but Barney Forge. He played with Montreal in 1941, when I was with Baltimore, so we knew each other. He shook his head. "Well, I'll be a SOB. I thought I was crazy by becoming a manager, but you're crazier than I am—you're an umpire." He asked how long I'd been umpiring, and I told him I was taking the wraps off that day. Barney was very nice to me. "Well, Jim," he said, "don't worry about it. I'll make sure my boys don't abuse you one bit no matter how bad you may be." But the manager of the Milford club, Walt Millies, a former Phillies catcher, said, "That doesn't go for me. You better bear down."

Now Horsey told me to work the plate. I didn't know for nothing about umpiring, so I said, "Gee, Hans, maybe if I work the bases, I'll be able to watch you." But he said, "No, I'm an old man. I shouldn't even be out there on the bases. You work the plate, and if I think you're doing something wrong, I'll help you out."

I was under the impression that you had to tell everybody whether it was a ball or a strike, so by the sixth or seventh inning my throat was hoarse from hollering so much. But nobody bothered me. I didn't get a beef from the fans or the players the whole game.

After the game I was sitting on the running board of the car, changing shoes, when a distinguished-looking gentleman came over and said, "Young man, how long have you been umpiring?" I told him that it was my first day but that I'd improve as the season went on. He thought I was kidding, so he asked Hans. When Hans told him I had just come down from Baltimore, the man tapped me on the shoulder and said, "You stay with it, young man. You've got a hell of a future ahead of you." I thought he was the owner of the Milford club because they won and only the winners congratulate umpires. Hans said, "Hell no, he's your boss." I said, "That's Tom Kibler?" He said, "No, that's Bill Carpenter. He's the head of all minor league umpires."

The next day Mr. Kibler was at Horsey's house with a contract. He made me a fabulous offer of $200 a month. I told him that was quite a letdown because I was making $700 a month with the Baltimore club.

"Well," he said, "if you want to be an umpire, this is the kind of salary umpires get." After a long talk, I signed the contract because I was fascinated with umpiring.

That's how I got into umpiring. I've always believed that people have a calling to be a certain thing. Umpiring was my calling. I have no other way of describing it. It hit me that morning while I was shaving. I hadn't given it any thought before then. It was the Good Lord's way of letting me know to be an umpire.

I was born and raised in Oneida, Schuylkill County, Pennsylvania, a little coal-mining town about fifty miles west of Allentown. My parents were from Czechoslovakia. They settled in Oneida, got married, and raised a family. I was the last of eight children, five boys and three girls. My father was a coal miner. The mines were his death. He lost his legs in a mining accident and then died when I was only six months old. We had a tough row to hoe. I depended a lot on an older brother for guidance because I had no father. And my high school football coach, Jim Harrigan, took a liking to me and talked many times about rights and wrongs. One thing that was instilled in me as a youngster was always to respect my elders. I think that's one of the biggest problems we have today is the lack of respect for people, especially with the younger generation.

Things were tough in those coal-mining towns, especially for a large family without a father. We had to struggle. As my brothers got old enough, they got jobs in the mines to support the family. Fortunately I didn't have to do that. During the Depression we didn't always have shoes or good clothes. When we got dressed up, it was in a pair of overalls. Today overalls seem to be the thing, but in those days it was all we had.

I was interested in athletics as far back as I can remember. My older brothers played semipro baseball, and they kept throwing balls at me, so baseball became my number one love. I also enjoyed playing pickup football games. I was big and fast for my age, and one time, when I was still in elementary school, the Hazelton team asked me to play with them in a game against Sheppton. My mother didn't approve of it. She was always worried about one of us getting hurt because the finances weren't there to take care of injuries. But I played anyway in my work shoes and overalls. I could walk all over those fellows even though they were adults, so the word spread that there was a phenom down in Oneida.

The next thing I knew Jim Harrigan, the West Hazelton High School coach, came down and tried to get me to go to his school. He had also seen me play baseball once when I had an exceptionally good day hitting. My family couldn't afford the bus transportation out of the district, but he promised to arrange for transportation and practically camped on my doorstep until it was time to register that fall. Hazelton Township High School didn't have much of a sports program, so I went to West Hazelton.

I finished my last year in high school at New Mexico Military Institute at the instigation of Pop Warner of Temple University. I was gaining a reputation as a football player, and a lot of schools were recruiting me. Pop wanted to get me away from the other coaches, so I went out to New Mexico with the agreement that I would attend Temple on an athletic scholarship. At Temple I played fullback, which in the old double wing formation was similar to quarterback today. I graduated in June 1940 with a B.S. degree in education.

Football helped get me through school, but baseball was my game. While I was going to Temple, I played on weekends and holidays with the Limeport team in the semipro East Penn League. My last two years in college I played for Burlington in the Northern League, a college league in Vermont, with fellows like [George] Snuffy Stirnweiss. I was hitting the ball real well, so the Baltimore Orioles signed me.

I played for Baltimore in the International League in 1941 and then went to Panama to play winter ball with the Balboa team. Our season started in November, and of course, in December war broke out. The manpower was immediately frozen in the Canal Zone. I wanted to play ball with Baltimore, but I couldn't get back to the States. I got stuck down there for twenty months. After the baseball season was over, I taught social studies and general science in junior college and high school.

Things eased up in 1943, so I was allowed passage back to the States, provided I would go into the service. I registered with the draft board, but since they didn't know when I'd be called, I got in touch with my manager, Tommy Thomas, who told me to meet the team in Jersey City.

I was in pretty good shape because of playing ball all winter long. The first night I joined the club, Tommy put me in as a pinch runner. When I got to third base, I told him I thought I could steal home on Dick Fowler, who had pitched for the A's. He said okay, and I did. It was the only run of the game.

I had a real good year, so the Cleveland Indians, who had a working agreement with Baltimore, bought my contract. I was to report to them on September 15, right after the end of the International League season. But Uncle Sam had first call, and on September 1, I went into the Navy. While in the service, I was in gunnery and did nothing but patrol duty at sea for three years.

I got out just before spring training in 1946 and reported to the Baltimore club. Cleveland had canceled my contract because I was in the service so long. I hadn't touched a ball in three years, and besides the inactivity, the couple of dislocated shoulders I got playing football meant that my arm was very poor. I could hardly throw, but they thought I could help the club once I got back into shape. But of course, after a couple of months I went off to umpire.

I never had any problems with umpires as a player. I never abused an umpire, was never in a rhubarb, and got fined only twice.

I got fined once for fighting. One time Herman Franks, the catcher for the Montreal club and a pretty rough ballplayer, deliberately went for the spike with the ball when Doug Jones tried to score. That sort of caused a rumble. Two or three weeks later in Baltimore I was coming home, and he did the same thing with me. I came up swinging and got fined $50 for it.

The other time I got fined involved an umpire. One time in Jersey City Fred Dehaney called one of our guys out at home on a close play. Half the dugout was on the field, and Tommy Thomas was calling him everything—"you thief," "you SOB," "you steal." I thought it was shameful the language he was using on the man. I was standing in the on-deck circle and said to Steve Gromek, "He doesn't have the guts to chase Thomas out of the ball game." Dehaney overheard me and said, "No, but I heard what you said, and you're out of the game." He chased me, and I got fined $25.

A few years later I ran into Dehaney, and we got to talking about it. I asked him why he picked on me, and he said, "Jim, I had to pick on somebody. I couldn't chase Thomas because whatever he said was the truth. But I had to get somebody, and when you opened your mouth, you were the fall guy."

I think my previous relationship with umpires and my experience as a player helped me in my umpiring career. At any rate, I was fortunate to make rapid progress in the profession. It wasn't two weeks after I started in the Eastern Shore League that Jim McCloud, the Centreville, Maryland, manager, came over to me before a ball game and said, "Congratulations. I hear that the International League bought your contract." I laughed and told him it was news to me if they did. The rumors were quite persistent, and I finally did get a call from Frank Shaughnessy, the president of the league. He said,

"Jimmy, I'm very interested in you, and I want you to work in my league. I want you to buy your contract from Tom Kibler. Find out how much he wants for it, and if it's in reason, you buy it, and I'll reimburse you for it."

So the first time I saw Kibler, I said, "By the way, Tom, I'd like to buy my contract." He laughed and said, "No way." He asked who put me up to it, and not wanting to embarrass anybody, I said, "Nobody. I just want to become a free agent at the end of the season." He told me there was no way I was going to become a free agent and that I should call Shaughnessy back and tell him I would cost him $2,500. He knew all along.

Well, Shaughnessy asked me if I could report September 1, the end of the Eastern Shore season. I told him no because I had committed myself to serve as an assistant football coach with Howdie Meyers at Johns Hopkins University. To me a commitment is a commitment. Kibler wanted me to work the play-offs, but when September 1 came around, I went off to coach football.

The next year I worked the International League. And I almost made it to the major leagues in one season. One night in early August, after I had had a real good game at Roosevelt Stadium in Jersey City, an elderly little gentleman with a Scottish brogue came into the dressing room and introduced himself as Tommy Connolly, the supervisor of American League umpires. He asked me to meet him the next day at the Commodore Hotel in New York for lunch. During lunch he said, "I liked what I saw last night, and I want to recommend you to Mr. Harridge to be an umpire in the American League." We talked for a while, and then he asked me how long I'd been umpiring. When I told him that was my first full year, you would have thought I jabbed him with a knife. "Whaaat?" "Whaaat?" He said there was no way he could bring me up to the American League because the ballplayers would not accept anybody with only one year of service. I told him that I thought it was unfair, that if he liked what he saw and thought I was capable of doing the work, that was all that mattered. Well, he said he would explain things to Mr. Harridge, and while they might pick up an option on me, they'd never take me with one year's experience.

In my second year in the International League, I became a crew chief. Everything went along just fine, and again there were rumors that the American League was interested in me. One day I ran into Artie Gore, who by then was umpiring in the National League. He told me that he had heard good reports on me and that Ford Frick had expressed an interest. Artie was a personal friend of Tommy Connolly's, so he wrote a nice letter of recommendation for me. I worked the play-offs that year and then had a real good Little World Series between Montreal and St. Paul, both of the Dodger chain.

After the Series I met Mr. Harridge for the first time. He said the American League didn't have an opening, but he liked what he saw and would try to convince the club owners to add a fourth man to one crew. After the winter league meetings, he called to tell me that the owners weren't sure about a thirteenth man, so he couldn't send me a contract but would send me to spring training.

I was assigned to work with the New York Yankees that spring. Tommy Connolly was with me every day, talking nothing but baseball. My first eight hours in Florida were spent with him on the beach, talking rules and regulations and diagramming plays in the sand. I later found out that the owners had agreed to a thirteenth man but that they weren't sure who it would be.

I'll never forget the way they tested me. About halfway through spring training I was scheduled to work the plate for a Yankee–St. Louis Cardinal game in St. Petersburg. Just before the game Tommy told me that under no circumstances was I to put anybody out of the game. I couldn't figure that out. It just didn't make sense.

Well, from the very first pitch, and I mean from the *very first* pitch, that Yankee dugout got on me. Every time I called a ball on a Cardinal they hollered. Every time I called a strike on a Yankee they hollered. I got damned aggravated because of the constant yelling. I wanted to do something about it but couldn't. I was so burned up inside I was ready to explode. And wouldn't it be my luck that the game went thirteen innings!

Finally, the damned game was over—I don't remember who won, I was so damned mad and disgusted. When I got to the dressing room, Tommy Connolly was waiting for me. I took my mask, dug it into the ceiling knocking off some plaster, and told him where he could stick the American League. He sort of snickered. (You had to know the man to appreciate him. I appreciated him more later, but not at that time because I was *fuming*.) I said, "Yeah, you got a big kick out of it, sitting in the stands, but I'm down there taking a lot of abuse for thirteen innings because you said I couldn't do anything about it. I would have cleaned them bastards out of there real quick. Well, I've got news for you. The American League can go to hell. I'm going back to the minor leagues, where at least I know I am a boss and I don't have to take this bullshit. I'm going to call my wife and go home tonight."

Connolly snickered some more in his little pixie way and said I should at least stop by his hotel for dinner before I left. I told him if he was paying, it would be the last thing I ever took from the American League. My biggest tormentor that day was Jim Turner, the Yankee pitching coach. He hollered every time I called a ball on his pitcher. While I was waiting for the elevator in the hotel, who should I run into but Turner. He tapped me on the shoulder and said, "Nice game, Jim." I said, "Go fuck yourself."

After dinner Tommy and I went for a walk, and he told me about the whole thing. Seems they wanted to see whether I could take abuse, whether I could work under pressure. Since I hadn't had any trouble all spring, they worked out a test with the Yankees. The next morning Mr. Harridge offered me a major league contract.

I opened the 1949 season in St. Louis with Bill Summers, Bill Grieve, and Johnny Stevens. I made the first four-man team in the majors. I looked up Stevens the day before because I knew him from when he worked our games at Temple. I met Summers and Grieve in the dressing room before the game. Summers, who was the crew chief, said, "Kid, how long you been umpiring?" (He always called me kid; three or four years later he was still calling me kid.) When I told him two years, he exploded. He took off on me in no uncertain terms. "Mr. Harridge must be going crazy. How in the hell could he bring a kid like you in the league with only two years of experience? It's a shame. I spent eighteen years in the minor leagues." I said, "Mr. Summers, just because you spent eighteen years in the minor leagues doesn't say that I have to spend that long. If you have any complaints, you take them to Mr. Harridge." That exchange sort of deflated my ego. I figured I was in trouble if I had to work with a guy who resented me from the very beginning.

I was in awe when I went onto the field. It wasn't the size of the crowd, but the players. The Browns had nothing to speak of at the time, but the Cleveland Indians had won the World Series the year before. I was awed being on the same field with fellows like Bob Feller, Bob Lemon, Mike Garcia, Early Wynn, Lou Boudreau, Kenny Keltner, and Joe Gordon.

The next day I was at second base. Boudreau came over and offered congratulations. "Good luck, kid. You've come up to the big leagues, and you're going to find it a lot easier to work up here than in the minors." Then he tipped me off about their famous pickoff play. "When I'm down on my knees and my glove is open, it's going to be a pickoff. I'm going to count to three, and I'll be at second base. But if I'm on my knees and my glove is tucked under, then there is no play on. I want you to be alert, but don't give me away." I appreciated that very much.

After I got to the major leagues, I toned down my style a bit. In the minors I had good motion, really threw out that right arm to the side on strike calls, especially on the third strike. That emphasis was my way of letting the players as well as the fans know that I knew what I was doing back of the plate. After I signed my contract with the American League, Tommy Connolly and Mr. Harridge had a long session with me. They told me not to emphasize the strikes, just to raise my arm over my head on all strikes. They said, "We want you to be seen but not to be heard. You are not what the people come out to see; they come out to see the ballplayers perform. If, when the game is over, the people don't know that Jim Honochick umpired the ball game, then we know you worked a good game." I switched, and that's the way I worked for twenty-five years. I resented it a little at the time they changed me because I was doing what came natural to me. But after I got into the habit of doing it, then it did become natural with me.

Of course, times have changed. Showmanship is increasingly popular with umpires. Mr. Harridge would never have tolerated Emmett Ashford. Personally I don't think it is good for baseball. Not because I didn't do it but because as one of the so-called old-timers I had it instilled in me that people come to see ballplayers perform and not the umpires. I'm completely in accord with the view that the players are making the big money because they are who people come out to see. Why should an umpire take anything away from the superstars?

I concentrated so hard on umpiring that I could not really appreciate what was happening on the field. If you're looking to see what players are doing, then you're not concentrating on your work. If an umpire is dedicated to his work, there is no way that he can know everything that is going on about him except what he is involved in. I worked four no-hitters in the majors and never knew they were no-hitters until the news media started questioning me in the dressing room. In fact, I didn't even know about one of the greatest games I ever worked until it was over. On May 15, 1952, in Detroit, Vic Wertz hit a home run off Bob Porterfield in the ninth inning to win the game, 1–0. When I walked off the field, all I knew was the score and that the Tigers had won. In the dressing room I found out that Porterfield had pitched a four-hitter and Virgil Trucks a no-hitter.

Sure, there's a lot of pressure on umpires, but maybe I'm of a different nature because I never had to unwind. I worked with a lot of fellows who couldn't wait to get to the nearest bar and take a few slugs to calm themselves down. I never drank, had never smoked. I'd tell them if umpiring got me so uptight that I had to take a drink to calm down, then I'd quit the profession.

I really enjoyed umpiring, no question about it. True, there were days when I didn't feel like going out on the field. Maybe I didn't feel so well; maybe I had called my wife and learned one of the kids had an accident or something, and I'd be thinking I would rather be home. But I never suffered from nerves or got uptight. What's there to get uptight about?

Of course, I definitely got worked up more for important ball games than the ordinary ones. I don't know just how to describe it, whether it's butterflies or anxiety. I call it an intense feeling that you have inside that you have to put out the very best you can. You know if you have a play-off game, or an All-Star game, or the World Series how much it means to each and every player. You can't afford to make mistakes. And since you're being watched by millions of people, you're going to try a lot harder than you would for just another game. A regular game didn't faze me until I got to the ball park. As I would get ready to work, rub up the balls or something, the pressure would start building up. But something like the World Series stays with you every day. You just can't make a mistake.

I had something of a record for umpires in the World Series. I worked six Series, and each of them went seven games, meaning that I worked forty-two World Series games. I don't know of any other umpire who broke in after World War II who worked that many Series or games. The first one was 1952, the Yankees and the Dodgers; the last was 1972, Oakland and Cincinnati.

The seventh and final game of the 1955 World Series was truly a monumental game for me. Johnny Podres beat Tommy Byrne and the Yankees, 2–0, to give the Dodgers their first championship. I was scheduled to work the plate, but sometimes the senior man gets the call for the final game. Even though I was the youngest umpire in the crew, I worked the plate with the world championship on the line. It was my biggest thrill in baseball.

The least memorable World Series I had was the one in 1972. I couldn't satisfy the Oakland A's one bit. It started in the very first game, when I had a lot of bang-bang plays at first base. Dick Williams kept coming out and putting on a show, carrying on like a big baby, like you had taken candy away from him, kicking dirt and so forth. The umpires were hampered because the great commissioner, Bowie Kuhn, would not let us eject anyone during the Series. (I think that was a lot of BS because if a ballplayer or manager gets out of line, he has no business being out there, World Series or no.) So I went to the commissioner and told him that if he wanted us to keep control of the game, Williams had to be fined to show him that we weren't going to tolerate his foolishness. The next day he got fined, and from then on Dick Williams had no use for me. The Oakland club, at Williams's instigation, had it in for me. It was obvious that they were out to get Honochick, to give me a going-over every time I had a close call.

It was also that first game that I had a run-in with Gene Tenace. Joe Morgan was on first base, and Blue Moon Odom kept throwing over trying to get him tired so he couldn't steal. A couple of times Tenace deliberately sat down on Morgan, again trying to wear him down. Finally, I called him on it. I didn't penalize him, but I told him that I knew what he was up to and that I didn't want to see any more of it. Tenace said, "He tripped me." I said, "Who in the hell are you kidding? I'm standing here looking at you, and he hasn't come close to tripping you." He grumbled but cut it out.

I had no problems in the second game, when I worked the plate, but in the next game at Oakland there was a big rhubarb at third. Bobby Tolan of Cincinnati stole third base. Sal Bando had the ball in time, no question about it, but he didn't get it down quick enough to make the tag. Bando put on a show, jumping around, and the great Williams came out wanting to know how in the hell I could call a play like that. Again my hands were tied. The next inning Bando wanted to apologize because he said the instant replay showed that I was right. I told him where he could stick his apology and that went for his manager, too. That was a tough Series, a lot of bang-bang plays, and I was mighty glad there was such a thing as instant replay on television because it showed that I made the correct decisions.

After the Series I got a very nice, complimentary letter from Sparky Anderson, even though his club lost. He said he didn't have a habit of writing to umpires complimenting them on their work, but that he felt my work had been so outstanding that he had to write. Needless to say, I appreciated that very much.

The funniest experience I ever had was in Anaheim in 1970, when our equipment failed to arrive for an Angels-Red Sox game. Finally, at the last minute we borrowed some clothing from the Angels— white sweat socks, dark blue windbreakers, light blue usher's pants, and baseball caps. Since I was working the plate, I had to borrow some catcher's equipment. I felt ridiculous and uncomfortable because my pants were too small. We were a sight when we walked on the field, but the fans cheered us. I guess they realized that without the umpires there could be no baseball. And our most important concern was that the game be played.

Cooperation among umpires is essential. You have to work as a team out there. There is no question that the four-man crew has made umpiring a lot easier and more efficient because you have to run only one position. But there are situations on balls hit to the outfield when you operate as a three-man team on the bases. We had signals to help each other. I always believed in being open and aboveboard on that; I didn't permit hidden signals, and I think the players appreciated that. As a crew chief I always told my men, "If you look at me, my head is shaking all the time. I'm saying yes or no, so there is no delay and everyone can see that I've made a decision." Of course, there are instances where, with certain umpires, they wouldn't help you get out of a jam one iota.

I had that happen to me in my second year in the league. Bill McGowan was the oldest man in the league at that time. He was resentful of young fellows coming in because he was at the end of his career. One day in Chicago, McGowan was going to work the plate. Before the game he asked Ed Hurley and me to do him a favor by calling the balls hit down the lines. Well, Chico Carrasquel hit one down the line. I motioned it fair, and he wound up on second base. All of a sudden McGowan said, "Foul ball." The White Sox's manager, Johnny "Red" Corriden, who was a real nice fellow, gave him hell about it, but McGowan said I had no business making the call because it was his decision. Then Johnny came over to me, and I explained what had happened. I said, "It was a fair ball, and it will be a fair ball until the day I die." He said, "I know, but what can you do about it? He's a sick man."

I was still fuming after the game. He had showed me up in front of everyone in the park. I told McGowan in the dressing room, "If you were a younger man I'd beat the daylights out of you right here and now. I respect you for your age, I respect you for the umpire you have been, but don't ever ask me again to help you out on a ball field again." He said he didn't see me make the call. Bullshit. The next day I got a call from Mr. Harridge wanting to know why there was a double decision. I explained things, and he told me just to go about my business.

As mad as I was with Bill McGowan, I still admired him. I caught him when he was on the way down, and at the end he was a very sick man. But even with his age and sickness, I consider him the very best umpire that I worked with. There were days when he was so sick he shouldn't even have gone out on the ball field. He was a diabetic and had only so much energy in him, but if he wanted to give you a game, he'd say, "You want to see an exhibition? I'll give you one today." Then he'd go out and really bear down behind the plate. The man was uncanny on balls and strikes. When the game ended, he was completely exhausted. He couldn't do anything on his own. You had to help take his coat off. The worst thing he could have was Coca-Cola, but he'd drink six bottles before he removed his clothes to take a shower. He was drained, physically and emotionally drained, but he had given you the best game of umpiring you'd ever seen. After McGowan there were only good and bad umpires. He was the greatest umpire I have ever seen, a superstar.

If I were looking over a young man umpiring in the minor leagues, the first quality I would look at would be his judgment. Judgment—balls, strikes, safe, out—is better than 50 percent of umpiring. If he has bad judgment, what's the sense of looking beyond that point? After judgment I would go to his actions, how he handles himself on the field. Then I would take into consideration his physique: How impressive does he look as an umpire? Size is important in the extreme. You wouldn't want to bring in a fellow 5′ 5″ or a big guy who weighed 300 pounds.

As to what makes the good umpire, I guess some people are just born to it. I've always said you either have it or you don't. Making the calls is strictly judgment—some can do it; some can't. To know the rules is one thing; to apply them is another. I think all the really good umpires have that something called intuition or instinct. A lot of umpires, especially the young ones today, are mechanical umpires who stand around flat-footed and wait for something to happen and then make a decision. The good ones don't exactly anticipate, but they just seem to know that there is a possibility of certain things happening in certain situations so they are prepared in advance for the play.

One time my intuition got me in trouble. Back in the early 1950s I was working the plate at Fenway Park. There were two men out, Billy Goodman was on first, and Teddy Williams was at bat with a count of two balls and one strike. As I waited for the pitcher to come in with the ball, it hit me that Goodman was going to steal second base. As the pitch came in I watched Goodman break for second out of the corner of my eye. That's a big no-no for an umpire, but I did it. As I watched to see if he was going to make it, I forgot I had to make the decision on the pitch. The ball was way up in Williams's eyes, but I called it strike two. I realized the mistake right away. In the meantime, they threw out Goodman to end the inning. Williams never said a word. He just tossed his bat toward the dugout and trotted to the outfield. I had heard what a great guy he was, and that proved it to me. If it had been Nellie Fox or Sal Bando or Gene Tenace or one of those guys, I would have had to put them out of the ball game because they would have stood there and argued. Ballplayers today start bellyaching before they even step in the batter's box.

The next inning Williams was the leadoff hitter. As he was swinging the bat to get loose, I walked over and said, "Teddy, even if I'm not supposed to tell you, I sure blew the hell out of that pitch." He laughed and said, "No, you didn't, honey." (He always called me honey.) "I knew Goodman was going to steal, and I should have swung at the damn pitch to help him, but I didn't, so I'm more responsible for it than you." Now can you fault a guy like that?

As a crew chief I had a problem with Jim Odom, a young umpire who didn't have good baseball instinct. We were working a game in New York; I was at first base; he was behind the plate. Al Lopez, the White Sox manager, who was a real stickler, kept accusing Whitey Ford of throwing a spitball. Every two or three pitches he'd holler, "Look at the ball!" Odom would look at the ball and throw the damned thing out. By the end of the first half inning, he had thrown out maybe a half dozen balls.

Now that was wrong. If you have to throw a ball out, it meant that Whitey Ford was doctoring it and you should get rid of *him*. If he was not doctoring them, why throw them out? Before the half inning was over, I started to shake my head no. But Odom didn't grasp it. So when the Sox went out, I went in and told him not to pay any attention to Lopez and not to throw out any more baseballs regardless of what he said. See, when the game was over, Lopez would have counted the balls thrown out and claimed Ford had thrown that many spitters.

When the next inning started, Lopez hollered again. But Jim now said no. The White Sox picked it up right away, so Lopez came out asking what right I had to tell Odom not to throw out baseballs. I said, "Al, you know better than that. You know you want to crucify the guy when the game ends. Now when you think Ford is throwing a spitball, you holler at me, and I'll go in and check the ball." "Well," he said, "the hell with it," and walked away.

Afterward in the dressing room I brought it up, and Odom, who was highly emotional, jumped all over me. "Don't you ever tell me what to do back of that plate again. I'll run the game the way I see fit." I told him I was only trying to save his neck because I knew what Lopez was doing. He said, "Yes, but I don't want you to ever come in and tell me what to do." I said that was fine with me.

It wasn't a week later we were in Baltimore when something happened while he was working the plate. He was looking for me to come up and help, but I thought, no way. I just let him stand back there and take it. After the game, he came out of the shower and called me an SOB for not helping him. I reminded him about what he had said in New York and told him that he had to make up his mind whether he wanted help or he didn't. I said, "If you want help, I'll help you, but if you want help, you're going to listen to what I say." That's the way it was from then on.

The only way to handle a rhubarb is with honesty. A rhubarb starts only because somebody thinks that you did wrong. Now maybe you did, no one ever knows for sure. Who can say for certain on a judgment call? I always felt that if a man felt he had a legitimate beef coming, he was entitled to tell me why he thought my decision was wrong and that I ought to listen to him. I've had players, managers, even general managers tell me that I was a fellow that they could talk to. I felt I was a good listener, and I considered it a compliment. When I played ball, that was the way I wanted to be treated, so that's how I acted as an umpire.

I didn't have that attitude "I never do anything wrong." No way. I'm a human being, and human beings make mistakes. Nobody had to tell me when I made a mistake; maybe I wouldn't admit it to anyone, but I knew it deep down inside. I was always willing to listen to somebody point out my mistakes, but if he did it in a harsh or abusive way or used profanity, he was gone. I chased a lot of guys, but I always felt that I never personally put anyone out of a ball game. There are certain rules and regulations you must abide by, and if a player or manager violated those rules, he ejected himself.

Sometimes you'd have a rhubarb because many players and managers do not know the rules. That was the cause of the first rhubarb I ever had. It was during my first year in the league. The Cleveland Indians were in Washington. The score was 0–0 in the eighth inning. Eddie Robinson, the Washington first baseman, was on third with one man out. Somebody hit a ground ball, and they got him in a rundown between third and home. As Robinson tried to score, he ran smack into Early Wynn, who was standing right in the baseline without the ball. Immediately I put up my arms and yelled, "You score!"

Next thing I knew twenty-five Indians and their coaches were all around me, everyone shouting at the same time. I told Lou Boudreau, the manager, that there was no way I could explain the play with all that shouting going on. After he cleared them away, I told him I had called an obstruction play: Wynn had obstructed the runner because he didn't have the ball. Well, Boudreau said that he had never heard of such a rule and that Wynn hadn't interfered. I tried to explain the difference between an obstruction call, which does not kill the ball, and an interference play, which does. Finally, he said, "Jim, I think you're sincere. You're new in the league, and I'll let you get away with it today. But if you're wrong, I'm going to get you out of the American League." I said that was okay with me. The game continued, and as it turned out, Washington won, 1–0.

The next day we weren't in the dressing room ten minutes when there was a knock on the door. It was Boudreau. He said as long as he had been in baseball, he never knew there was such a thing as the obstruction rule. He said, "Jim, I have to give you credit. You know what the hell you're doing out there. We made fools of ourselves. You'll never have to worry about me ever giving you any trouble again."

He had no sooner left than Joe Kuhel, the Washington manager, knocked on the door. He did not have a good reputation among umpires because you could never satisfy Joe Kuhel. He said he didn't know what had happened on the field last night, and he wasn't going to say anything because it was in his favor, but for his own information he wanted to know what it was all about. Bill Summers said, "The kid was right," and told him about the obstruction rule. Kuhel said he didn't know the rule and had never seen it called before.

Every umpire has a mental book on people, who the good and bad fellows are. But it's not the same for everybody. The National League umpires talked about how Eddie Stanky was no good, but I never had any trouble with him when he came over to the American League. He always acted like a gentleman. The same thing with Bobby Bragan. Some umpires couldn't tolerate him, but I never had problems with him when he was at Cleveland. Birdie Tebbetts was another. I'll never forget him. When I first broke in, he was catching for the Boston Red Sox. When you first come into the big leagues, you're awed by the surroundings and you get a little excited, so you have a tendency to call too many strikes. Birdie helped me adjust to the big league strike zone. If I called a pitch that was maybe a little high when he was catching, he'd never let the batter know, but he'd say, "Jim, bring that pitch down a little more." Later, when he was managing Cleveland, he would always come out to me first when he had a fight with one of my crew. There were some umpires he couldn't stand and vice versa, but we got along just fine.

You cannot, however, be overly friendly with ballplayers or managers and expect to be a good umpire. The friendlier you are with them, the more they try to take advantage of you, and that makes you a bad umpire. I've seen it happen many times. I worked a lot of games with Eddie Rommel. Eddie told me that he and Jimmy Dykes roomed together as teammates on the Philadelphia A's, but that Dykes was the one man who got him in trouble all the time after he became an umpire. He said he couldn't satisfy Dykes no way, that Dykes was after him the minute he walked on the field, although they had been the best of friends. I've always maintained that the guy you are extremely friendly with is the guy who is going to give you the most trouble, so I was never social friends with players. You can say "hello," "how are you?" give them the time of the day, that sort of thing, but never hang out with them off the field because when they get to know you, they feel they can get away with anything.

I always felt that Yankee Stadium was the best park to work in because you didn't have only the diehard rooters for the home team. You had a cross section of people who came to New York just to see a ball game. Outside New York, I would say Chicago and later Anaheim or Dodger Stadium had a nice cross section of fans. The tough ones were towns like Boston, Baltimore, and Philadelphia, where there were only the diehards, who would really give it to you every time there was a close decision. You had to set yourself mentally for that. If I was wrong, I expected a certain amount of abuse and was entitled to it. But by the same token if you work for the people, hustle for them, let them know you're doing a good job, then you have no real problems.

I don't care too much for baseball games on television, but I do make it a point to see a few ball games each summer. I watch the umps more than the game. The thing that annoys me more than anything else about ball games is the constant turmoil of people walking around, buying a beer or something. What in God's name do they come for? If they want to drink, why not go to a bar? Why come to the ball park if you're not going to watch the ball game?

Of course, those are the people who abuse umpires. Probably 75 percent of the people who go to ball games don't know baseball. The people who really know the game are not the people who will abuse you. I can see that now when I go to games. It's the guy who has a few beers and wants everybody in the ball park to think he's a big shot that raises hell with the umpires. As an umpire I wasn't aware of that, but now that I see how some people behave in the stands I can understand why the umpires get abuse on the field.

It's the same thing with the media. The reporters sit up in the press box, eating and drinking and everything else. Half the time they don't see the ball game. But the next day, when you read the headlines, it's the umpiring that lost the game for the home team. It is always that close decision that determined the game, never the fact that a player made a crucial error that cost his team the game. When you have a close play like that, the reporters come into the dressing room with pencils and paper to take quotations from you. You tell them exactly what took place, but when you read it the next day, it is not what you said; it's what they wanted to say. The umpire is strictly a scapegoat. We are forgotten people. We are remembered only if we happen to make a bad call.

In all my years in baseball, I don't think that umpires could have been treated any better than we were by Calvin Griffith in Minnesota. He was Class A-1 as far as treatment of umpires was concerned. He couldn't do enough for you. That was not true of every park. Of course, they all had a cooler or refrigerator where they'd have soft drinks. And after the game some of the clubs would put beer in there for you. But in some places, Dodger Stadium, for instance, you couldn't get a drink of water unless you put your mouth under the hydrant. And if you had a run-in with the Pittsburgh club, they'd treat you like a dog. I remember one time we had a run-in there, and Fred Haney, the general manager, took out the water cooler, the soft drinks, everything. He even told the clubhouse boy that under no circumstances was he to do any favors for the umpires as far as getting us anything to eat or drink. That's fine. We could be men enough to go out and get whatever we needed.

I've seen great changes in the umpiring profession during my career. With the old-timers, baseball was their whole life—on the field, off the field. We didn't stop baseball because the game was over. We'd sit and talk in the dressing room for maybe an hour, hour and a half, especially if we had a problem on the field. You'd talk baseball at dinner, in the lobby of the hotel, or just walking the streets. You'd talk about rules, experiences—anything about baseball. You don't get that with the present-day umpire. I don't know why, but it seems they're interested in working the ball game and getting the hell out. In my last five or six years as a crew chief, it completely changed. I'd want to talk about certain things that happened, and they'd say, "I'm not interested in why it happened," or, "Leave the game on the field," or, "It's over with." It's a different group altogether today.

Just because a man has a uniform doesn't mean he is an umpire, even though that's his profession. There are umpires, and then there are umpires. In the first category of umpires are the fellows who are in it because of the social life, the salary and pension, the fringe benefits. There are quite a group in that category. Then there is the umpire who is truly dedicated to his job, who lives and eats and sleeps umpiring, does everything to benefit the profession, and is proud of the profession. I think I was in that category of umpires.

When I broke in, there was no Umpires Association and no pension to speak of. Every umpire went his own way. You had to fight for what you thought was right. If you felt you were entitled to more money, you had to go to the league president and explain things to him. Today it's all cut-and-dried. The guys know how much they are going to get along the way. The organization is good because it has improved the position of umpires, but on the other hand, if an umpire is bad, they have an awful time getting rid of him after he's been in the league a few years. I think that's wrong. If a ballplayer is not up to par, he should be demoted to the minor leagues, and that should also be the case with umpires because there's nothing worse than having a weak link in your crew.

There are definitely some things that should be done to better the umpiring profession. The situation in the minor leagues is terrible. Umpires in the minors are grossly underpaid. Also, they do not get adequate supervision. They work practically without any supervision, which means they do not get proper guidance. Each minor league ought to have someone knowledgeable in umpiring, maybe a retired major league umpire, as a supervisor to observe and assist these young men. Neither Fred Fleig nor Dick Butler, the supervisors of umpires for the National and American leagues, ever played the game of baseball or were ever involved with the umpiring profession. They are administrators. Fleig was connected with Warren Giles, and Butler was Commissioner Chandler's right-hand man. These fellows know the requirements of an umpire, but can they judge whether or not an umpire has the necessary savvy? It seems to me someone with a working knowledge of umpiring would be better able to evaluate minor league umpires and promote them.

Another thing that is lacking is uniformity. There will always be differences in style and technique among umpires. The rule book states that the strike zone extends from the armpits to the knees, but just about every umpire has a different interpretation of "armpits" and "knees." And some will prefer inside over outside protectors. I myself always used the outside protector for health reasons—unless you are foolish enough to stick your arms out, there is no way you're going to get hurt with the outside protector. (Lou Jorda, who I thought was a real good umpire, got hit one day at the Polo Grounds over the heart while wearing the inside protector; it damaged his heart, and he was done for life.) But I don't think there should be independent National League and American League umpires. There should be major league umpires with basic uniformity in the way they work. After all, there is a Major League Umpires Association, so why not organize umpires under someone knowledgeable of the profession? Mr. Harridge used to say, "I could never be an umpire. I could never live the life you fellows have to lead. I don't know how you do it." That's my point.

I have also seen some important changes in the game itself. I saw the beginnings of integration as a player and an umpire. I was with Baltimore in 1946, when Jackie Robinson broke in with Montreal. We had quite a few southern boys on our club who were contemplating not going on the field if he showed up, but the night Jackie Robinson was due in Baltimore each one of us got a telegram from Mr. Shaughnessy which said that anyone who did not take the field against Montreal would be suspended from baseball for life. Everyone played, and there were no problems with him that year. I could never understand why there was a problem with integration in the first place because white teams had played exhibition games and toured with colored teams for years.

During my early years in the league there weren't many colored ballplayers. Larry Doby and Minnie Minoso were the most famous. There was nothing ever said among umpires about race, just whether someone was a good ballplayer or not. Integration was much slower coming to the American League than the National League, but I don't know why. Maybe it was because our league was the dominant league, so things were kept as they were, while the National League did everything they could to get out of the doldrums. It worked. By signing so many of the good black players, the National League greatly improved and came to dominate the All-Star games.

Television came in during my career, and I have always felt that it was a big boon to the umpiring profession because the instant replays showed we were right 99 percent of the time. Before that, you had only still pictures in the newspapers, and because of the angles, you were always being crucified for having been wrong. By the same token television has hurt baseball in two ways: the ballplayers and umpires who became actors all of a sudden. I remember one day I had an open play at second base, but Sam Dente, the Washington second baseman, gave me a beef. I said, "Sam, you must be kidding." He said, "Jim, I know this game is televised. I've been fishing, and I want my wife to see that I got to the ball park." Strictly show. That's why you get certain rhubarbs.

There have been some changes in the game I do not approve of. Artificial turf is exactly what the name says—it's artificial, and the game played on it is artificial. Evidently only one architect has designed the new stadiums because they all look alike. The closeness of the fans associated with the old ball parks is gone.

When I first came into the league, almost all our games were day games. Then it got to the point where they played two night games a week, Tuesday and Friday. That wasn't bad, but you found that if you worked a Tuesday night game, you didn't have the same energy Wednesday afternoon. Then the A's and Washington started going to more night games, and the next thing you knew it had gone to night ball. I personally feel that baseball should be played in the daytime like in Wrigley Field. I don't think the lighting is important. The lights are good enough so there's no deception. But the mode of living is so much better with day games. You can live more like a normal human being.

Now I do think the designated hitter is good for baseball because most people like to see a wide-open ball game with lots of hits and runs. Of course, 75 percent of the people that go to the ball park don't know baseball; but they are in the majority, and you have to satisfy them.

By 1970 I went with the Baltimore club on a tour of Japan. It was a lot easier to work as an umpire over there. The Japanese players and fans had no time to abuse the umpires. There was a lot of commotion between innings, but from the time the pitcher threw his first pitch until the third out you could hear a pin drop in the park. The only time there was any abuse was when Earl Weaver got excited, and he got excited quite often because he didn't think the umpires' judgment was that good. He was probably right because they didn't get much instruction, and they stood upright behind the plate so there was no way they could call the low strike.

After the tour I wrote a report to President Cronin. I said it then, and I still believe, that you will eventually see Japanese baseball played in the United States as part of the major league complex. Maybe there will be baseball in Hawaii as a stopping-off point; the mode of transportation today makes it possible.

I retired at the suggested retirement age of fifty-five. Needless to say, I had hoped to stay in baseball. I contacted every club in the

American League, looking for a job as a scout or something of that sort. Bob Short was going to take me on as a scout, but then he sold the Texas ball club. The others never even gave me the courtesy of replying. So what did I get out of it? Other than my pension, nothing. That's the nature of the job. You're in it, and then you're out of it. You only get out of it what you put in: I put in twenty-five years.

Shag Crawford observes André Rodgers of the Cubs
tagging out Met Ron Hunt at second base during a July
1964 game in Chicago. Courtesy National Baseball
Library & Archive, Cooperstown, N.Y.

Shag Crawford

☒☒☒

Henry Charles Crawford
Born: Philadelphia, Pennsylvania, August 30, 1916
Height: 6′ 1″
Weight: 175
Playing career: minor leagues, 1937–38
Umpiring career: Canadian-American League (C), June–September 1950; Eastern League (A), 1951–53; American Association (AAA), 1954–55; National League, 1956–75
No-hit games: none
All-Star games: 1959 (first game), 1961 (first game), 1968
World Series (games): 1961 (5), 1963 (4), 1969 (5)
Championship series: 1971

Everybody seems to think that my nickname came from shagging fly balls, but it didn't. My old man didn't make too much money, so we didn't have very much. We had enough to eat, but our clothes were a little bit on the shabby side—holes in the pants, holes in the shoes, and so on. The kids used to call me Shaggy because of my appearance. My mother objected to it very much; but the name stuck, and as I grew older, it was shortened to Shag.

I was born in West Philadelphia, August 30, 1916. We had a good-sized family. There were six kids. I was number four. My father was a barber for sixty-nine years. We didn't have a lot of money, so after a couple of years of high school I dropped out to earn my keep. The truth is I wasn't a very good student. I was sort of limited in what I could do, so I got a job building steam engines for Baldwin's Locomotive Works in Eddystone, Pennsylvania.

My father is the one who got me interested in sports. In my day as a kid all there was were Babe Ruth and Jack Dempsey, so my father wanted me to be either a fighter or a baseball player. But he was really a great baseball fan, and that sort of pumped me up to do something in baseball.

After I left high school, I started playing semipro baseball. Patsy O'Rourke, a scout for the Phillies, signed me around 1936–37 and sent me to Centreville in the Eastern Shore League. I had a cup of coffee there and came back home. A year later I went down to Joe Stripps's baseball school in Orlando, Florida. Knoxville of the Southern Association picked me up and farmed me out to Hutchinson, Kansas, in the Western Association. I was there long enough for another cup of coffee before I got cut.

I must admit that I was a pretty feisty ballplayer. Not too many decisions by the umpires set right with me. See, I played with great intensity and drive because I loved the game and wanted to do well.

I was a catcher. I just loved to catch. I was a pretty good receiver and could throw the ball, but I just wasn't too much with the lumber. I just couldn't hit the curveball well enough to make it.

After I got released, I went back to Philadelphia and started playing semipro ball again. When World War II came along, I went into the Navy for a little over two years. When I got out, I went back to delivering milk and playing semipro ball. I loved the game so much I just couldn't let it go.

Now when the Korean War broke out and the Army started drafting guys, I suddenly discovered that I was the grandpop on the team. I was in my mid-thirties, so I figured it was about time for me to get out of the playing part of the game. I loved the game so much I didn't want to lose touch with it, but I didn't know what I could do.

Then one day I saw an ad in the Philadelphia *Inquirer* offering some umpiring equipment for sale. I told my wife that I thought I'd try umpiring, so I bought the equipment and started out working some fairly good sandlot games in Philadelphia. Now, when I got the equipment, it was not with the intention of becoming a professional umpire. I did it strictly to keep in touch with baseball, to be around the kids and the sandlot games.

But as it turned out, it started me on a whole new career. A lot of the guys thought I was a pretty good umpire, and they kept urging me to take a shot at professional baseball. Johnny Stevens, who was then umpiring in the American League, saw me work and recommended me to George McDonald. George was then a minor league umpire supervisor; he later became president of the Florida State League. George looked me over and sent me to the Canadian-American League, Class C, in June 1950.

I spent the rest of that season in the Canadian-American League and moved on the next year to the Class A Eastern League. I stayed in the Eastern League for three years; then in 1954–55 I worked the American Association. The call to the big time came in 1956.

I never went to an umpire school. I was plucked right off the sandlots. Today it's just an impossibility to get a job like that, but back then the schools were just starting to come to the fore. I was very fortunate because if I had been required to go to umpiring school, I would never have made it. I would never have been able to go because it cost too much money. I was married and had three kids, so it would have been an impossibility for me to attend the school.

If I had it to do over again, I would go the same route. My sandlot and minor league experience provided me with a good, fundamental background in baseball. There weren't too many things that happened to me in the big leagues that didn't happen to me in the minors. I had had a pretty good background when I went to the big leagues, so I was confident that I could do the job.

Those years in the minors were tough financially, especially in the lower leagues. The money was horrendous. When I broke into the Canadian-American League, I got $250 a month. I had to send that home to my wife and kids. I lived on $100 a month expense money, which meant I was paying $1 or $1.25 a day for a room. There was always a lot of company in those rooms—bedbugs and what have you. I used to look for restaurants that served a lot of bread. That's the truth. If they served lots of bread, they had me for a regular customer.

I did everything in the off-season to make ends meet except rob a bank, and I was on the verge of that a few times. It was difficult to get a job because nobody wanted to hire me on a part-time basis. I'd tell a few little white lies about quitting baseball so they'd hire me, but away I'd go when the bell rang for the following season. I kept running out of jobs, so I had to grab anything I could. I worked as a milkman, delivered bread, swung a sledgehammer, and drove oil trucks. I drove a cab the three years I was in the Eastern League.

My last year in the Eastern League I almost quit umpiring. I had been in the league three years and figured I should be advancing to

AAA ball, but there was no sign of me moving up. After the season I told my wife that I thought I would wrap it up. She encouraged me to give it one more year. That was good advice because during that winter the American Association offered me a contract, and a year later the National League purchased me. All told I was only in the minor leagues five and a half years, but I was getting pretty impatient because of my age.

I was almost forty years old when I finally went up to the majors in 1956. The National League had released Lon Warneke, the old "Arkansas Hummingbird," a great pitcher who had put in seven or eight years as an umpire, and they hired me as his replacement.

You need help to make it to the major leagues. You need people in your corner who will put in a good word for you. A couple of guys in the American Association helped me a lot. Mike Higgins, who managed the Louisville Colonels, and Kerby Farrell, who managed the Indianapolis Indians, were real good boosters of mine. They didn't tell me directly what they thought of me, but I heard through sources that they were pumping me up pretty good for advancement to the big leagues. There are so many good umpires in the minors that sometimes a little boost like that makes all the difference.

I was in high heaven my first big league game. It was in Milwaukee. The Chicago Cubs were in town. When I walked out on that field with those 47,000 or 50,000 people in the stands, why, it was just a great feeling. I broke in at third base. Boy, that was a cold day. The temperature was around 38 degrees at game time, and it snowed during the last three innings. I had one guy slide into third; I was so stiff and tight I almost didn't get my hands up to call him safe. We got the game in, but then we couldn't get out of the hotel for three or four days because of the snow. That was my introduction to the big leagues.

The first time I went behind the plate was definitely a big day for me. It was in Chicago. I can still remember the pitchers. Johnny Klippstein, a big, hard-throwing right-hander, pitched for the Cincinnati Reds and Russ "Mad Monk" Meyer pitched for the Cubs. Of course, at that particular stage of my career I wanted to be as sharp as a tack, so I really prepared mentally for the game. Even though I had never seen either of them pitch before, I knew what they threw, and I sort of pictured in my mind calling curveballs, sliders, whatever. After you're in the league awhile, you don't have to do that because you know the pitchers. All I did later on was stand behind the catcher during the warm-up pitches and call them to myself to get my timing. When the first pitch of the ball game came, I was ready to go.

Anyway, I really prepared mentally for that first game. I was especially concerned about the Mad Monk because he was the kind of fellow who would blow a fuse real quick. We went twelve innings—I think Cincinnati won it—and I had a real good day behind the plate. Monk never murmured a word or an objection of any kind, and neither did either catcher. The next day, when I came out on the field, Meyer said, "Kid, you worked a hell of a ball game yesterday." That made me feel very good.

I truly loved being a major league umpire. A lot of fellows didn't like all the traveling, but I didn't mind traveling at all. In fact, I enjoyed it. Milwaukee was a great town to be in, and I liked Chicago, New York, and then Los Angeles. The only town I didn't particularly care for was San Francisco. It is definitely too cold up there.

I never got tired of the ball parks. In my opinion Dodger Stadium is the best ball park in the world. Not even the new installations that have been built in recent years can compare with Dodger Stadium. It's a good place to work a ball game, and it's a park that is meticulously kept up. It is just beautiful.

Now the greatest spot in the world is Wrigley Field in Chicago because there you have afternoon baseball. The game was made to be played in the daytime. But I must say that the lighting systems in the modern ball parks are better than daylight. You have no problem whatsoever with the lights, provided they are adjusted properly.

The Astrodome was a tough ball park to work at first because you would lose sight of the ball on account of the glare from the roof. The old Crosley Field in Cincinnati could be very tough at times because of all the ground rules. They kept building extensions on the fence so that if a ball hit the wall at a certain place, it was a home run; if it hit someplace else, it was a double. Those kinds of ground rules make it hard on umpires.

I guess I'd have to say I didn't like any ball park that had artificial turf. It has definitely changed the game. It has almost completely taken the bunt out of the game, and it has changed the defensive play because of the way the ball scoots through the infield and bounces over an outfielder's head. And Lord, when you stand on that stuff for a doubleheader, your legs are like planks. The heat's unbearable sometimes; I'll bet the difference between the official temperature in a town and the heat on that turf on a hot summer day is 30 to 40 degrees. Artificial turf is beautiful to look at, but it ends right there. I'm definitely for eliminating it.

The only tough thing about traveling was being gone so much at a time when the kids needed their father around. I've always lived in

Philadelphia, so I was home whenever I worked a Phillies series. Otherwise, I was on the road for long stretches at a time. But you have to make sacrifices in whatever job you take up in life, and traveling is one of the drawbacks in the umpiring profession.

I was fortunate in that Vivian, my wife, did a great job acting as a mother *and* a father to four kids. She let me make all the decisions on the ball field, and she made them at the house. My son Jerry umpires in the National League, Joseph is a basketball official in the NBA, Henry III, who we call the Bunk, drives a tractor-trailer for A&P, and my daughter, Patty, is married and has three great boys. I'd say Vivian did one hell of a job.

My wife wasn't too much of a sports fan. She was greatly interested in baseball because I was in it, and she saw to it that the kids were playing ball and things like that. But she would almost never come to the ball game. And she went on the road with me only once or twice because she didn't like to travel.

My kids were never treated as celebrities because they had a dad who was an umpire. It might have been different if I had been a ballplayer. And they never objected when people got on me during a ball game. They could sit there and watch the games and keep their mouths shut. They were pretty observant; they knew what was going on out there.

One night, while we were eating dinner, Jerry said, "Dad, I would like to go to that umpiring school." I was really surprised. I never thought he was interested in umpiring. He used to go to the ball games with me and hang around the dressing room, but never once did he mention umpiring before that night. I guess he got the idea from umpiring Little League games. He was managing a team, and when they needed an umpire one time, he did it. Apparently he liked it.

I thought it was great that he decided to try umpiring because I have the greatest admiration in the world for professional baseball umpires. I don't think there is any better profession to get into, provided you are successful at it. Anyone who has moxie should try it. I did tell him the pitfalls, which he pretty much already knew, and I tried to make the point that he had to be honest with himself. You have to have confidence in yourself even to try to make it as an umpire. At the same time the competition is keen out there, and if you can't hack it, then you've got to get out or you'll just waste important years of your life.

I didn't try to assist him too much when he started out in the minor leagues. In fact, we didn't see very much of each other during the baseball season because we were both on the road. We talked a little baseball during the winter, but there's not much you can tell another umpire. You can't make decisions for him. A position that is comfortable for you might not be comfortable for him. Your way of handling situations might not work for him. So Jerry's progress was due to his own efforts. After six years in the minors, he replaced Tom Gorman in the National League in 1976. We are very, very happy about it. And proud.

I'm also proud that Joe is doing a good job in the NBA. I never refereed basketball, so he didn't get it from me. But I did sort of give him the incentive to become an official. Joe always loved basketball but didn't have enough height. So I told him, "Look, you love this game. Pick up the whistle." And he did.

The best thing about umpiring is seeing the best in baseball every day. I really enjoyed the ball games. The cardinal rule of umpiring is to follow that ball wherever it goes. Well, if you watch the ball, you can't help seeing somebody make a great catch, watch it leave the ball park, or see somebody strike out. That's what makes umpiring so much fun.

It was a pleasure being on the field with all those great players, Hall of Famers. Willie Mays, Roberto Clemente . . . I could go on all day. But to me the guy who stood out so plainly above all the others was Pete Rose. He's the greatest player I ever saw in the big leagues. A total ballplayer. Quite a few guys had more talent—could hit better, run better, field better, throw better. But in totality, nobody could do it better than Rose. The effort he puts into the game is remarkable; that's what made him the most remarkable player in my time. He played the game the way I think it should be played, the way I would want to play it. I'd pay ten dollars to see Pete Rose play; he's worth every cent of it.

As far as pitchers are concerned, I saw a lot of great ones: Robin Roberts, Sandy Koufax, Bob Gibson, Tom Seaver, Don Newcombe. But the greatest craftsman was Warren Spahn. He could do everything required of a pitcher. He could even win his own games with a home run or a key base hit. He had good stuff, outstanding control, and a great pickoff move to first base. He was an artist out there on the mound.

Of the managers I worked with Walter Alston has to be rated tops because of his record. But Gene Mauch was a hell of a manager, a terrific manager in fact. I thought Birdie Tebbets was also a good manager.

Sure, there were lots of scuffles with some guys. But I'm not the type to do any criticizing. That's all water over the dam anyway. I'm trying to obliterate all that from my mind.

Umpires? Lee Ballanfant broke me in. He was my first crew chief. He helped me a lot—polished me off with different techniques, eased me in and out of different situations, and so on. He was a fine umpire and a great guy. Al Barlick, Augie Donatelli, Jocko Conlan, and Larry Goetz were all outstanding umpires, guys who controlled the game. Goetz was tremendous, a really great umpire. Some of the younger fellows were also very good. They were not as grizzled as the old-timers, but they ran the game in their own way. Eddie Vargo, Doug Harvey, John Kibler, and Andy Olsen are excellent umpires. Bruce Froemming is also a very, very good umpire who really controls the games he works.

The most memorable game I ever participated in was the Marichal-Roseboro incident on August 22, 1965. I'll never, never forget that moment. It was a frightening situation, a serious stigma on the game.

There had been bad blood between the two teams for quite a while. The Dodgers and Giants had been battling for first place most of the season, and then the Dodgers came into San Francisco for a crucial series. There were several incidents in the first two games that got tensions pretty high—catcher's interference, brush-back pitches, things like that—and then for the final game the two best pitchers in the league, Sandy Koufax [21-4] and Juan Marichal [19-9], squared off for the first time that year. It was a Sunday game, so the largest crowd of the year was at Candlestick Park.

The thing blew up in the bottom of the third inning. Los Angeles was ahead at the time, 2–1. All of a sudden Marichal, who was at bat, hit Johnny Roseboro, the Dodger catcher, over the head a couple of times with his bat. Marichal never said a word, just hit him with the bat. Marichal later said that Roseboro tried to hit him in the head when he threw the ball back to Koufax.

Anyway, Roseboro went down with blood pouring from this nasty gash in his head. The whole thing happened three feet in front of me. I couldn't believe it. Everybody—the fans, the players, the managers—was completely flabbergasted. Naturally both dugouts emptied. Charlie Fox, the Giants' third-base coach, came running over. So did Tito Fuentes, the on-deck hitter, and Koufax. We finally got Roseboro away, but then Marichal went crazy. He went down the first-base line, swinging the bat like a wild man. The Giants were in front of him, and the Dodgers were behind him, but nobody would make a move on him because of the bat. I came up on the home-plate side, trying to get a shot at him. I waited until he raised the bat to swing again; then I dove at him. I hit him around the neck, grabbed the bat, and we both went down. That's when both teams dove on him. And me, too—I got cut up and bruised pretty good.

When we finally got the thing straightened out, there were policemen cordoned in front of the stands in foul territory from foul pole to foul pole, one cop about every ten to fifteen feet. Tony Venzon came in front of first base and said, "Shag, don't you think we ought to get these cops off the field? It looks like everything is under control." I agreed that it didn't look too good playing a ball game with all those cops on the field, so I explained how we felt to Inspector English of the San Francisco Police Department.

He took me by the arm and said, "Shag, listen. You take care of the baseball game, and I'll take care of the police." The cops remained until the final out. I kept thinking how Deacon Delmore, who used to umpire in Cuba before Fidel Castro took over, would tell about how the field would be cordoned off with soldiers with machine guns. I knew how he must have felt because that's how I felt that particular game.

Wouldn't you know, we no sooner got the game under way again when Willie Mays hit a three-run homer? The Giants finally won the game, 4–3.

After the game I made out a long report on the incident to Warren Giles, the league president. He suspended Marichal for eight games and fined him a record $1,750. That was pretty stiff, but the Dodgers didn't think it was stiff enough. Ron Fairly said he should have been suspended for 1,750 games.

Believe it or not, I had a game worse than that one: the Cubs against the Pirates in Pittsburgh on October 2, 1974. That was a big ball game, even though the Cubbies were in last place because if Pittsburgh won the game, they would be the champions of the Eastern Division of the National League; if not, they would have a one-game play-off with St. Louis.

The Cubs got four runs off Jim Rooker in the first inning. The Pittsburgh fans weren't too happy about that, but when John Kibler called Richie Zisk out at home trying to score on a fly ball in the fourth inning, all hell broke loose. The yelling and screaming was okay, but when they started throwing bottles and stuff at the Cubs when they went out in the field for the fifth inning, things got a little mean. José Cardenal almost got hit with a whiskey bottle out in left field.

I was the senior umpire, so I had to take charge. I had had enough experience to know not to make an announcement right away about the bottles and the debris because that would just bring more stuff out of the stands. I went in and told Danny Murtaugh, the Pittsburgh manager, that we had to stop it but that we shouldn't make an announcement yet. Then I told the Cubs' manager, Jim Marshall, that I would try to take care of the situation. I had it in my mind that this was such an important game it had to be played; I was certainly not going to forfeit the game to the Cubs because of some nitwits in the stands.

Things calmed down a little, but when the Pirates scored a couple of runs, it started again. I don't know why; it didn't make any sense to me. Anyway, in the eighth inning a bottle landed near Jerry Morales in right field, and the Cubs walked off the field. Oh, then it really came down.

I didn't have any choice then but to announce over the public address system that any further disturbance could result in the Pirates' forfeiting the game. Well, you can imagine how the crowd reacted to that. Danny Murtaugh even went out to second base and waved his hands for them to stop, but it didn't do any good. It took fifteen to twenty minutes to clear the field of all the debris. I had to persuade Jim Marshall to get his ballplayers back on the field. Marshall was very cooperative. He told me that he realized the game should be played but that he didn't want any of his men to get hurt. I told him I didn't want any of them to get hurt either, but I emphasized that we had to get the game in. I said, "I don't care if we have to chase all the people out of here and it's two o'clock in the morning. We're going to play if we have to play it before an empty house." The Cubs finally went back on the field with the outfielders wearing batting helmets.

We went to the bottom of the ninth with the Cubs leading, 4–3. Bob Robertson came to bat with two outs. Rick Reuschel struck him out on a low curve, but somehow the ball got away from the catcher, Steve Swisher, and Al Oliver came in from third base with the tying run. The Pirates went on to score a run in the tenth to win the ball game.

That was the most extraordinary game I ever saw. It was unbelievable how Pittsburgh came back to tie the game and then win it. I was never so relieved to have a game over. The behavior of the fans was the worst I ever saw. I give Jim Marshall a lot of credit. He took more than most clubs would have—or even should have. But we got it in—I guess the Good Lord was with us.

Naturally my biggest thrill in baseball was working my first World Series. That's tops in anybody's career—players or umpires. It so happened that there was a lot of extra attention focused on my first

Series because it came the year [1961] Roger Maris hit sixty-one home runs to break Babe Ruth's record. As was the custom at the time for umpires working their first series, Bob Stewart and I worked the foul lines.

No question the adrenaline gets flowing a little more rapidly before an All-Star or a World Series game because of the publicity from the press buildup. But that doesn't, or at least it shouldn't, have any effect on an umpire. You're aware of the fanfare, but once you're out there you let it rip. You call a World Series game the same as a regular-season game. You can't change the strike zone; you can't change the safes and outs. I've always believed that you work the same in April as you do in October.

That belief got me into a little controversy during the 1969 World Series. I threw out Earl Weaver, the Baltimore manager, for arguing a called third strike in the fifth game. Commissioner Kuhn was not very happy about that because the front office doesn't like to have anyone ejected from a Series game. I knew nobody had been thrown out of a World Series for a long time [thirty-eight years], and I didn't want to break the precedent. But Weaver questioned a strike call, and the rules say that is an automatic ejection, so I unloaded on him. What else was I supposed to do? Ignore the rules? If I had let him get away with it, I wouldn't have been doing my job. I don't think an umpire should be told to compromise his authority for anybody or any game. A ball game is a ball game, and the rules are the rules. When you go out on the field, you have to use your natural instincts and judgment; if you water it down, you're not doing the job right. Besides, how could you live with yourself if you did otherwise?

For me the most difficult call to make was the sliding play when you had a good base stealer and a fielder with quick hands—somebody like Maury Wills and Ken Boyer. Boyer had unbelievably quick hands; he'd take a throw and, bing, make the tag in a split second. A guy like Wills was so adept at sliding; you never knew which way he was going, and he could just nick that bag so quick. No question, that bang-bang tag-slide play was the toughest to call.

Even though I was confident behind the bat, 1 was pretty tense when working the plate. It's a self-inflicted tension. You have 250 or so decisions to make, and you want to be pinpoint perfect. But you know you won't be, and you know that the ones you miss will cause who knows what kind of fuss. I thought about those things; that's the reason for the tenseness.

I always left the ball game on the field. When the game was over, it was over. As soon as I left the ball park, I had dinner and a few schnapps. I usually went out with my crew. I was fortunate in that I always had good relationships with all my crews. I enjoyed the company of the guys I worked with, especially if they liked to go out and have a few schnapps.

The only time I hated to go behind the plate was the second game of a doubleheader. It was especially tough late in my career. After being out there for three hours the first game, I really had to pump myself up to get behind the plate. That's hard work. Also, in the first game of those twi-night doubleheaders you'd get the shadow of the grandstand moving from home plate toward the pitcher's mound as the sun went down. That makes it very tough to pick up the ball sometimes. Tough on the hitters, too.

I would say that I was a pretty good ball-and-strike umpire. Each umpire has his own built-in strike zone because of the position he assumes behind the plate. It's that simple. Even though the strike zone varies from umpire to umpire, the key is that an individual umpire be consistent in calling the pitches. I did all right back there because I had pretty good consistency.

I adopted my style of umpiring behind the plate from Art Passarella, who I thought was one good umpire. I understand he is now a stand-in for Karl Malden. When I was in the minor leagues, I happened to be in Hartford, Connecticut, one night when the Yankees were in town. Passarella worked the plate. I was really impressed with him. He didn't stand up and throw his arm up like a lot of umpires; he stayed down and moved his arm out to the side from his hip. It was a very easy motion. I said to myself, "That's a beautiful motion. That's for me." From then on that's how I did it.

I had a real good strike call and was just as flamboyant as Emmett Ashford. I think an umpire should put it on. He should try to develop a good ball-and-strike call, a good call on outs and safes.

There's a saying that an umpire has done a good job when the people leave the park and don't know his name. Well, the only people who make that kind of statement are the baseball executives, not the people on the field. I don't think umpires should be submissive to the executives. I think umpires should let the fans know who they are and what they are.

Now you can go too far in putting on a show. I think Ron Luciano over in the American League is completely out of line. He's out there talking to people in the stands, shooting the players out like he has a gun, and all that stuff. That's totally ridiculous. It's undignified and disgraceful.

To be a good umpire, you have to be flexible in applying the rules.

It's not the knowledge of the rules that's so important—anybody can learn them—but the application. There was a minor league umpire—I can't think of his name—who was a great, great rules man. The major leagues used to refer questions to him to be solved. But the poor devil got fired from every league he was in because there was no flexibility in his rendering of the rules on the field. You simply cannot call every play the same way. Say the first baseman pulls his foot off the bag a little before he catches the ball. If it has no bearing on the call, if the runner is out a mile, you let it go. But if it is related to the play, like it's a bang-bang situation, then you call it. You have to have flexibility on each particular play.

After I got out of umpiring, I kept hearing how umpires enforce this and that rule in Little League or the minors, but they let it go in the majors. I got sick of hearing that. I finally wouldn't listen to that anymore. Major league players are so much smoother; it's just a different game. You have to be flexible; you have to adapt the rules to the game that's being played.

Now I am completely in favor of the fraternization rule. I wish the leagues would back it up. It is a shame the way the ballplayers fraternize with each other. All that hugging and fraternizing with guys who are supposed to be your opponent doesn't look good. Besides, it's not necessary. A visiting club is in town for three days, so invite a guy to dinner or something. Spend a few bucks on him if he is such a good friend, but leave him alone on the field.

It's a shame the league won't enforce the rule. I personally have turned in eight ballplayers at one time. They should have been fined $50 automatically for fraternizing, but they just got a warning. That's not right. What's the point of turning them in if the league won't do anything about it?

Besides, I don't think it should be the umpire's job to watch for fraternization. The ball clubs should do it. They should fine their own players for fraternizing with the opposition. But the club doesn't want to antagonize their ballplayers, so they put it on the umpires' shoulders. Of course, then you have ill feelings between the ballplayers and the umpires.

One of the things that makes baseball a great game is that the rules haven't been changed in so many years. Most of the rule changes are sort of superfluous; there is nothing really solid about them.

The only change I didn't like as far as the umpires are concerned is the automatic appeal on the half swing. I'm against that. I don't believe in it. You should just call it as best you can and go on from there. It's the plate umpire's call, and he should make it.

Another important ingredient in umpiring is being able to handle situations. You can't fall apart in a crisis. You have to control the game. You do that by getting the respect and confidence of the players. You don't do it by being good buddies with them. That's the way Goetz was. He was a bear out there, and everybody knew not to crowd him. He didn't like that "nice guy" umpire, and I tend to agree with him. It's always been that way. The strong ones, the not-so-strong ones, and the easygoing guys all had to be forceful in their decisions and control the game. The only change I can see in umpiring over the years is that the old-timers used hairbrushes and the guys today have hair dryers in the dressing room.

Rhubarbs are spontaneous things, so you have to handle each one differently. I was pretty feisty at first, pulled the trigger quite a bit on the ballplayers. But then as I got more maturity, more experience, I calmed down a little.

I think the correct approach for an umpire in handling a rhubarb is to react to the player or manager according to the way he approaches you. If he comes out charging at you like a bull, get him gone real quick; if he comes out wanting to give his opinion or get an explanation, then you talk with him.

I would not tolerate them cussing me or trying to show me up. Now, you have to realize that some guys are just foulmouthed: every other word is a cuss word. And baseball is a game of frustration—a guy strikes out, four-letter word; I miss a play, four-letter word. That didn't bother me at all. A guy could curse from now to doomsday over a play as long as he didn't direct his curses at me. I figured: Go ahead and curse; Satan will get you.

I kept a book on players in my head. I knew what they were capable of doing, how they behaved. Sure, I told my partners, especially a new guy, what I thought. But I always put in this note: "I think this guy will do this or do that, but you treat him as he treats you. You wait until he does something before you form your opinion about him."

You have an easier time when the kick comes away from you. Say I was at third base and a hell of a rhubarb breaks out at first base. I'd take a slow walk toward first, and while the argument was going on, I would try to figure out what happened and what I should say when I got over there. You should never rush over and jump into it unless there was a fight going on that you have to break up. The better you prepare yourself for the situation, the better you will handle it.

Over the years the rhubarbs decreased quite a bit. I'm not sure why. Maybe it's the diplomacy of the officials. Maybe it's the education the umpires received in those umpires' schools; they're sort of like finishing schools, aren't they? Or maybe it's just their unerring accuracy.

Sometimes you know you kicked one, but I think it is a very, very poor policy for an umpire to tell a guy that you blew it to relieve the pressure. The shortstop doesn't come to you and say, "Sorry, I kicked the ball." He kicked it, that's all; everybody knows it, and you go on with the game. The same thing with an umpire; if you kick it, you just handle whatever arises from your error of judgment and go on with the game.

It might be obvious that an umpire kicked a play, but that umpire still might think that he called it right. That happened to me. I'd ask one of my partners in the dressing room how a particular play looked, and I couldn't believe it when he told me that I kicked it. I'd swear I had it right. When you analyze old Bill Klem's famous statement you have the answer: He said he didn't miss any in his heart, but he didn't say anything about his lamps.

The booing and all never bothered me. I figured the people paid their way to get into the ball park, so they had a right to yell what they want. Now sometimes it can get to you if you get someone who is real abusive with the bad language. But if you have a crowd of, say, 60,000 or 70,000 people, it's just one loud noise; you can't tell who's yelling what. You know, you can hear those sixty voices in the two dugouts very clearly, but as far as the fans are concerned, you are pretty much oblivious to them unless something really serious happens in the stands so that the ball game has to be halted.

I accepted whatever happened to me at the ball park as a matter-of-fact thing, but I did object to people being smart when I'm off the field. Sometimes, when you go to a party or someplace, people try to show off, tell you something you haven't heard, try to impress you with how much they know. I realized they were just trying to be friendly and all that, but it sometimes got to the point where I finally put in the earplugs.

There is a professional jealousy among umpires, no question about it. It's very visible with some guys. I was never envious of any of my partners; I never worried about whether or not they were better umpires. I just went out there and did my best. The Good Lord gave me whatever ability I had. What else could I do?

Fortunately the National League did not have a supervisor of umpires like the American League, or there would have been more competition and jealousy. Fred Fleig, the secretary-treasurer of the league, acted as an overseer for us. He was a terrific guy to work with. He would come around and talk with you to see how you were getting along, scout you a couple of ball games, especially in your first few years, and that was about it.

I think a lot of umpire supervisors create turmoil in order to keep their jobs. They are always looking for trouble because if there are no problems, there is no need for a supervisor. I think they tend to create little frictions where there shouldn't be any.

We were a lot more colorful, more individualistic than the guys in the American League. That's because they had a supervisor. Cal Hubbard kept a pretty tight rein on them; he made them umpire the way he thought they should umpire.

In the National League the crew chief is the boss. His deportment is reflected by the whole crew. We were pretty much free to do what we wanted on the field and off. You could go out after a ball game with your crew chief and have a few drinks without worrying about somebody telling the front office that you'd gone to this place, done that thing, or whatever.

I definitely do not like the talk about lumping all the umpires together under the commissioner or some independent supervisor. They talk about it as an economy move, but I think it's just that Bowie Kuhn wants to control the whole of baseball. Mr. [Charles S. "Chub"] Feeney and Mr. [Leland] MacPhail do a very good job of running the umpires in their respective leagues, so there is absolutely no reason to change.

Besides, I want to be known as Shag Crawford, National League umpire. There is great pride in being a representative of a particular league. I'm sure the guys working today in the American and National leagues feel the same way I do. The pride and competition between the leagues are good for baseball.

I know some people say that umpires in the two leagues should use the same positions and techniques. Maybe. But the point I have to make is that we in the National League think our way of doing it is the best way. The fellows in the American League probably think the same way. I'll concede that the balloon is more protective behind the plate, but other than that, I see no reason for it. A lot of the American League umpires today are wearing the inside vest protector. I think we can see the outside corner and the high pitch just as well from our position behind the catcher, and I think our position on the infield with a runner on first base is definitely better because you get a better look at things like juggled balls at second.

Now it is definitely a good thing for all the umpires to be part of the

Major League Umpires Association. There is no question that before we organized the association in 1964, umpires were neglected financially. During my first thirteen years in the major leagues I drove tank trucks for the Sinclair Oil Company. It was a good job for me because the heating oil season complemented the baseball season. The company wanted to hire drivers in the late fall and lay them off around the end of February, and of course, I wanted to be away umpiring from around March to October. Since the association the profession has made tremendous strides. The salaries are terrific, and the fringe benefits—hospitalization, dental care, the pension—are the best.

It all started when about eight of us got together in Los Angeles to propose an association. I think one crew had a day off, so they laid over to meet with the next crew that came to town. There was Jocko Conlan, Augie Donatelli, Al Barlick, Eddie Vargo, Bill Jackowski—I can't remember everyone who was there. Anyway, we sounded out each man on the staff about an organization, and they were all for it. We tried to get the American League umpires on board, but they were reluctant at that particular time, so we went ahead and presented our demands to Mr. Giles. Naturally there was a little bit of resentment by the owners. They were receptive to some things, unreceptive to others, but they finally approved the salary schedule and a package of fringe benefits.

We were aware that trying to organize the association might cost us our jobs. But the league couldn't really dump all twenty-four of us at one time. Oh, I guess they could have if they really wanted to get nasty about the thing. But there were some really great umpires with outstanding reputations involved, so I think they didn't have much of a choice but to sit down and talk to us.

We were so serious about the association that we went out on strike during the 1970 play-offs. It was the first umpire strike in history. The association had presented our demands to Mr. Feeney and Mr. Cronin, but they did not acquiesce to them. So we struck on October 3 at both Pittsburgh and Bloomington. We had pickets at Three Rivers Stadium, but not in Minnesota. The National League got four AAA umpires to work the Pirate-Cincinnati game, while a couple of minor league umpires and retired major league umpires worked the Baltimore-Twins game.

We didn't want to strike, but it was one of those situations where we had no alterntive because the leagues tried to back us against the wall. We realized there was a risk in what we were doing. We knew there were a lot of guys in the minor leagues just itching to go up to the majors. But we figured the leagues couldn't fire us all because there were some pretty big names involved. Besides, we were only asking for what was right.

The next morning we met with Mr. Feeney. There was John Reynolds, our lawyer, Harry Wendelstedt, the president of the association, Augie Donatelli, and me. Augie and I were on the board of directors of the association. About an hour before the second game we reached an agreement. We got a pay increase for the championship series from $2,500 to $4,000. The salary for working the World Series went up from $6,500 to $7,500, and the fee for the All-Star game went from $500 to $1,000. We made out pretty good.

Toward the end of July 1975 I sort of sensed that I might be at the end of the line, that it might be my last year. I hadn't heard anything specific about it. I just had that feeling. The last game of the season was in St. Louis. The Cardinals beat the Pirates, 6–2. I was working at second base, and after the last out of the game, I thought to myself: Well, this might be the last major league ball game I will ever work. I normally ran off the field, but that night I walked off to experience the full feeling of being on a big league umpiring staff. Sure enough, after the season I got a letter saying that I had been retired.

I was reluctant to let it go, but the powers that be said otherwise. I had planned on resigning after the 1976 season anyway. The strain of getting up and down behind the plate was getting a little tough on an old goat like me. But I was in pretty good physical condition—still am. I ran a lot in the off-season to keep in shape; jumping in and out of those tank trucks and hauling those heavy hoses around were a pretty good workout, too. I wanted to hang on through the 1976 season because I was scheduled to work the World Series that year. It cost me quite a bit of money to be retired, but I've got no beef. Besides, I've got my son up there now.

The Umpires Association put in the recommended retirement age of fifty-five, and I had a four-year extension, for which I am grateful. I think the fifty-five year retirement is a good thing, especially for the young guys. If my son stays with it, he will have put in twenty-five years of calling them by the time he reaches fifty-five. That's enough; then he has time to travel, to have a good time in life. Of course, the guys like me who go up at a later age would rather have retirement at sixty or sixty-five.

It's the abruptness that gets you. Baseball is such an integral part of your life. It was my life on the field and off the field. I talked baseball all the time with the umpires, and when I'd be introduced to somebody outside the game, they'd want to talk baseball. Then, one day, it's over. They tell you, "Shag, we are retiring you." There's nothing you can do about it. Nothing. It's over. There is no way to come down slowly, like a player who can go to AAA ball or something. Bang! It's over. That's what makes it hard.

My interest in baseball is still very keen. I'm not a fan in the sense that I go to the ball park. I hardly ever go in to see the Phillies play because the traffic is so bad. But the first thing I do when I get up in the morning is get out the sports page and check the box scores and what-have-you.

I hoped I might get a shot at managing. George Moriarty managed after retiring as an umpire, and if he could do it, so could I. I've handled players in their worst moments, when they were really on the rampage. I'd seen it all. I could have coped with any situation that could possibly come up. But I never got the chance.

I even tried [1978] getting into professional softball as the general manager of the Philadelphia team, but I quit after a couple of months because it was taking up too much time. I'm retired. What do I need with a job that keeps me busy five days a week?

What did I get out of umpiring? A very rewarding career. I loved it. I was able to provide well for my family and also got the satisfaction of being in the big leagues. As a kid my ambition was to be a big league baseball player; I finally realized that ambition, although it came as an umpire.

If people would say, "Shag Crawford was a good umpire," that would be sufficient for me. I wouldn't want any superlatives other than that. If people say, "He was a son of a bitch, but he was a good umpire," that would be enough for me. I'm satisfied with my career and the great people I met; there is nothing I could add to that.

Ed Sudol registers the finality of the out as Pirate Kurt
Bevacqua registers disbelief during a home game with
the Dodgers in 1974. Courtesy National Baseball
Library & Archive, Cooperstown, N.Y.

Ed Sudol

ප්‍රප්‍රප්‍ර

Edward Sudol
Born: Passaic, New Jersey, September 13, 1920
Height: 6′ 2″
Weight: 210
Playing career: minor leagues, 1940–43, 1945–53
Umpiring career: Tri-State League (C), July 1953–54; Interna-
            tional League (AAA), 1955–June 26, 1957; Na-
            tional League, June 27, 1957–77
No-hit games: Juan Marichal, June 15, 1963; Jim Bunning, June 21,
            1964 (perfect game); Bill Singer, July 20, 1970
All-Star games: 1951 (second game), 1964, 1974
World Series (games): 1965 (7), 1971 (7), 1977 (6)
Championship series: 1969, 1973

I retired after the 1977 World Series between the Yankees and the Dodgers. My wife and I talked about it while I was home during the championship series, resting up for the World Series. I told her then that it would be my last year. Chub Feeney, the league president, had kept me on two years beyond the retirement age of fifty-five called for by the association contract because he felt I could still do the job. But I knew even if I was offered another contract that I couldn't go on fooling them anymore. Only Debbie knew the terrible pain I'd been suffering in my hip. Over the years the constant crouching behind the plate caught up with me; I couldn't stand the excruciating pain any longer. That November, right after the Series, I had an operation to remove my right hip joint and replace it with an artificial one. What better time to retire than after my third World Series? I had been looking forward to it for the last six years. For an umpire, it's like going out on top.

I worked the plate for the last time in the second game of the Series. I was a little worried before the game because I had never seen Catfish Hunter before. But Nestor Chylak said, "Ed, don't worry. You can sit in a rocking chair and call his pitches. He has beautiful control." As it turned out, I didn't get to see too much of him because he got bombed. Burt Hooton pitched a beautiful game, and the Dodgers won, 6–1. I was in excruciating pain during the game. Only my wife knew how I was suffering. I knew then that it was over.

I'll never forget the final game. I was at second base, so I had a real good look at the pitches Reggie Jackson hit for those historic three home runs. Charlie Hough threw him a tremendous knuckleball; I don't know how Reggie even got his bat on it, let alone hit it about 420 feet. The other pitches were also tough ones—good corner pitches. Deep inside, I got into the excitement of the crowd. I marveled at those home runs; you have to admire the man's fantastic ability. After the final out I had to run as fast as he did to get off the field. I was bumped by several spectators pouring out on the field from the stands looking for a souvenir—a base, a piece of turf, anything. I can't describe the excitement. It was electrifying.

It was a moment in history that will not be repeated for me because I knew that it was my last ball game. It was sad. And yet it was exhilarating to think that I was finally going to live like a normal human being. I was really going to notice the trees turning green and hear the birds singing. I had no time for things like that before because I was working so hard to make a living, to provide security for my wife and me, and to make something out of myself.

All those thoughts and many more flashed through my mind. They say that in your dying moments everything appears before your eyes like a movie. That's what happened to me. It kept going through my mind as I sat in the dressing room being congratulated by Bowie Kuhn, the commissioner of baseball, for a job well done. I knew it would all be gone, that it would belong to the past forever. I'd never again feel the excitement of the games, the adulation of the fans, and the friendship of the people I'd met in twelve cities over the years. I knew I was going to miss it.

I am grateful that the Good Lord gave me the strength, the courage, and the endurance to make it to the major leagues and stay for twenty years. I had lots of firsts, lots of thrills, lots of memories. I was blessed with friends from all walks of life who I will never forget. Most important, I had accomplished what I had set out to accomplish: I had realized my lifelong dream of reaching the big time in baseball.

I was born on September 13, 1920, and raised in Passaic, New Jersey. My parents were from Warsaw, Poland. There were five children, all boys. My father operated a tavern in Passaic for forty-six years. We didn't have a great deal of money, especially during the Depression time, so I had to quit high school at age sixteen to go to work to help the family with expenses.

Interestingly, by quitting school, I got more involved with baseball than before. I first started playing ball with the local American Legion Post No. 200; we won the state championship. Anyway, the place where I worked, the American Can Company in Jersey City, had a team in an industrial league, so I furthered my baseball experience by playing after working hours.

Mike McNally from Paterson, a scout with the Baltimore Orioles, signed me to my first baseball contract. He saw me catch a semipro game in Garfield, New Jersey, one night. It turned out that Alex Yoda, an All-State pitcher, threw a no-run, no-hit game. McNally credited that performance to my proper handling of the pitches, so he signed me. At the time Baltimore was in the International League, part of the Cleveland Indians organization.

My father was my staunchest supporter. Mother wanted me to stay in the factory and get that weekly paycheck. You couldn't blame her because there wasn't a great deal of money at home, and as the bulwark of family life, she wanted to hold everybody together. But Dad was very sports-minded, particularly about baseball. His favorite team was the New York Giants. When his older sons participated in high school and semipro ball, he attended every game, and when I had an opportunity to be a professional, he said, "Go on and take a crack at it. If you never make it, you can at least say you had a chance to try for it." When I became a success in baseball, he was very, very proud.

I think my background helped me in my baseball career. Whatever field of endeavor you pursue, I think it is best to start from a poverty background because you have such a drive to get out of that ghetto and better yourself. Not that you blame your parents for things that happened to you or that they couldn't give you a college education to better yourself. It's the motivation to move up that's important. I credit my background with pushing me to achieve what I wanted to achieve. It gave me that super energy or strength to go on and make it to the top. If I had had an easy family life as a youngster, I don't believe I would have been very successful at anything.

When I broke into professional baseball, getting from the minor leagues to the majors was like trying to reach the moon. It was almost unheard of. There were fifty-six minor leagues with eight teams in each league and only two major leagues of eight teams each. The odds against your making the big time were tremendous. But I never gave up trying. Even when I was thirty-two years old, when most ballplayers are washed up, I still had that determination to make it. Eventually I got there, but not the way I had hoped when I signed that first contract.

I broke in with Pocomoke City, Maryland, in the Class D Eastern Shore League in 1940. I was released after the first month of the season because I was hitting only .201. I was the highest-paid player on the team, and they didn't think I had a high enough batting average to justify my salary of $100 a month. I wouldn't take a pay cut, so they let me go. But I was still determined to pursue my dream because I had proved to myself that I had the ability to be a professional ballplayer.

During the winter John Polk Whalen, who had been my manager at Pocomoke City, contacted me about playing again. He had been appointed manager of the Tarboro, North Carolina, club in the Coastal Plain League. He said that he had confidence in my ability and that the Baltimore front office wanted me to take another crack at it. I had a wonderful year for Tarboro—played first base and hit .311.

The next spring I made the big jump from Class D to the Baltimore Orioles. I didn't last very long because I got beaned by Rufus Gentry in Buffalo. I finished the season with Wilmington in the Inter-State League, Class B, and Jacksonville in the Class A South Atlantic League.

I went to spring training with the Orioles again in 1943. I had a deferment from active duty with the United States Army Signal Corps because I was going to radio operator's school. After a few games with Baltimore I was sent to Wilkes-Barre in the Class A Eastern league. There were lots of future stars up there like Gene Woodling, Bob Lemon, and Allie Reynolds. Woodling and I battled for the batting championship. He broke his leg and missed the last month of the season; he beat me out of the batting title by three points, .338 to .335. I was ready to report to the Cleveland Indians, but Uncle Sam tapped me on the shoulder.

After I got out of the service in 1945, I went to spring training with the Orioles but got shot down by the numbers game. It seemed thousands of discharged ballplayers were scrapping to get their jobs back. The competition was fierce, and many of us found that our timing and reflexes weren't the same as before the service. I got beat out for first base by big Eddie Robinson, who later starred for several big league clubs.

To make a long story short, I drifted into the lower minors all along the East Coast, the South, and the Southwest. I was hitting pretty well, usually around .300 or better, and led the league in fielding a couple of times. In 1952 with Pampa in the West Texas-New Mexico League, I hit .293 with twenty-one homers and eighty-five RBIs. At the end of the season Charleston of the South Atlantic or "Sally" League bought my contract.

That winter I was at a crossroads. I still hoped I could make the majors, but I knew that at thirty-two years of age I soon had to find another road that would lead me to a better living.

One night, after driving a beer truck through the snowy and icy streets of Passaic, I sat down before dinner to read the new issue of the *Sporting News*. I turned like always to the back of the paper—"Caught on the Fly" and sections like that to catch up on news about my old colleagues. Well, the first page I turned to that cold winter evening in December carried the picture of a beautiful girl in a bikini leaning against a palm tree by the ocean. The ad read: "Bill McGowan's Umpire School, Daytona Beach, Florida. Enjoy the beautiful girls and the climate under a six week course of tutoring to become a professional umpire." I was tired and disgusted with the snow and beer trucks, and I knew that at my age I couldn't play ball much longer. That ad seemed to be telling me something; right then and there I made up my mind that I wanted to be an umpire. The school was going to open in a couple of weeks, so that night I mailed a letter which read: "Dear Bill: Count me in."

Off I went to attend umpire school with the great Bill McGowan. Al Somers was the chief instructor. I loved it. My ballplaying experience helped a lot, and I finished as one of the two best students out of a class of 196. Instead of starting out at the bottom of the ladder, I got a contract in Class C ball.

Things looked great, but there was a problem: I was still under contract with Charleston. I really had no business going to an umpire school because I was under contract with a ball club, but I went anyway. When George Trautman, the president of the National Association of Professional Baseball Leagues, heard about it, he called me in Daytona. He told me to honor my contract with Charleston, or he would see to it that I didn't play ball or umpire. I immediately said, "Yes, sir, Mr. Trautman. I will do what is right. I will do whatever you say." But I went ahead and bought a full set of umpire's equipment—just in case something worked out.

That spring I reported to Charleston. About a month into the season I got beaned and went on the disabled list for two weeks. The club figured I was through, so they sold me to Rock Hill, South Carolina, in the Class C Tri-State League. Around the middle of July I got beaned again. I knew then that I wasn't going to make it as a ballplayer, that I was about to get the pink slip. I had come to the end of my rope, all washed up after twelve long years in the minors. I was really down in the dumps.

The night before I was to be released, I was sitting around with my roommate, Kirby Higbe, the former Brooklyn Dodgers' pitcher, feeling very low when the telephone rang. It was Bobby Phipps, the president of the league. Mr. Phipps had heard I was being released, and he wanted me to replace one of his umpires who had gotten sick. I told him I had my umpire's gear in the trunk of my car and was ready to go. He said, "All right, report to Charlotte, North Carolina. You start umpiring tomorrow night." I said, "Oh, my God!" Who was playing in Charlotte that night? My ex-teammates.

When I got to Charlotte, Red Simpson, the crew chief, put me behind the plate in my first professional game. Wouldn't you know the pitcher for Rock Hill was my roomie, Kirby Higbe. I was scared, believe me. Fortunately, it was a rocking-chair game.

So I went from ballplayer to umpire in twenty-four hours. I not only opened behind the plate but also worked the game with my former teammates and roommate. I guess you could say my umpiring career began under some very unusual circumstances.

I stayed in the Tri-State League through 1954, then moved up to the International League, which was one step away from the big time. I was in the International League two and a half years.

It was frustrating at times in the minors. The pay was low. I got $175 a month when I first signed in the Tri-State League; my salary increased to $400 when I moved to the International League. Even though we had to pay our own expenses, I had an advantage because I was not married. Having only myself to take care of was a tremendous advantage financially, and of course, I didn't have the emotional burden of worrying about a family away from home. The fans were very, very vicious at times, but it was nothing like I had expected. No rough stuff—bottles, fights, and so on—like the old days. Things had settled down quite a bit. Still, there were days when I wanted to pack my bags and go home. But because I had that driving determination to be successful, I stayed with it.

Actually, I rose very rapidly as an umpire. It was only four years from my first minor league game to the majors. I'm certain that my experience as a ballplayer helped me get to the big leagues so quickly. I was used to the tension and yelling in the ball park. As an ex-player I could anticipate various plays and understand the different dispositions and temperaments of ballplayers. I was temperamental as a player, so I would take a little more than some other umpires because I knew how the player felt, what he was thinking. I never took any profanity or abuse, but I would take enough time to listen to gripes.

I remember when I got the call to the majors like it just happened yesterday. It was Thursday, June 27, 1957. I was at the Cadillac Hotel in Rochester, New York, preparing for the ball game that evening. About an hour before I was to leave for the ball park, that would be about five-thirty, I got a call from Mr. Fred Fleig, secretary-treasurer and supervisor of umpires for the National League. He said, "Ed, are you ready to work? I want you in Chicago tomorrow." I said, "WHAT?" I was so excited I jumped up on the bed and hit my head on the ceiling. I was stunned, speechless. Mr. Fleig finally said, "Ed, can you hear me? Are you still on the phone?" He told me that Dusty Boggess had suffered a heart attack and would be out indefinitely, so he needed someone to work the series between the Dodgers and the Cubs. He said, "Can you be in Chicago tomorrow?" I told him, "I will be there if I have to walk."

The next day I was at Wrigley Field. I remember my feelings exactly as I walked on the field. I said to myself, "Ed Sudol, it took you sixteen years. You couldn't make it as a ballplayer, but you finally made the big time as an umpire." The feeling was so overwhelming that I just thanked God through the tears coming down my cheeks.

I joined Tom Gorman, Ken Burkhart, and Hal Dixon. Gorman replaced Boggess as the crew chief. They really broke me in real fast. I worked third base my first game; nothing much happened. We were rained out on Saturday, so we had a doubleheader on Sunday. Instead of working the bases, they put me at first base in the opening game and behind the plate in the second. The Cubs won the first game, 3–2, in eleven innings. Then I had my real test.

I wasn't nervous at first base, but I was really nervous before the second game. Although I had worked some spring exhibition games, I knew I had a tough job ahead of me. I had heard from the veteran umpires that Roy Campanella could be real rough on a rookie umpire. Jim Fanning, who for a number of years was the general manager of the Montreal Expos, was catching for the Cubs that day.

I had quite a ball game. Danny McDevitt pitched for the Dodgers, Moe Drabowsky for the Cubs. I got through it all right, but I had a few arguments. I got initiated because everybody tests a rookie. Fanning was a sweetheart, but Campy gave me a rough time, especially when I called a crucial balk on McDevitt.

The Dodgers were leading, 1-0, in the sixth inning when McDevitt quick-pitched the batter. He tried to get the batter off-balance by not taking his normal stretch—that's a balk with men on base. There were runners on first and third at the time, so the balk brought in the runner from third with the tying run. The Dodgers broke it open in the eighth with three runs and won, 5-1, but that was a tough call for me the first time behind the plate.

As it turned out, I became the first "fifth umpire" in the major leagues. I had done real well since going up, so I felt pretty good. Then one hot night in late August, when I was standing in front of the Netherland-Hilton Hotel in Cincinnati, a cab pulled up to the curb, and out stepped Dusty Boggess. I didn't know whether to congratulate him or get mad because I'd have to go back to the minors to make room for him. But the league was so pleased with my performance that they kept me on as the fifth umpire in the crew. For the rest of the season I alternated working the foul lines.

Tom Gorman and the other fellows in my crew helped me a great deal when I broke in. They encouraged me, built up my confidence, gave me suggestions, and helped get players and managers away from me during rhubarbs. But they could not make the decisions for me. You either can do it or can't. When I joined the National League, Warren Giles, the president, said, "Ed, you're not a full-fledged major league umpire until you have had about seven years of experience. It takes that long to get the confidence and the respect of the ballplayers." That's very true. The first five years or so are crucial in determining whether you stay around. Like any other field, the more years you put in, the more experience you get, the better you perform. You cannot beat experience.

I don't know what it is that makes an umpire. It's something you cannot define correctly in words. It's something inside of you like a soul, and nobody can define the soul. You have to be born with the temperament and ability; you can't make someone an umpire. Young men have come into the profession out of umpiring school with all the tools, perfect knowledge of the rules, and mastery of the mechanics, but they'd freeze, make the bad decision, when the chips were down on the field. It takes guts or in a finer term, intestinal fortitude.

Even though I worked in the National League, I used the American League technique. I started out with the balloon at McGowan's school and stayed with it. When I went up to the majors, Jocko Conlan and I were the only ones in the National League using the outside protector. I changed over to the inside protector in 1957 but continued to work over the catcher's head instead of down over the shoulder on the inside. I preferred the American League technique because I had the view of the whole plate and had a good shot at both corners.

As to whether the National League is a low-strike league and the American League is a high-strike league, I don't really know. I've heard that from hitters and pitchers, but I cannot evaluate the point. Actually, the strike zone is exactly the same in both leagues. You can look it up in the rule book.

On the bases—that is, at second base—I loved to work in the outfield behind the bag. But Fred Fleig, our supervisor, insisted that it was better to work on the inside of the diamond for this reason: If the second baseman juggles the throw from the shortstop on a double play, you can see it from the diamond but not from the outfield. That is true because it happened to me once on a nationally televised ball game. Davy Johnson, who was playing second for the Atlanta Braves at the time, juggled the throw from the shortstop before relaying the ball to first. I didn't see it because I was behind him, so I called the runner out. I was told by the third-base umpire that Johnson dropped the ball, so I had to change my decision. On that particular play it is better to stay on the inside, but I like the outfield better for trapped balls and other calls.

The fellows you work with are important because you are only as good as your crew. If you have one weak umpire on your crew, they won't point to that particular person. They'll point out the crew. It's Sudol's or Gorman's crew that's making all the blunders. Consequently, you appreciate good calls and good performance by your fellow umpires.

I worked with a lot of good umpires. Frank Dascoli was probably the best. He was very flamboyant and very serious all at once. He was beautiful to watch call balls and strikes. He was so sincere and intense and honest and hardworking that I had the greatest respect for him. I was working with him when he got fired after twelve years in the league. Frank just let his emotions go uncontrolled off the field, and it hurt him. But he was a good umpire, an exciting umpire to watch, an umpire with tremendous ability.

My style of umpiring changed considerably over the years. During my formative years, meaning my first ten years, I was a mechanical umpire. I wasn't demonstrative. But from about my twelfth year to the end of my career I got very demonstrative, especially on balls and strikes. I wasn't trying to be a showboat. It just came out naturally because I was more relaxed. I was very confident; I was becoming a master of my profession. I guess it made me more colorful, but I wasn't putting it on; it just came natural.

I think it is good that umpires are getting more demonstrative and colorful so long as it doesn't interfere with their ability to call pitches properly and make proper decisions on the bases. I don't care if a man does a somersault calling a bang-bang play at first base if the play is called right. Of course, he'll look like a damn fool if he is flamboyant and misses the call.

My technique for calling balls and strikes was first to size up the size of the ballplayer and his batting stance and then, in my mind, project a mental image of my strike zone according to the size of the ballplayer and his batting stance. I called a lot of outside pitches strikes on batters who were bending over the plate. I'd get a lot of argument on it, but the pitch was a strike according to their stance.

You might say I was a pitcher's umpire because I loved to call those strikes on the corners. If I had a close pitch on the corner, I always rang them up as strikes. It's like the great Rogers Hornsby told his players when he was managing in the big leagues: If it's close enough for the umpire to call it, it's close enough for you to swing at it. That's true. I had some of the best hitters in the game strike out swinging on bad pitches and turn around and ask, "Ed, was that a strike?" See, the players themselves, even the great hitters, don't really know on a lot of pitches.

The National League had so many great pitchers during my career, but the one who really stands out in my mind is Warren Spahn. He was one of the greatest left-handers of all time. He still holds the major league record for victories by a left-handed pitcher, 363. Spahn had extraordinary control. He could throw that ball exactly where the catcher put his glove. Robin Roberts was another one with super-human control. Those two were unbelievable. It was a picnic to work behind pitchers like those two.

As far as managers are concerned, Preston Gomez would go at the top of the list. He was a very good manager, and to go along with his ability was a temperament that made him particularly outstanding to work with. Gomez would never argue viciously or be demonstrative for the television cameras and newspaper photographers. (You know, it's funny: we have more rhubarbs during nationally televised games than at any other time.) He never used profanity, never. I don't remember ever seeing him thrown out of a ball game in all his years at Houston and San Diego. He was, in a word, a gentleman.

I admired Stan Musial the most as a batter. He had fantastic reflexes and an extraordinary eye. Willie Mays was another great hitter and a wonderful all-around ballplayer; he could do it all. Those two come immediately to mind, but for a good, steady hitter you couldn't beat Pete Rose. He didn't hit with too much power, but you could always count on him making contact. He is definitely destined for the Hall of Fame.

I always had butterflies, always had a little fear when I walked on that field. And not only behind the plate—you can get plays on the bases that can be crucial in deciding the ball game. But there is no question calling balls and strikes is the most difficult job. All that crouching is hard physically on your back and legs. Then there is so much tension from the mental concentration in judging instantly several hundred balls traveling 90 to 100 miles an hour. I can't find the words to explain what's involved in executing behind the plate, but sometimes I marvel at the whole thing myself. I was physically and mentally drained after calling balls and strikes; it would take me almost an hour to recover after a plate game. It was even more strenuous with that TV monster that goes into everyone's living room—my God, you have millions of umpires making the calls with you. Of course, television shows those fans that we are right 99.9 percent of the time.

Most people just don't understand what it's like to be an umpire. Sure, it's lots of fun to be around baseball and watch the greats of the game. But it's hard work, too.

People say, "You've got a great life, Sudol. You only put in two and a half to three hours at the ball park." That's true, but I prepare for that ball game mentally from the time I get up in the morning until game time. You prepare yourself just like a prizefighter. You study the players' strengths, weaknesses, tendencies. If it's a plate game, you ask yourself: "Does the pitcher have control or is he wild? What does he throw? What's his motion?" If you're on the bases, you check the lineup to see who has the speed to give you the bang-bang plays at first, who likes to steal, and so on. You must prepare mental notes for the game.

Then they say, "It must be nice to travel all over the country, visit exciting cities, live in the best hotels." Yes, but the constant traveling, the constant routine of packing and unpacking gets a little boring. You're always living by the clock, so you can't relax socially. You're always worrying about making it on time to the ball park or catching a plane or something; it's difficult to visit friends or see the cities with that kind of time schedule. And it was hard to do the things normal people do because as an official of the National League, as a representative of major league baseball, you have to watch where you go, what you do, and who you associate with. You've got to live like a preacher; if you don't toe the line morally, you won't stay around long.

I never really felt lonely. Bored, sometimes, but not lonely. I knew how to handle my spare time because I was a professional ballplayer for so many years. And because I was not a family man, I didn't have the pressure of worrying so much about home. I didn't get married until my third year in the league. My wife, Debbie, traveled with me for several years, but she got tired of the big-city life and the constant moving every three days. Finally, she stayed home. She said, "Whenever you have twenty-four hours, hurry home." I couldn't have survived as long as I did without Debbie's prayers, encouragement, and long-distance phone calls cheering me up and building up my confidence to continue.

I had many, many thrills during my twenty years in the major leagues. I worked three World Series, three league championships, and three All-Star games. I also worked the first championship series in 1969. I closed up the Polo Grounds in 1957, worked the last series before the Giants moved to San Francisco. I was in Atlanta the night Hank Aaron hit his 715th home run to beat Babe Ruth's record. In fact, I worked second base, so I called that historic home run. I saw Reggie Jackson hit three home runs on three pitches to win the World Series. And I called three no-hitters, including a perfect game.

Every World Series is a special thrill for an umpire. There's an excitement, an intensity that is just awesome. For me nothing can match walking out on the field for my first World Series in 1965: the Dodgers and the Twins. I can't find the proper words to describe my feelings that day.

I can describe my feelings the day I worked the plate the fourth game in Los Angeles: nervous. I was very, very nervous. I knew that maybe 100 million people all over the world would be watching on television. I kept thinking: My God, if I make a mistake, the whole world will know about it. You could blow your whole career with one bad call in the World Series because people will always remember that one bad call. Eddie Rommel, the former A's pitcher who umpired in the American League for eighteen years, got to the point where he refused to work the World Series. He said, "Number one, I don't need the money. Number two, if I make one mistake, my whole career is shot."

In addition, you always worry in a World Series or All-Star game about seeing pitchers from the opposite league for the first time. You talk about pitchers with the umpires from the other league, about speed, rhythm, control, and so on, so you have an idea of what to expect. After an inning or two you know him pretty well. But you worry about that before the game.

By the time we went to the plate to get the lineup cards I was really nervous. I continued being nervous, not until the first pitch was thrown, but until the first inning was over. It took me an inning to get into the groove and get relaxed mentally so I could make my calls with confidence. Even after that I was in sort of a daze. But it was a great game. Don Drysdale struck out eleven and beat Mudcat Grant, 7–2, to even the Series; the Dodgers went on to win it four games to three. Afterward I had a delayed reaction. It didn't really hit me until I was back in my hotel room that I had actually worked behind the plate in a World Series. I had to run for the bathroom; I almost vomited.

The highlight for any umpire working behind the plate is a no-hit, no-run game. I was fortunate to call three of them. The first one was on June 15, 1963, when Juan Marichal of the Giants beat the Astros, 1–0. The last one I had was July 20, 1970, when Bill Singer and the Dodgers beat the Phillies, 5–0. Those were outstanding pitching performances and games I will never forget.

But the game that stands out most is the perfect game Jim Bunning pitched against the Mets at Shea Stadium on Father's Day, June 21, 1964. The Phillies won, 6–0. Bunning was sensational. He struck out ten and had only four balls hit out of the infield. I was about as excited as he was when he struck out Johnny Stephenson to end the game. Working a perfect game behind the plate was a supreme thrill. I would put it almost in the same category as working my first World Series. Perfect games—no runs, no hits, no errors, no walks—are so rare; Bunning's was the first one in the regular season in a long time [forty-two years]. It was fantastic to be a part of that accomplishment.

I knew all along that he had a perfect game going because that mammoth scoreboard was staring right at me. That's what made me so extra-tense. I wanted to be perfect, too. I didn't want to be responsible for a blunder that would ruin a perfect game. What if on a full count, three-and-two, the batter doesn't swing on a pitch that could go either way? The adrenaline was really flowing. And it was real hot—in the 90s with high humidity. I was so exhausted after the game that I left the dressing room an hour after my partners had gone. I was drenched with perspiration and exhausted by all the mental notes from that pressure-packed game. I sat there reliving all those moments. It took a lot out of me.

I had so many marathon ball games that I was known as the extra-inning umpire. I was in the longest day game, the longest 1–0 game, and the longest night game in history. The weird thing about it is that I was behind the plate in each game, the Mets were involved in each game, and the length of the games increased in succession from twenty-three to twenty-four to twenty-five innings.

The first long ball game was the twenty-three-inning game between the San Francisco Giants and the Mets in Shea Stadium on May 31, 1964. Besides being the longest day game ever, it was part of the longest doubleheader in history, nine hours and fifty-two minutes, and the most innings played in one day, thirty-two. (Bunning's perfect game came three weeks later, so that was an exciting time for me.)

It was the second game of a Sunday doubleheader. The Giants won the opener, 5–3, in two hours and twenty-nine minutes. The second game went seven hours and twenty-three minutes before the Giants finally won it, 8–6. I thought it would never end. Great defensive plays kept snuffing out rallies. The Mets' shortstop, Roy McMillan, was sensational. He made a lot of great stops and started a triple play in the fourteenth inning. Bill Wakefield started for the Mets and Bookie Bolin for the Giants, but Gaylord Perry [ten innings] and Galen Cisco [nine innings] pitched full games in relief. There were thirty-six strikeouts and forty-seven hits; lots of guys got to bat ten times. Willie Mays wound up playing shortstop for the Giants. We might still be playing if Del Crandall hadn't broken the tie with a double down the right-field line.

It was a long day. I left my parents' house in Passaic about 10:00 A.M. and arrived at the ball park at 11:00. The first game started at 1:00. We had a half hour break between games and then went back on the field. The second game ended at 11:25 P.M. My wife and I left the ball park at 2:30 A.M. the next day. My brother had taken the car home because he had to go to work the next morning, so we caught a ride to the Port Authority Bus Station on Forty-second Street in the back of the Railway Express truck that was handling our luggage. We got home at 5:30 A.M. My next assignment was that night—in Milwaukee.

That was a grueling experience. I was exhausted from the mental strain of concentrating on calling about 800 pitches and was getting a lot of cramps in my calves, thighs, and around my hip joints from the constant crouching. But I never left the field because I was in condition.

Most people don't realize the extraordinary wear and tear on the body involved in working behind the plate. The muscle strain is tremendous. Up to my very last year as a National League umpire I suffered severe cramps after every plate game I worked. Sometimes the cramps were so terrible I had to get up three or four times during the night. The only way I could relieve the pain was to walk on the tile floors the hotels had in the bathrooms. The shock of the cold floor would accelerate the circulation and ease the cramps.

I conditioned myself like a fighter, so I would never have to leave the field during a ball game. I didn't drink too much liquid or eat much food before a ball game. If you overdo one or the other, either you have to go to the bathroom or you get logy. I never ate a thing between games of a doubleheader. You have to know how your body reacts to tense situations and long periods of time, then train yourself. After a while your body gets sort of computerized and does just what you want it to.

The second long game, the longest 1–0 game recorded in the history of baseball, involved the Houston Astros and the Mets in the Astrodome on April 15, 1968. Even though it was an inning longer than the Mets-Giants game, it was shorter in time—six hours and thirty-six minutes. The two starting pitchers were magnificent. Tom Seaver went ten innings for the Mets; Don Wilson went nine for the Astros. It ended at 2:37 A.M. when, in the twenty-fourth inning, the Mets' shortstop, Al Weis, let a ground ball hit by Bob Aspromonte go through his legs.

That game was even more difficult for me physically because of the Astroturf. The artificial turf is just murder on your legs and feet. It's like standing on concrete. And it's hot. I've worked games in St. Louis and Pittsburgh where the temperature was 96 degrees, but down on the artificial turf it was about 120.

The longest night game came on September 11, 1974, the Mets and the St. Louis Cardinals at Shea Stadium. It began at 8:00 and went until 3:13 the next morning, seven hours and four minutes. We played twenty-five innings, one short of the major league record. [Brooklyn and Boston played a twenty-six inning 1–1 tie in 1920.] A record 202 batters came to the plate. Fifty players got into that game. I ejected Yogi Berra, the Mets' manager, about 1:30 for arguing on a half swing; I think he got home before the game ended. Bake McBride finally scored the winning run from the first base on a wild pickoff throw by Hank Webb and a dropped throw at the plate by Ron Hodges. When it was over, a reporter asked how I felt. All I could say was: "Why me?"

After the game my brother, a friend, and I stopped at a diner in Passaic. We got there about five o'clock. They went in to get something to eat, but I couldn't join them because I had such terrible cramps. I had to walk around the parking lot for about thirty minutes before I walked them out. I finally went in, got a bowl of soup, and called it a long night.

One time I almost didn't make it to a ball game. My crew was to fly from Philadelphia to Los Angeles for a night game in 1959, but our plane had mechanical problems. They finally got another plane ready, but by the time we landed in Los Angeles it was only thirty minutes until game time. A police escort rushed us to the Coliseum, but we were still late getting out on the field. We arrived at the ball park five minutes after game time; by the time we got dressed and got to the plate it was 8:25. The 82,000 fans on hand for the Giants-Dodgers game started to boo us as we walked out, but then they cheered. I guess they finally realized that you can't have a game without the men in blue.

They got their money's worth. Sad Sam Jones almost pitched a no-hit, no-run game. The one hit the Dodgers got was a questionable one. Carl Furillo hit a grounder to deep short, and Andre Rodgers's throw pulled the first baseman off the bag. Sam was very unhappy about the official-scorer's ruling, as he made plain in a headline story the next day. I personally thought it was an error, but I'm an umpire, not a scorer.

There have been a lot of changes in umpiring over the years. In the old days there was great rivalry between the leagues. It's still there with the players, but not as far as the umpires are concerned. The Major League Umpires Association covers all umpires even though they are in separate leagues. In the old days, umpires and ballplayers were a rough-and-tough bunch of fellows. Now you have a more refined, college-bred community of fellows in every facet of the sport. There are still arguments, but the vocabulary is 100 percent better now. The front office doesn't allow vile language from players or umpires, especially umpires. Umpires used to get away with using profanity, but not anymore. In the old days umpires had to worry about controlling the game. Today the name of the game is "keep it moving."

There is no doubt that the formation of the Major League Umpires Association is the most important thing that ever happened to advance the umpiring profession. It started out as the National League Umpires Association, chartered in the state of Illinois in 1964. Four or five years later the American League umpires joined.

Prior to the association, umpires had very little security. Under the old plan you got about $100 for every year you put in—a pension of $2,000 for twenty years of service. It would have gone up some without the organization, but not very much. With the association we gained tremendous benefits in the form of a thrift-plan annuity coupled with a pension plan. Now after twenty years you can leave the game smiling, without fearing where your next dollar is coming from.

The association also got us better per diem expenses and better traveling accommodations. Instead of going economy, we fly first class. We don't have to lug our heavy equipment bags along with our personal luggage anymore; Air Express handles it. Now when you get to a new city, your bags are already at the ball park and your clothes are hanging in your locker. We now have a good salary scale which increases according to years of service. My first major league contract was for $6,500; a rookie umpire now gets more than double that figure.

The association, which negotiates a new contract every three years, also made great changes in the compensation for special assignments. When the championship play-offs began in 1969, we got $1,500; in 1978 it was about $7,000. In 1977 we got $10,000 for working the World Series. Compensation for the All-Star game went from $500 to $1,250. In one span I didn't work an All-Star game for ten years because I felt it was more worthwhile to spend my three days with my family since there was no compensation for working in the game.

The association is also responsible for the rotation of assignments for the All-Star games and the World Series. I didn't work my first Series until I had almost nine years in the big time. The league always wanted veteran umpires, so the old-timers were constantly in line for the cream. If there had been a rotation plan when I broke in, I might have had two more World Series.

The one rule change I did not like is the appeal on the half swing. It was not a unanimous decision to put in that rule; a couple of managers were responsible for it. It's a bad rule for several reasons. First, who is closer to the play than the plate umpire? They say, "Sometimes he gets blocked out." Well, that can be true on any play. Besides, if he is in the right position back there, he shouldn't be blocked out. Second, I don't like to be put on the spot. Say the bases are loaded, full count on the batter, and I'm at first base. The plate umpire wants my help on the half swing. He is putting me on a hell of a spot. Everything hinges on my decision. It's 90 feet from home to first base, and we take our position 10 feet beyond the bag. I'm going to tell him whether the batter checked his swing from 100 feet when he is 2 feet away? I don't have a good angle on it anyway. Whenever I was asked about half swings, I had to guess on it. I had to make a decision, so I did. But I guessed.

I miss baseball. But I still have my scrapbooks, mementos, and memories. Baseball has been good to me. Besides the thrills and financial security, it gave me an opportunity to travel. Not just across the United States, but also in other countries. I played winter ball in the West Indies, the Dominican Republic, and in Panama in both the Canal Zone League operated by the United States and the Panama City Professional League run by the Panamanian government. As an umpire I worked in Colombia, South America, in Barranquilla and Cartagena. I ran umpire schools in Mexico City for the State Department in 1959 and 1960, training umpires for the Mexican League.

In 1958 I toured Japan with the St. Louis Cardinals. I was the only American umpire there, so they made me work the plate all the time. The Japanese officials were afraid that they wouldn't do a proper job calling balls and strikes on major league players. We played ball in about sixteen cities, and everywhere we went there was a welcoming committee to greet us. A group of women would come out before each game and present flowers to the umpires. An umpire enjoys quite a revered position in Japanese baseball. The Japanese players wouldn't think of arguing about a call. You are looked upon practically like an emperor. It was quite a change from American baseball. It was an unforgettable experience.

I hope I'll be remembered as a good umpire, as a man who was conscientious in his work. Twenty years in the major leagues is quite an accomplishment. I've received lots of recognition. The Al Somers Umpire School named me umpire of the year in 1977, and the St. Louis Baseball Writers Association selected me in 1978 as the Official of the Year, an award which embraces all sports. An award which really surprised me was the one presented by the New York City Police Department in a pregame ceremony at Shea Stadium on August

5, 1977. They gave me a beautiful plaque which reads: "The Man in Blue of the Year. Honored by the Men in Blue."

I received another honor which I will always cherish as one of the highlights of my career. A few years ago a group of six youngsters stopped me as I was heading toward the dressing room at Veterans Stadium in Philadelphia. They asked me if they could start an Ed Sudol Fan Club. I thought it was some kind of joke, but the fellow who started it, John Langenstein, said they were serious, that I was their favorite umpire. They showed me newspaper clippings and lots of other things about me and the club. I was overwhelmed; I almost choked up. Usually ballplayers get all the accolades and adulation. Here some fans decided to give some of that to an umpire, the unsung hero of baseball.

Bill Kinnamon, American League umpire, in 1966.
Courtesy *The Sporting News,* St. Louis, Missouri.

Bill Kinnamon

◈◈◈

William Ervin Kinnamon
Born: Lincoln, Nebraska, May 13, 1919
Height: 6′
Weight: 210
Playing career: none
Umpiring career: Sooner State League (D), 1953; Pioneer League
            (C), 1954; Eastern League (A), 1955–June 1956;
            American Association (AAA), June 1956–Sep-
            tember 1960; American League, September
            1960–1969
No-hit games: none
All-Star games: 1962 (second game), 1968
World Series (games): 1968 (7)

K nowing what I know now about how tough it is to become a major league umpire, I doubt if I would have left a good job with the Internal Revenue Service to be an umpire in Class B baseball for $250 a month. Today I know that maybe one out of 100 will make it. Some guys won't have the ability. Some will find out that they don't really enjoy umpiring. Finances will drive out others; how many guys, especially those with a family, can make it on $800 a month for five or six months living away from home? And some guys won't have the temperament; it's tough to stand there, be called an SOB and worse, and take the abuse without fighting back.

Why do fellows with a college degree throw away promising careers to come to my umpire school? For the same reason I did. I loved the game and wanted to be part of it. I didn't want to be tied down to a desk at that stage of my life. I went to umpire school thinking that nobody could be any better than I was. I never gave it a thought that I couldn't make it. Desire and confidence: that's why you do it.

I was born in Lincoln, Nebraska, May 13, 1919. When I was two years old, the family moved to Casper, Wyoming. When it was time to go to high school, we moved back to Nebraska. I lettered in football, basketball, and baseball at Lincoln High, was All-State in baseball as an outfielder.

After graduation I went to the University of Nebraska, where I majored in business administration and lettered in football and baseball. I caught for the baseball team and played single-wing quarterback and defensive halfback for Potsy Clark's Cornhuskers. In the middle of my college work, the National Guard unit on campus was mobilized. It was December 1940. We were supposed to be in only a year; but then Pearl Harbor happened, and I remained in the service four and one-half years more. After the war I returned to the university. My athletic eligibility had expired, so I got a substitute teacher's permit and for two years taught physical education and coached the baseball team at Lincoln High. I also coached American Legion ball during the summer.

I graduated from Teacher's College in 1949 and took a job as an Internal Revenue agent in Wyoming. The next four years I played a lot of local basketball and softball. I just loved sports, especially baseball; couldn't stay away from it.

One day—it was in 1953—Don Rogers, a boyhood friend, and I were sitting around reading the *Sporting News* when I got the idea that it might be fun to go down to Bill McGowan's Umpire School in Daytona Beach, Florida. At that point I had never umpired a baseball game. I had refereed football and basketball games at the junior and senior high school levels but had never umpired baseball because I was always playing.

Anyway, we made arrangements to go. I got a leave of absence from the government. But at the last minute Don couldn't go because he was married and had six kids and just couldn't take off. So my wife and I headed for Florida and six weeks of umpire school.

I attended the second class McGowan ran that year. There were around 220 students in the class. Since I was thirty-three years old, far beyond the average age of the students which was about twenty-three or twenty-four, I decided that if I was going to do anything in baseball, I'd have to do it quickly. So I set a goal of being in the major leagues in five years; if I wasn't, then I'd quit, take the rest of my CPA examination or whatever.

There were about fifty minor leagues at the time, so there were quite a few umpiring jobs open each year. But since there were far fewer umpires in the majors then than there are today, McGowan made it clear the competition for advancement would be keen. He always said that if you weren't the best umpire in your league, you wouldn't move to a higher classification.

I went to the school determined to do the best I could. I worked hard and kept accurate notes on everything we did during the day on the field and in the evening classroom meetings. With about a week left in the school, I worked a Cardinals' exhibition game over in Deland. Afterward, McGowan stood me up in front of the whole class and said, "This man will be a major league umpire." From that point on, I felt I had something to prove to him and to myself.

Bill McGowan was a tremendous individual and one of the really great umpires the game has ever seen. He worked ten years in the minors and thirty in the majors—there wasn't anything about baseball he didn't know. Bill's only problem was that he got in trouble with the front office from time to time, like the time he got suspended for throwing his ball-strike indicator at Bob Porterfield. I have a favorite picture of him that says it all. It shows him surrounded by five or six big guys, all giving him hell. The caption reads: "He knew when to walk, but he never ran."

After graduating from the umpire school, I got a job umpiring in the Sooner State League, Class B ball, down in Texas and Oklahoma. I got $250 a month plus eight cents a mile for driving my car. Halfway through the season, I wrote McGowan telling him that I would be interested in coming back next year as an assistant. He wanted me back (in fact, he had earlier raised the possibility), so I assisted him by taking care of the equipment and illustrating mechanics on the field. That second year at the school helped me a great deal because I could better understand the principles and situations they were trying to get across. Since then I have always believed umpires should work a year and then go back to school or a clinic.

I made good progress in the minor leagues. I worked the play-offs in the Sooner State League my first year. I also worked the play-offs in the Pioneer League in 1954 and moved on to the Eastern League in

1955. I reached the American Association in 1956. All that time I continued to sharpen my umpiring skills through the schools. Bill McGowan died in November 1954, but I worked for his son as an instructor for the next two years. When Al Somers took over the school in 1957, I continued as an instructor for him.

I didn't consider umpiring a challenge. I hate the word "challenge." Every time somebody says a job is a "challenge," he soon loses it. I considered umpiring an *opportunity,* and I was determined to make the most of it.

An umpire must have ability to advance, but he must also have self-discipline and determination. You have to be willing to give 110 percent every time you walk out on that field, even if you don't feel like it. In the Pioneer League we'd drive from Salt Lake City to Billings, Montana, 600 miles, for a game. We'd drive all night, get in about ten in the morning, sleep for four or five hours, and head for the ball park. I was not mentally alert or physically ready, but I knew that for two and a half hours I had to give it all I had. That's the kind of thing that motivates the successful umpire. He doesn't worry about his wife or family or financial situation or what happened yesterday or anything else. For two and a half hours he is worried only about what is happening on that ball field.

When I reached the American Association, I began to really feel the pressure for the first time. There were eight guys in that league who were every bit as good as I was. Two of them were under contract with the majors—Tony Venzon with the American and Bob Stewart with the National. Now I had to evaluate them and do an honest evaluation of myself. What do Venzon and Stewart do to make the majors want them? What am I doing or not doing that would influence my progress? I even umpired winter ball a couple of seasons to work with major leaguers.

In the winter of 1959 Cal Hubbard and Joe Cronin watched me work in Caracas, Venezuela, and in the spring the American League picked up my contract. I went to spring training with the American League in 1960 but was optioned back to the American Association. Later that year I was called up to work the last twenty-three games of the American League season. When the league expanded the next year, I kept the position. I remained in the American League until an injury forced me to retire at the end of the 1969 season.

I went up to the big leagues under very unusual circumstances. One day toward the end of the American Association season, I got a call from the league president, Edward S. Doherty, Jr. He said,

"Where are you going when you leave Louisville?" I told him I didn't really know and asked if I would be working the play-offs. He said I shouldn't worry about the play-offs because I couldn't work them anyway—I was to report to Kansas City the next day.

I later found out what had happened. Two umpires were involved in a blackmail situation in Washington. They called in Eddie Rommel, an old-time umpire, and the three of them decided to turn the guys in. They put the FBI on the case, but in the meantime, the league sent the umps home for the rest of the year with pay. The FBI moved in and arrested the blackmailers, and the umps went back to work in the American League. It was a courageous thing for them to do.

Anyway, Harry Schwarts and I, the replacement umpires, joined John Flaherty and Al Smith in Kansas City on September 8. Washington won, 7–0. I didn't have a call during my first game in the majors. About the sixth inning someone hit a foul ball down the left-field line. I was at third base, so I went down the line and, even though it landed in the seats, gave it the old "gray" call. I mean I poured it on as if it was six inches foul. The bullpen down there started hooting, raising their hats, and everything. But I thought: Hell, if that's the only call I'm going to get all night, I'm going to call it right. I've got to earn my money.

The next series in Detroit was something else. Now major league umpires don't handle their own baggage. It's handled by Railway Express. When we got to the Detroit ball park for a doubleheader with Minnesota, there were no bags. No umpire's equipment in Detroit. Well, the Detroit trainer gave us some of his white shirts and pants; we borrowed caps from the Tigers, borrowed shoes from the players. We looked like a bunch of rinky-dinks going out there—four guys dressed in white wearing Detroit caps.

I was scheduled to work the plate, but the American League had a rule—actually it was one of Cal Hubbard's rules, which I never understood—that prevented a rookie umpire from working the plate his first time in a park. Since I had never been in Detroit before, Flaherty jumped ahead of me, and I worked first base. About the fifth inning, the batboy told us that our equipment had arrived. We finished the first game the way we were and then went in to get ready for the second game.

My bag was not there. Only three bags had arrived. Well, I borrowed shoes from Al Smith, pants from somebody else, coat from another guy, jockstrap from somebody else—everything I had on to work that game was borrowed. I worked my first game behind the plate in the American League without one piece of equipment that belonged to me. The shoes were too big; the mask was too small. The only thing that fitted was the chest protector.

The point is that I couldn't let it bother me. If you are going to be a successful umpire, nothing can distract you from what you're doing for two and one-half hours. And it didn't upset me. I just went out and concentrated on my job. After I got through, we laughed about the whole thing, but believe me, it wasn't funny at the time.

Working the plate is by far the most difficult task for an umpire. It is not only difficult to do, but it is crucial for the game. The man behind the plate controls the ball game. A base umpire usually has only a few tough calls, and even if he blows one, there is usually not too much importance attached to it. But if the umpire behind the plate has a bad day, then it will be a poor ball game. You can make or break the game back there: *that's* pressure.

To work the plate successfully, you must prepare mentally for the ball game. I worked with guys who would line up pitchers four days ahead, trying to figure out who they were going to get. Each man approaches the job according to his personality. Johnny Stevens was one of those guys who got very quiet the day they worked the plate. Johnny is a quiet man anyway, but if you talked to him the day he was working the plate, it would be a monologue because he wouldn't answer you. Larry Napp was just the opposite. Larry would laugh, sing, tell jokes, try to be real loose to get rid of the tension. Myself, I don't believe that I consciously felt any different on the days I worked the plate. But I would think about the game that day, especially about the pitchers.

Every umpire has a mental book on pitchers. You get to know pretty soon what kinds of pitches a guy has, how he throws them, and what you can expect them to do. For example, anybody who has an exceptional curveball generally will not have a consistently good slider, and vice versa. The slider is thrown with a motion in between the fastball and the curve, and most pitchers can't consistently control them both because of the difference in speed. You don't get into the habit of looking for patterns of pitches like a batter might, but getting to know what you can expect from a pitcher makes your job easier. Of course, it's easier to get to know some pitchers than others.

Hoyt Wilhelm was as tough as any pitcher who ever lived. He was so difficult to call because there wasn't any way his ball couldn't go. You never saw everything he had because the ball never did the same thing twice. When he released the ball, only the Good Lord knew where it was going. He never tried to finesse you—throw it low or high, inside or outside. He just threw it right at the center of the plate, and the ball did whatever it did. You had to wait until after the catcher caught the ball before making the call. I've seen him throw balls that were head-high and then all of a sudden drop down for a strike. He was by far the best knuckleballer who ever lived. Wilbur Wood and Phil Niekro are good, but nothing like Wilhelm. I've seen him throw one right down the pipe and have it wind up three feet outside. One time catcher J. C. Martin of the White Sox got hit on the knee with a pitch. You wouldn't think a man could throw a pitch and hit you on the shin guard before you could get your glove on it.

Mickey Lolich was an outstanding pitcher who was also very diffi-cult to call because his ball would really move. Just about the time you'd make up your mind on the ball, that slider would bust in there. His ball would also ride a little bit. Nobody throws a ball hard enough to make it jump up, but a few can throw it hard enough to make it ride a little. Lolich could do that. When the ball is thrown, gravity takes over so it will follow a certain plane. But Lolich could throw a ball that would suddenly break its plane, ride up. The ball would look like it was going to be down and yet it wasn't. If you made up your mind on Lolich eight to ten feet in front of the plate, you'd probably miss it. I finally got to where I was calling Lolich very well. It was all a matter of timing.

If you treated Sudden Sam McDowell like just another pitcher, you were definitely going to be in trouble. He was something else, a very tough pitcher for hitters *and* umpires. He had a real herky-jerky mo-tion and could throw the ball like a bullet. And his ball *moved*. You always had to be especially alert for him; he was so quick that there were times you weren't quite ready to call the pitch. And he *never* threw the ball down the pipe; he'd have a 3–0 count on somebody and still throw a questionable strike. I had him one night in Oakland when he struck out fifteen. When Danny Cater came up to bat the last time, he pretty well summed up what players thought of Sam when he was throwing the ball right: "There should be another league for him."

Although he was a great pitcher, we called him Sad Sam McDowell because he didn't accomplish as much with the wonderful talent he had as he should have. I have seen him throw a lazy, change-up curve up there, and a guy'd double on it. Damned if he wouldn't throw the change-up on the guy the next time up, and he'd cream it again. The problem was that Sam always felt he could get a guy out by thinking instead of challenging him with his best pitch. Every time he threw a curve or change-up he did batters a favor; even if they had to adjust to hit it, they still had a better chance of hitting it than his fastball.

Camilo Pascual was the best right-handed curveball pitcher I ever saw. Never saw anybody who could compare with him. Pascual had three or four different curveballs that would break anywhere from six inches to a foot. Just about the time you thought you had him down pretty well, he'd come up with a different kind of curve. You didn't know Pascual until you worked him ten, twelve, maybe fifteen games; that's how good he was.

I never saw a pitcher who had everything going for him the way Denny McLain did in 1968, when he won thirty-one games. You didn't really have to prepare when he pitched because you knew there was a 95 percent chance the pitch would be a strike. That particular year he threw more different pitches for strikes than anybody I ever saw. That was the key to his success. He was an amazing pitcher who had a fantastic year.

I had Bob Gibson in the fourth game of the World Series that year. McLain and Gibson, the two best pitchers in baseball at the time. It rained all day. It rained real hard in the morning, and I remember waking up thinking: Why me? After all the time I had spent in the minors and majors, it rained on the day I was going to work the plate in a World Series. Up to then every day had been beautiful. It cleared up some that afternoon but started raining about the third inning. I went out to Gibson when it started to sprinkle and told him to put the rosin bag in his pocket to keep it dry. He said, "Man, I don't use that stuff. Give me the ball." He was absolutely superb. I have a lot of admiration for the way he played and the way he pitched that game.

Whitey Ford was a great pitcher. He wasn't a big man, but he could hum it pretty good. And he had perfect control. He was one of the smartest pitchers who ever played the game; he'd take advantage of any edge you gave him. Also, he was one of the nicest ballplayers I have ever known. He never said a word to an umpire when he pitched.

Whitey loved to throw that dirty ball. One day, late in his career, after he had had surgery and was trying to hang on, he came off the mound in the second inning and said as he walked by, "Hey, don't throw them out too quick. It's going to be a long day." I think umpires went along with him a little bit because he had been such a great performer. You wouldn't intentionally allow anything other than what you normally would, but there were times when you might give him another pitch with a ball that is just a little bit dirty or something along that line.

Whitey dirtied the ball on only one side. That meant that when the ball was rotating on its way to the plate you had an optical illusion— you saw only half of the ball. Once, after we had thrown out three or four balls on Whitey in an inning, I told Bobby Richardson that I didn't think there was another human being on earth who could get a ball dirtier than Whitey Ford. Bobby looked at me and said, "You know, I've been playing with him a long time, and I don't really know how he does it myself. Just about the time I think I know exactly what he's doing, he'll change and do something else."

My first year in the big leagues I threw a new ball out to Whitey in Yankee Stadium. Yogi went out, Richardson and Tony Kubek came in, and they had a little conference out there, all the time rubbing the ball. I didn't know what was going on. Finally, they went back to their positions, and Whitey got ready to pitch. The batter, Charlie Maxwell, "Always on Sunday" they used to call him, stepped out and asked me to look at the ball. I said, "I just threw him a new one."

He said, "Yes, but I know this guy better than you do. Check it."

When that ball came in, I could not believe it. In a matter of a minute or a minute and a half at most, he had gotten that ball so dirty you couldn't possibly play with it. I had to throw it out and give him a new one. He just stood there, grinning and rubbing it up again.

In his later years he got help from the catchers. The Yankees never wanted an umpire to throw the ball to the pitcher; they wanted you to give it to the catcher. Now when you handed a ball to Elston Howard, he all of a sudden had the worst hands in the world. You could *lay* it in his hand, and he couldn't hold it. Of course, when he went to pick it up, he'd drag it in the dirt for about eight inches, which meant that he had loaded the seams on the bottom of the ball. Then he would run out and *hand* the ball to Whitey, who'd put enough slime or something on it to get half the ball dirty by the time Ellie got back to the plate.

Many catchers whom umpires consider outstanding because they were easy to work behind are not well recognized by the public for their ability. Umpires loved to see the guy who didn't cry a lot, who didn't bother you on the pitch, and who could catch the ball.

Paul Casanova of Washington gave me the best look at the plate of any catcher I worked behind. He was a big, tall, lanky guy, but he absolutely *laid on the ground*. He would give the signal and then disappear; you wondered where in the hell he went, that's how low he stayed. If the pitch was a little high, he never came up with his body; just the glove would come up and pick off that pitch. Casanova was a right-handed hitter, so he alternated with Jim French, depending on the pitcher; umpires used to check to see who was pitching the Senators, hoping they'd get Casanova.

Bill Freehan of Detroit was a fine catcher and a swell guy to work with. Freehan never got excited, cried, or complained. Sometimes, when Mickey Lolich was throwing, if I made up my mind maybe an instant too soon, Freehan would turn his head and say, "We've got to have that pitch, Bill." Now if Freehan tells me it is a strike, I'm going to have to take another look because he is not a crybaby. When a guy like that says something to you, it means a bit more.

Of course, you pay no attention to the chronic complainers. Sammy White of the Red Sox had the reputation of being one of the best catchers in the American League. But he could cause you trouble hollering and crying back there, and a lot of umpires who regarded him as a great receiver didn't like him as an individual.

Yogi Berra was as good a receiver as I ever worked behind. He had as good an arm as I've ever seen and an innate ability to catch the ball. He was the best ever on a bouncing ball in the dirt. He absolutely never gave you that nonchalant swipe at the ball. He'd be down right in front of it. I never saw a ball hit the dirt and get by him to the backstop. If the ball was close, he would get it. He was so quick back there—not fast, but quick.

To illustrate the point, Bert Campeneris was on first base in Kansas City one day. Campy could fly, and he got a jump on a pitch like you couldn't believe. The batter foul tipped the pitch, and I'm telling you before it ever got to Yogi's glove, he opened that glove. The ball hit right in that glove and fell to the ground. I'll swear on a stack of Bibles that if Campy hadn't been running, Yogi would have caught that ball. Catching a foul tip is pure reflex; you can't control it. Now Yogi didn't *drop* the ball because if he had, I would have left Campeneris at second base. He didn't *catch* the ball, and I swear he did it on purpose.

Of course, Yogi was not the most delightful guy to be behind because he chattered all the time. Every time his pitcher threw the ball it was a strike, and when he was hitting, every pitch was a ball. I mean *every* pitch. One time a pitch bounced up there, and he said, "Wasn't too bad, was it?" Fortunately, when he was batting, he swung at an awful lot of bad pitches. He was such a good hitter he could pick them out of the dirt and double them off the wall.

Almost every umpire agrees that a half swing is the most difficult call to make. The knuckleball can be a difficult pitch to call, but it is called entirely by an individual umpire who sees everything there is to see. If he missed it, it was because of bad timing or something along that line. But the trouble with the half swing is that there is no possible way that you can see exactly what happens. There is no problem with the half swing that is low. But when the half swing is chest- or shoulder-high—and that is where 99 percent of your half swings come—the catcher's glove comes up and blocks your vision, and you lose the last three or four feet of the ball. It is the most difficult call in baseball simply because you are blocked out of the crucial part of the play.

That is why the appeal rule was a good innovation. When it was first adopted, a lot of major league umpires, especially some of the old-timers, hated to think that they couldn't handle every call. But it has proven of benefit. At least it takes some of the heat away from the home-plate umpire.

There is another thing that makes the half swing so difficult to call. You can generally get an excellent picture of a particular play from television replay because one of the camera angles is going to show you exactly what happened. But replays do not prove anything on a half swing. If a batter gets halfway through a swing and then quits on it, just relaxes, the last part of the swing means nothing. In other words, the bat might sweep across the plate area, but if there was no intention to hit the ball, it is not a swing. Frank Robinson was the best I ever saw at giving you a real good start and then quitting on the ball right in the middle of the swing and letting the bat trail through. Now the replay will not show you exactly where he quit going after that ball; it only shows where the bat went. It's tough to determine where and whether he definitely quit on the ball.

When I first went into the American League, Johnny Rice told me that the toughest call an umpire has to make is not the half swing; the toughest call is throwing a guy out of the game after you blew the hell out of the play. That's true.

Sometimes, when you kick a play, you don't get a lot of heat out of it, but sometimes it brings you all kinds of problems. When that happens, you've got to be nine feet tall, just swell up like a peacock, and say, "No," "No way," "Absolutely," "That's the way it's going to be," and so on.

Now there's a technique for handling rhubarbs. If you will let the manager or player come out without antagonizing him, without challenging him, without forcing him to go into a vicious diatribe, you've got a pretty good chance of him arguing about the play without getting run out. If you let him do all the talking, it isn't going to be very long before he will start to repeat himself. How long can he talk about a play without starting to repeat? When he starts to repeat is the time you move in and say, "Look, Skip, we've been over this before. Come on, it hasn't changed. It's going to stay that way. Let's go from here."

Above all, you must be calm. When a guy is absolutely sure he's got a good beef and he's boiling mad, that's when you've got to be the calmest. When he's at his worst, you must be at your best. If you get mad, there is no way you can keep him in the ball game. You're going to run him if you challenge him. The easiest thing in the world is to set up a player or manager and chase him; the toughest thing is to keep him in there without bending your own convictions or rules.

Now, if you blew the call, you are going to take a little more from him. I saw a home run in Detroit that if it wasn't twelve feet fair, I've never seen one in my life, but the umpire called it foul. Don't you know a situation like that dictates that the player is going to get a little more time with you and you will turn a deaf ear a little bit longer? Certainly you are not going to challenge him. If he is going to be ejected, you make sure that he throws himself and that you do nothing to help him leave.

But if a guy comes out with a half beef, one he's not really sure about, that's when you really go after him. You let him know that you're sure about the call and that he has no real beef.

I think the rhubarb is good for baseball. I know Joe Cronin did. When he was president of the American League, he would come up to the dressing room after there had been a big rhubarb with everybody hooting and hollering and three or four people having been thrown out and say, "Oh, that was a good one, you guys." He loved it. He felt it was good for the game. It is a good rule that a man cannot leave the dugout or coaching box to argue balls and strikes because that just slows up the game over something that isn't going to change anyway. But not to allow people to voice an opinion or protest on a play situation or question your interpretation of a rule would destroy an integral part of the game.

Other than the automatics—the magic word, thrown equipment, physical contact, and the like—you eject someone 99 out of 100 times because of what he says, not his actions. Every umpire draws his own line, things he will not tolerate, based partly on individual temperament and partly on the situation.

I remember a fellow umpire in the American Association, John Mullen. Now if someone walked up to almost any umpire and said, "You are horseshit," that guy would be gone before he even got the words out. But it didn't bother Mullen to be called horseshit. Somebody would say, "John, you are horseshit," and John would say, "Yeah, I was horseshit yesterday, I'm horseshit today, and I'll probably be horseshit tomorrow." It's a matter of temperament.

Now situations can change that. One night we had a game with Minneapolis and Denver. Minneapolis was leading, 1-0, in the top of the ninth inning. Mullen called a pitch, and Eddie Stanky, the Minneapolis manager, came up on the bench and yelled, "Bear down out there!"

Mullen turned into a raging maniac for a minute or two. He tore off that mask, charged the bench, and got as violent with his talk as I had ever heard him. He was still fuming after the game. When we got into the dressing room, he threw his mask against the wall and said, "Can you imagine that son of a bitch saying that to me? I've got a one-to-nothing game, I've been working my tail off all night long, and that SOB has guts enough to yell, 'Bear down.'" The situation had changed. You could call John horseshit and it wouldn't bother him at all, but when Stanky said, "Bear down," after he had been bearing down for eight innings, it was too much.

Temperament is so important. An umpire has to take a lot of abuse from players, managers, and fans. You do not have to take personal abuse, and you should not take personal abuse. But you must have the thing in perspective. There are lots of things said to an umpire that are not personal, that are not directed toward him—"bear down," "get with it," and so on. You hear that a thousand times, and it doesn't mean anything. A guy might mumble under his breath after being called out on strikes. If those kinds of things start bothering you, you're going to get into trouble. There are some things you just don't have to hear. You have to distinguish between personal abuse or abuse directed toward you and the things that are impersonal and routine. Not everyone is able to do that.

Some guys have unbelievably short triggers. When Bruce Froemming was in the Umpire Development Program, I wrote a report on him which was as good a report as could have been written on anyone. But on the bottom I said, "The only thing I would question is whether he can control himself. If he can, he is a big league umpire." Bruce has thrown sportswriters off the field. He has even thrown an announcer out of the press box. Bruce's temperament was entirely different from another umpire in the program, Jimmy Quick. It doesn't mean that one of them isn't doing the job; they are just doing it different ways.

I broke in with crews run by Jim Honochick, Ed Hurley, and John Flaherty. Honochick and Flaherty were very easygoing. Hurley was entirely different. Eddie Hurley saw everything, was always ready to jump on everybody. If a guy dropped a jacket on the ground in the bullpen, Eddie would see it clear across the field. He was a tough, outstanding umpire, and he helped me out several times.

The first time it happened was when Minnie Minoso raised all kinds of hell when I called him out on strikes in my first year in the league. He went to the dugout, yelling a lot of things in Spanish. I was concerned about the game, so it didn't bother me. But it bothered Eddie, who was working third base. The next inning Eddie followed Minoso all the way out to left field. The veins in Eddie's neck were sticking out like ropes. The next time Minoso came up, he said, "Me big league twelve year. You big league one year. Me no say nothing to you." He never said another word, and Minnie and I became good friends. The point is: Hurley ran his crew, and if somebody was picking on a member of his crew who wasn't in a position to handle it, Eddie took care of it. I was young, inexperienced, so Eddie took care of a potential problem right then and there. Ballplayers had a lot of respect for Eddie Hurley.

Another time he helped me by ejecting a guy. I called Johnny Temple out at first base on a close play. There had been a collision at second, and it took a few minutes to get Chuck Schilling back in the game. Meanwhile, Temple stood at first. When we were ready to resume play, I said, "Hey, you were out." Well, he reared and raved a little and then ran toward the third-base dugout. I turned my back to the situation and, when I turned around, could see a bunch of dirt in the air, a cap floating down, and Eddie Hurley throwing him out.

Of course, I got chewed out pretty good when we got upstairs because anytime an umpire has a situation like that, he shouldn't turn his back on the player. I did not know that when Temple ran across the mound, he had scooped up some dirt and thrown it and his cap in the air. I didn't see it, but I should have. It should have been my first ejection in the majors. But Eddie didn't chastise me for not ejecting Temple; he chastised me for not seeing what had happened. As an umpire you can't handle a situation unless you see it. You simply must see it.

I was always easy to get along with, had an even temper. I rarely got hot under the collar and felt I could always control myself no matter how tough the situation. I did, too, with one exception, and it was a bad one.

The incident happened in Toronto with a manager who is now very successful in the major leagues. At that time he was not in con-

trol of himself, and he did a very poor job of handling men. He was
disliked by just about everybody concerned. I think the incident occurred because the man simply had an intolerable situation with the
ball club.

The trouble began during the first game of a doubleheader. Toronto
had runners on first and second with one out when the batter hit a
drive to deep center field. As the batter-runner tore around first base,
he passed the runner who had stopped to see if the ball would be
caught. As it turned out, the ball hit the wall, and when the action
stopped, a run had scored, and runners were at second and third. I
had called the batter-runner out the instant he passed the previous
runner, but nobody in the park saw the play because everybody was
watching the fly ball in the outfield. Well, the Toronto manager came
out screaming, and I had to remove him.

When we met at home plate to begin the second game, he was still
hot. He said, "I've got proof that you lied about that call." I said,
"What are you calling me? A liar?" Well, for twenty minutes I was
subjected to every abusive piece of filth that could come from a person's mouth. He scooped up dirt with his hands and piled it a foot
high on home plate. I ejected him from the game, but several times
after he had gone to the bench, he came back out on the field. There
was no way to fight back, no way to get rid of him except to throw
him out bodily. I could have forfeited the game, but I'd never have
given the little SOB the satisfaction of having gotten me into that position. I looked for help from the police, but they wouldn't come out
and get their own manager; if we had been anywhere else, the police
would have nabbed him after the first outburst.

The grounds keepers wouldn't even come out and remove the dirt
from the plate. I couldn't do it because I had only a two-inch wide
brush; besides, I *wouldn't* do it because of the principle of the thing.
So I told the batter to step in and hit. He said, "Where's the plate?" I
told him it was underneath the dirt, and if he stood where he was,
he'd be all right.

Finally, a man jumped out of the box seats onto the field and introduced himself as the owner of the Toronto team. He assured me that
the manager would not come out again and that the grounds keepers
would be out in a minute to clean up the mess.

The next day I wrote a report to Tommy Richardson, the president
of the league, detailing everything that happened, knowing full well
that the letter would be read by everybody involved in the incident.
You try hard when writing a report to wait until you cool off so that

you give only the facts of the case and don't let your emotions pour out on the paper. But I was still so burned that I told Richardson, "If this man ever says 'hello' to me again on the street, I'm going to punch him right square in the mouth." I told him that I didn't care if I ever saw the guy again and that if I never worked another game in Toronto, it would be too soon. That's how I felt about him. Spec kept me away from him for the rest of the year, which I obviously appreciated.

I don't think my letter had anything to do with it, but Toronto fired the guy at the end of the year. He was out of baseball for five years, and when he came back, the first thing he said was that he had done a lot of things he wasn't proud of, that he had learned from his mistakes, and that he wouldn't be the same man people knew five years ago. Only a couple of years later he was managing in the big leagues, and few men have been more successful at it than Sparky Anderson.

Eddie Stanky came to the American League with the reputation of being a real hard man to handle, a junior Durocher. But we found he wasn't at all difficult to work with because he was an absolute professional from the word "go." By that I mean when at home he never staged anything, never put on a big act, never threw violent tantrums, never did anything that would incite the crowd against the umpire. That isn't to say that he never got thrown out at home, because he did—for saying the magic word or something like that. He was a past master at getting teams and fans excited, and he would do it on the road. He'd do anything to get them worked up, come out on plays he had no business coming out on and things like that. People would boo him when he walked to home plate. The point is, the people were on *him,* not the umpires. You've got to love a guy like that. All of us had a lot of respect for him those years he was with the White Sox.

Ralph Houk was probably the most violent manager I ever worked with. But again, Houk was a professional. He really flew off the handle one time in Baltimore in 1961. The Orioles beat the Yankees in a doubleheader, and although it was the middle of the season, every game was for the pennant as far as Houk was concerned. Well, Ed Hurley called Hector Lopez out on strikes to end the second game. Houk came out of the dugout so hard and fast that if John Blanchard, the Yankee catcher, hadn't tackled him I honestly think he would have hit Eddie. In fact, there was even a lot of contact after he got up even with Blanchard holding him, and he was suspended.

The day he came off suspension we had him in Kansas City. He walked up to home plate, grabbed Ed by the coattail, and said, "Hey, we had a good go-round, huh?" That was it. When Houk got mad, it had nothing to do with an individual, nothing other than a particular play or situation. There is no one more violent on or off the field than Ralph Houk, but he doesn't carry it over. You've got to respect him for that.

Umpires respect the guys who never bring up yesterday, who want you to call a new game every pitch. Not all managers do that. And umpires do not respect the guys who chronically complain, chronically cry, and keep bringing up things that happened a long time ago.

Umpires probably have the worst seat in the house instead of the best because they can't watch the game. The first thing an umpire learns is that nothing can happen without that little white ball. As a result, you follow the ball during the entire game. You see things happen, but you're not really aware that the shortstop made a fantastic play in the hole or the center fielder made a spectacular catch. You can't see those things because you cannot take your eye off the ball; if you do, you're in trouble. You get so engrossed in your job that you don't pay any attention to how many strikeouts, hits or putouts a guy has. Besides, you're not interested in those things; you're there to work, not watch.

I enjoyed umpiring. Coming up to the major leagues was like going to a completely different world. Accommodations at the hotel and ball park are minimal in the minors, but first-class in the majors. You often had to drive between towns and take a cab around town in the minors, but in the majors you fly and have a car at your disposal. In the minors you tried to get by on two meals a day because meal money was short, but in the majors you eat in nice restaurants. Minor league towns get boring; major league cities never do. Minor league umpires buy their own equipment; major league umpires have everything furnished but masks and shin guards. The biggest difference is recognition and respect. It means a great deal to be a major league umpire, but it means absolutely nothing to be a minor league umpire. In the minors an umpire is nobody; umpiring in the minors amounts to being a second-class citizen.

And it is definitely much easier to work in the majors than the minors. Major and minor league baseball might look the same on paper, but it is not the same game. Major leaguers make it mechanically easier because they make a better play for you and because they are a little quicker, they force you to be a little more alert. It is also easier working with three other umpires instead of one. In the minors everybody is scrapping for promotion; but in the majors you have arrived, and your job is more or less secure as long as you perform. Also, every time you move up the minor league ladder into a new league, you have to prove yourself all over again. Players and managers are always testing you every time you walk out there until you gain their respect. Each year you're working with new players, new managers, new umpires, and you have to learn about them. As soon as you're established, you're off to a new league, and you start all over. In the big leagues they test you, sure. They'll take a few shots at you at first. But they soon know your ability and accept you. They don't try to knock you out of the box every night; they let you umpire.

It was over too soon. A chronic injury forced me to retire prematurely. I had been seriously injured in an automobile accident after graduating from high school—broke both legs between the knee and hip, broke three vertebrae in my back, and smashed my left hip. I spent a year in the hospital and on crutches but mended rapidly, as youngsters do, and went on to participate in intercollegiate athletics. But as time went on, an arthritic condition developed because I had lost the cushion in my left hip. By 1968 the pain was so great that it was clear I couldn't go on much longer. That year my crew covered for me so well nobody knew my problem; we rearranged our assignments so that another fellow would go out to cover the outfield so I wouldn't have to run so much. On June 22, 1969, I fell down during a game in Chicago, and I never worked again. The next spring I had surgery and now have a steel rod in my leg and a plastic hip socket.

But in a way I've never stopped umpiring. When things were looking bad for me in 1968, Ed Doherty, the administrator of the Umpire Development Program, offered me a job. I talked to Mr. Cronin about it, and he gave me permission to set up the instructional program for the first umpire school run under a subsidy of the American and National leagues. The school opened in 1969. We had a highly selected group of students, about thirty-four, and a handpicked instructional staff. Five students out of that first class are in the major leagues today; that is a fantastic record.

Ed Doherty, the guiding light behind the Umpire Development Program, was probably the only man who could have gotten it through. He was a veteran baseball man, well liked and respected. The program started because of dissatisfaction with the kind of umpiring they were getting in the minor leagues. We changed some of the basic things the umpire schools were teaching. Our purpose was to prepare rookie umpires to officiate with rookie ballplayers in Class

A instead of training them in four-man major league techniques. We gave them more classroom time, more field time, more preparation in dealing with players and managers.

When Doherty left the program to be Ted Williams's right-hand man with the Washington Senators, Barney Deary took over administration of the program. Joe Linsalata and I stayed on with him as supervisors. Our students didn't have to pay tuition, just room and board, so the program started getting a lot of heat from Al Somers, who felt that it was unfair competition with his school. He had a point because he had to charge tuition. It looked like there would be a lawsuit, so in 1973 they dropped the school entirely. They saved the $15,000 to $20,000 it cost to operate the school plus the salaries paid to Linsalata and me. That left Barney alone in charge of the program. He's still badly understaffed today.

Joe and I were now out of a job, so we decided that since applications had been made to attend a school and we were all set, we'd run our own. We worked together in 1974 and 1975; then I bought out Joe and have run it by myself since. I now hold classes in California as well as Florida.

In my school we try to emphasize technique and mechanics. You can't teach judgment. If a man has poor judgment, he's not going to make it as an umpire anyway. But a man with good judgment and baseball instinct can't umpire without good mechanics. The mechanics of a play should be correct regardless of whether the decision is right or wrong. Good mechanics—position—is the only thing that will keep you out of trouble. Consequently, we try to give as much on-field instruction as possible—walking through play situations, footwork, timing, working actual games. Mechanics are so important because until the majors, umpires work a two-man system.

A couple of guys in the big leagues today were not good mechanical umpires when they left the school, but we felt there was more there than we were getting. Terry Cooney came to the school with all the desire anyone could have, and yet he was as poor a base umpire as we ever put in Class A ball because he had a very bad habit of chasing the baseball. In other words, he just couldn't keep from taking a few steps toward where the ball was hit. He eventually overcame that and has gone on to be a good umpire in the American League.

The most important thing in calling plays on the bases is the angle, not distance. If you are thirty feet away with the right angle, you will get the play; if you are ten feet away with the improper angle, you will miss it. By moving toward the ball, Terry was losing his angle. Sometimes you must move *away* from the ball to get the proper angle. That's why mechanics, position, is so very important.

Timing is also crucial to the base umpire, and again you have to know the players. Take, for example, a ground ball in the infield. First, you have to know how fast a guy can run, just like fielders. Will he give you a close play at first base or not? When the ball is hit, you don't watch the batter-runner come down the baseline. You watch the fielder catch the ball and then release it. The next thing is to determine where the ball is thrown because that will determine the kind of play you will have—can the first baseman handle it, or is it off the mark so that there might be a swipe play? If the throw is on target, you take your eyes off the ball about the last third of the way over and direct them right at the bag. Now you've got to listen and coordinate the sound of the ball hitting the first baseman's glove and the batter-runner's foot hitting the bag. Whichever you hear first determines safe or out.

If you anticipate a call or if you make up your mind too quickly, you are going to kick some. If the first baseman drops the ball or even juggles it momentarily, you've got a completely different decision. Umpires have been seen with their hands in the air signaling a decision only to reverse it. That is bad timing. You must wait until a play situation is *completed* before making your decision.

I've caused trouble myself by being too quick. I was behind the plate in Detroit one day when Jim Gentile, the big Baltimore first baseman, came to bat in the seventh inning of a 0–0 game. He smashed the ball down, and it rolled out toward the pitcher. I came out from behind the plate signaling that it was a fair ball. They threw Gentile out at first, but John Flaherty came in from third base, yelling, "No, no, it's a foul ball!" Now we had an argument. Bob Scheffing, the Tigers' manager, said, "Bill, you pointed fair, so you must have seen that it was a fair ball." Now why the hell I had to get my arm out there so damn quick, I'll never know. All I had to do was stand there, let the play happen, and *then* make a call. But Flaherty said that Gentile had tipped the ball down off his foot, so it was foul. Of course, Jungle Jim said it definitely hit him on the foot. Finally, Scheffing went back to the dugout, and Gentile stepped back up to hit.

At that point Don Wert, the Tigers' third baseman, who had the ball, lobbed the ball in. (Players cannot throw a ball out of the game; only the umpires can do that.) It had a black smudge spot on it from where it hit Gentile's shoe! I *rolled* that ball into the Detroit dugout so

Scheffing could see it. Well, naturally, when you dig a hole for yourself, somebody is going to throw dirt in it. Gentile hit that ball nine miles in the upper deck, and the game ended, 1–0.

We emphasize working behind the plate because that is the most important and most difficult job an umpire has to perform. If you cannot umpire back of the plate, you cannot umpire at all.

We pioneered in using a pitching machine for plate instruction. We rigged up strings across home plate to mark the strike zone and turned on the machine. Although at no time does any pitching machine throw the ball the same way twice in a row—some are balls, most strikes—its real value is in working on position and timing. It is essential that the plate umpire have excellent timing on a pitch. The question of timing enters into a lot of different areas.

First of all, you must assume the set position at the proper time. You can't get down and get set when the pitcher is winding up or when he is getting the signal from the catcher. That's too quick. You can't get set when his hand is coming forward or when the ball is already released. That's too late. In other words, you can't be down as he releases or even a second or two before he releases; you must be down just *before* he releases. The proper time to be set for a particular pitch is just a fraction before you can see the white of the ball in his hand as his arm comes up.

It is important that you be there at just the right time because you aren't able to get a good look at the ball until you are perfectly still in the set position. As soon as you pick up the ball, you focus on it. You watch it leave his hand, watch it all the way to the plate, watch it right into the catcher's glove. Only when that ball hits the catcher's glove do you make up your mind and say, "Strike" or "Ball." You don't have to be fast. You can even give yourself another second after it hits the glove. There is nothing that says you've got to call the pitch when the ball crosses the plate.

There are many times as an umpire when you start with the strike motion and the batter hits the ball. The ball looked so good coming down the pipe that you say to yourself, "Boy, that's a strike. I'm going to jump on that baby." When that happens, it is nothing more than a complete breakdown in timing.

Calling balls and strikes is a tricky thing that is open to different interpretations. One thing is certain: The definition in the rule book is not the real strike zone. As I moved higher in classification, I found that the better the league, the more you squeezed the strike zone, brought it down the diameter of a ball or so.

You must be realistic in determining the strike zone. A batter cannot hit a pitch that is in the high part of the strike zone because he cannot swing level on a ball across the high chest. Dizzy Dean and Early Wynn made their careers throwing high, hard ones, A hitter's natural motion makes it easier to hit a ball, and hit it with more power, when it is lower in the strike zone than when it is up. In other words, if you get a ball exactly at the height of the strike zone as defined by the rule book, it will be very difficult to hit. Consequently, every pitcher will tell you that umpires don't call the ball as high as it should be according to the rule book. We are talking about only an inch or two, but the difference is important.

The same thing applies to the corners. An umpire can call a pitch a strike that is just off the outside of the plate, and nobody will know or care. A batter can't really judge the pitch out there, and besides, any hitter will tell you that he can hit the ball an inch outside, even that it is a good pitch for him to hit. But an umpire cannot widen the strike zone on the inside because he will take the bat right out of the hitter's hand. If the pitchers could get a pitch an inch or two inside, they'd saw off the bat. There would be no bat left. So there is a realistic difference on the outside corners; you have more margin on the outside.

In school we try to teach the strike zone as it is stated in the rule book. Later they can adjust to whatever strike zone prevails in the league they're working. We also try to get them to use as large a strike zone as possible because it is to the benefit of everybody in baseball to call strikes. If you miss a pitch, miss it for the pitcher, don't miss it for the hitter. Calling a ball a strike is a lot better than calling a strike a ball. By calling strikes, you force the man to swing the bat, and that makes for a better ball game. Fans like to see a guy up there swinging the bat. They don't like to keep hearing, "Ball four."

We also stress knowledge of the rules. It sounds elementary, but it isn't. Most players and managers do not know the rules. In any sport a man who spends his time developing skills to play the game leaves the rules and regulations to the officials; consequently, most players do not know the rules. Neither do managers, although Gene Mauch and Alvin Dark were good rule men. In general, ballplayers and managers know very little about umpiring. They do not understand position or mechanics. They don't know how an umpire does what he does, they only know the end results.

Cal Hubbard used to tell every young umpire who came into the American League: "Now look, your crew chief probably hasn't had a look at that book in ten years, so it is up to you to make sure every interpretation is valid because you are the one they are going to look to." That's true. Many of the veteran umpires don't know the rules.

They know the application of the rules but aren't able to recite the rule precisely. The young umpire coming into the big leagues is probably better prepared as far as rules and regulations are concerned than some of the old-timers. Nick Bremigan is by far the best I've ever had on rules and interpretations. He has a very methodical mind, lays everything out in black and white.

Of course, there are always differences of opinion on the interpretation or application of rules. That's why umpires and league officials have meetings on rules. Charlie Berry and I once disagreed about an obstruction call. With a runner on first, the batter bunted the ball toward third. The third baseman threw out the batter-runner, and as the runner rounded second to see if the play would be completed or whether someone would cover third, he ran into the shortstop. I was at second base, and I immediately signaled obstruction because the shortstop did not have the ball. Now an obstruction rule states that the play continues to completion and the offending team will then be penalized if possible by sending the runner to the base he would have gone to had there been no obstruction. I ruled that the runner should stay at second base because he was simply rounding second with no attempt to go to third, obstruction or not. After the game, Charlie, who was at home plate, said the only way to stop the obstruction of runners was to invoke the penalty and send the runner to the next base. It was my call, and I think I made it correctly. But there was certainly room for disagreement.

It takes experience to be a good umpire because you learn by doing. A young man can read about play situations in a book, see them diagrammed on a blackboard, and even see them demonstrated on the field, but until that play situation happens to him, he does not really understand it or retain it.

For example, in McGowan's school we were taught that in a two-man system the base umpire must not drift too quickly toward first base on a double-play situation. If a ball is hit directly to the shortstop, the umpire can drift early toward first base because there will probably not be a problem with the play at second base. But if the shortstop has to charge the ball, or goes into the hole, or bobbles it, then the umpire must hold his position or move toward second because there will likely be a close play there.

That very play situation happened in my first year in the Sooner State League. I was behind the plate; Milton Murphy was on the bases. A double-play situation developed, and Milton bailed out a little too fast on the play at second base. As he was drifting toward first base, the shortstop's toss pulled the second baseman off the bag; now

Milton ran toward second and emphatically called the runner safe. In his eagerness to call the play at second, Milton forgot to watch the throw to first base. Milton had already made two mistakes—he drifted too soon from second and failed to follow the play to completion at first—and now he made a third: Even though he hadn't seen the play at first, without looking at me he called the batter-runner safe. All hell broke loose because the guy was out by at least two steps. Finally, Milton asked me, and I ruled the batter-runner was out. Now the other manager came out yelling. Milton had made three mistakes on the play, but we caught it and rectified the decision.

But there was a fourth mistake. After the game George Johnson, a supervisor from the National Association who happened to be in the stands, came into the dressing room and dressed us both down. He gave Milton hell and then turned to me. "Bill, the instant you realized that your partner didn't call the play at first base, why didn't you call it?" He was absolutely right. I saw the play, and I should have taken the call, really poured it on to cover for Milton.

The point is that all the things that went wrong with that play had been covered at the school, but neither of us retained it long enough or well enough because we had not really experienced the play situation. When it did happen, we didn't handle it very well. But we never forgot it.

I don't believe minor league umpires receive enough supervision, especially at the Triple A level. Even though AAA umpires are only a step away from the majors, they shouldn't be left without a qualified supervisor who can evaluate their work, provide guidance, and assess their chances of getting to the big leagues. Barney Deary keeps tabs on umpires until they reach AAA; then their only supervision comes from the American and National leagues. There are several problems with that. First, Johnny Stevens and Al Barlick, the minor league supervisors for the American and National League respectively, are limited to the amount of time they can spend traveling around the three AAA leagues. Second, they are concerned only with the guys their league has an interest in—Stevens is not going to spend much time with an umpire optioned to the National League. He is not obligated to evaluate every AAA umpire. Third, a good, solid AAA umpire who has no real chance of going to the majors will not often be told that he has a limited future because the leagues want to keep all the good umpires possible.

It is not easy to umpire. It is a very difficult thing to do well. But if you have the ability, umpiring is a great career. And if you have it, the majors will find you. You can't hide a good young umpire any more than you can hide a good young ballplayer—the really good ones stand out in every classification.

I've seen some outstanding umpires over the years. Al Barlick was an outstanding umpire in the National League. I don't think there was probably ever anybody better than he was. Now the best umpire I ever worked with in the American League was Nestor Chylak.

Apart from ability, the thing that made Nestor "Nunny" Chylak so good was his attitude toward the game. He sincerely believes that umpiring is the only profession in the world to be in. To him nothing compares with being an umpire; there just isn't anything else. He is *totally* dedicated to his job. Nunny doesn't understand the young umpire who would do something to hurt his chances of becoming a major league umpire. He doesn't understand the umpire who would, say, show up with a hangover to work a ball game.

Nestor has mentally and physically prepared himself to do the very best job of umpiring that is humanly possible. He knows that he is the best umpire in baseball, that he is number one, and that's the way he umpires. He doesn't flaunt it. He doesn't go around telling everybody how good he is. He doesn't have to. Everybody who works with him knows it, feels that intangible something about him.

And the players and managers know it. One time in Detroit Bernie Allen of Washington pulled a ball out in right field with two men on base. It was clearly foul by eight or nine feet. I was at second base and yelled to the runner, "The ball is foul. Hold up." All of a sudden I see Nestor's hand going up, signaling a home run. Norm Cash, who was playing first base, nearly fell over; Al Kaline came running in from right field; and Bob Scheffing came roaring out of the dugout. I thought, Oh, Jesus, some rhubarb we're going to have now. But it didn't happen. Three runs scored on a foul ball, and the argument never got bad. Nestor got out of it because he was the most respected man in the American League. It was just one of those things that happen, and the Tigers respected him enough to recognize that.

In the dressing room after the game I said, "Nunny, let me shake your hand. I never realized you were human until you called that one." Some guys would drop you right there for telling him that he had kicked the hell out of the play, but Nestor accepted it because he knew what I was trying to get across. Up to then I wondered whether he really was human because over the years I had never been able to second-guess him. Umpires instinctively second-guess each other. The man at second base calls balls and strikes, you judge safe or out from across the field, and so on. I wouldn't say Nestor was 100 percent right on his calls, but every time I saw him make a decision it was what I would have called. I was across from him at second base twenty-five times that year, and I never in my mind changed a pitch on him. But when he blew that one, he had come back down to earth with the rest of us peons.

Johnny Stevens also got away with one like that once in Baltimore. They were building an extension of the grandstand for football, so there was a lot of scaffolding in the outfield stands. There was a huge sign about ten feet high and twenty feet wide with the name of the construction company on it that was a good twenty feet foul and only about five or six feet behind the foul pole. Well, somebody pulled a ball off that sign; it was clearly foul. Somehow Stevens called it a home run.

Now Johnny Stevens was a veteran umpire who was *absolutely* in charge at all times. I respected him very much because he was an outstanding umpire and because he always knew what was going on; he knew that league, every undercurrent, like the back of his hand. He was able to grasp situations quickly and maintain control.

Well, Billy Hitchcock came out screaming. But Stevens knew that the Orioles had a five- or six-run lead in the seventh inning, so the call didn't hurt him much. John said, "The last time I saw the ball it was fair." Billy said, "John, the ball hit that sign out there." "The last time I saw the ball it was fair." He just kept saying that. Finally, Hitchcock asked him to check with one of us, but John said, "No, it was my call. I'm not going to put pressure on anybody else. The last time I saw the ball it was fair."

Now I couldn't have gotten away with that. But Stevens did because he had been in the league for twenty years, because they respected him as an umpire, and because he had given them an honest answer: "The last time I saw the ball it was fair."

We no sooner hit the dressing room than the reporters swarmed in. Well, five or six different guys asked him five or six different questions about the play and every time he answered, "The last time I saw the ball it was fair." Now that shows the value of experience. A first- or second-year man couldn't get away with that. First, those reporters would crucify him, hang him out to dry. They respected Johnny Stevens too much to do that. Second, an inexperienced man would have started talking, and when you start talking about tough calls like that, you tend to lose composure and really get into trouble. John knew he could get away with it by simply stating the truth, and he did. The next morning the headline in the Baltimore paper read: THE LAST TIME I SAW THE BALL IT WAS FAIR.

Another example of a veteran umpire at work is the call Babe Pinelli made to end Don Larsen's perfect game in the 1956 World Series.
If that pitch was a strike, I'm a monkey's uncle. I was there, and I
know that ball was higher than Pinelli's strike zone. And I know a lot
of other people who have seen that picture a thousand times who say
the ball was high. But Pinelli got away with it; no criticism was ever
voiced about the fact that the ball could have been high. It was the
last pitch of a perfect game, and wherever Larsen threw it, it was a
strike three if the batter didn't swing. Dale Mitchell should have
never taken the pitch. Pinelli knew that, and he called it exactly the
way he should have. In other words, he handled it just like a veteran
umpire would have. Babe Pinelli has all the respect of me and every
other umpire because of the way he handled the situation.

I didn't work with Emmett Ashford very much. We weren't on the
same crew until into his second year, and then I retired two years
later. I liked Emmett. He was a very likable man. I think he was a
good umpire. On the bases and behind the plate he was no better or
worse than the rest of us, but it is no secret that his eyes weren't too
good when it came to balls hit into the outfield at night. The man was
about fifty years old when he came into the league, and I think Emmett would be the first to say that he came up after the peak of his
career. If Emmett Ashford had come up ten, fifteen, twenty years
earlier, he would have been one hell of an umpire.

He was good for baseball. I never saw him do anything detrimental
to baseball. No one ever found any fault with his deportment off the
field. He was a gentleman. And the people absolutely dearly loved
him. One night, as we were leaving Yankee Stadium together, some
kid all of a sudden yelled, "Emmett!" The next thing I knew, he was
standing there talking and signing autographs for a couple of hundred kids. Nobody recognized me; I just sat there on a railing and
waited. He signed an autograph for every last kid. That's the kind of
man he was, and that's the kind of feeling there was for him.

There was resentment toward him among the umpires. Everybody
knows there was. Emmett knew it, but he shrugged it off. Many guys
simply didn't accept Emmett. Politics or pull had nothing to do with
it. Some questioned his umpiring ability. And Emmett had his idio-
syncrasies—the cuff links, jumping over the mound on his way to
second base, his showmanship, things like that. (He was one fifty-
year-old guy who could move *very well*.) But mostly I think it was the
publicity Emmett got. Umpires are extremely competitive. When Ed
Runge was voted the best plate umpire in the American League, there

were nine guys ready to shove it down his throat. When Hank Soar was voted the best on the bases, some guys would talk about plays he missed. That's natural. And it's also natural for there to be resentment where there were five reporters around Emmett's cubicle and none around anybody else's. Everywhere Emmett went he was news, good copy. Emmett got more ink in one year than the top five umpires in our league got in their whole career.

I don't believe Emmett deserved a lot of the treatment he got. And I don't mean just from other umpires. Some players, especially members of his own race, gave him more trouble than they should have. That's not to say that black players should have accepted everything he did just because he was black. But I couldn't believe at times the unnecessary hell some of them gave him on play situations.

I sincerely believe that you cannot be introverted and be a great official. You must be extroverted to the nth degree. You must have the feeling that you are more than capable of going out there and handling the job. If there is any doubt in your mind, you are never going to make it. You have got to be able to meet people on any level of life and walk up to them as an equal. A major league umpire can walk up to anybody and not be cowed one bit. I think most every major league umpire feels the way Nester Chylak does, that they wouldn't be in any other profession and they are the best at their job.

I think longevity determines whether or not a man is regarded as a great umpire. Once you get to the major leagues, you've gone as high as you can go. I don't believe any one umpire has a great amount of ability over another; one or two might be a little bit better, but that's determined mainly by experience. A lot of the old-time umpires who are now remembered as great umpires probably weren't nearly as great then as they are now, just like some ballplayers all of a sudden have become a lot better than they were when they were actually playing.

Certainly I'll never be remembered as a great umpire. I was in a couple of situations that possibly some people will remember. For example, I was behind the plate when Roger Maris hit his sixtieth and sixty-first home runs. Actually, I had that historic experience because I worked out of turn. I had worked the plate the day before Maris broke Ruth's record, but just before the game Cal Hubbard, our supervisor, came into the dressing room and said to John Flaherty, "John, you've been around for a while. Let the young guy take it." I was lucky to be there. Of course, it's nothing to be especially proud of, and most people don't give a damn about something like that.

My contribution to baseball has to be the number of kids who have gone through my school and who have either become professional umpires or acquired a much better understanding of the game and themselves than they had before. I contributed something to baseball as an umpire, but I have contributed much more as a teacher. I'm proud of that.

Emmett Ashford in the middle of a called strike at
Comiskey Park in 1966. Courtesy National Baseball
Library & Archive, Cooperstown, N.Y.

Emmett Ashford

⊖⊖⊖

Emmett Littleton Ashford
Born: Los Angeles, California, November 23, 1914
Height: 5′ 7″
Weight: 190
Playing career: none
Umpiring career: Southwest International League (C), July
1951–July 1952; Arizona-Texas League (C),
August–September 1952; Western International League (A), 1953; Pacific Coast League
(AAA), 1954–65; American League, 1966–70
No-hit games: none
All-Star games: 1967
World Series (games): 1970 (5)

"**E**mmett's crazy! The man's crazy to leave all that security and go out in the desert to umpire."

That's what people said in 1951 when I quit the post office after fifteen years of service. I was almost forty years old, making $4,700 a year in the Payroll and Finance Division, and I'd just signed a contract with the Southwest International League as an umpire for $350 a month. What most of those folks didn't know was that I'd made up my mind five years before that, given the opportunity, that's just what I was going to do.

In 1946 I was at the Naval Air Station in Corpus Christi, Texas. I was lying on my cot one evening when the announcement came over the radio that Jackie Robinson had signed with the Brooklyn Dodgers. Right then I said to myself, "I'm going to be the first black umpire." And I did it! I said it then, and as luck would have it, it turned out that way. But then I'm getting ahead of my story and forgetting my youth.

Ah, those gracious days. I was born and raised in Los Angeles, California. My father left when I was a year old, so I never knew him. My mother raised the two of us boys alone. Because I was the oldest, I had to take the initiative and I worked most of the time after school.

There was a *Liberty* magazine in the old days. I took that magazine and worked it up to a route of 300, just walking and talking and selling. I got a lot of things that the other kids didn't have in those days, like a bicycle, because of selling those magazines. I also shined shoes on Saturdays and weekends and made good money at that. Later I went to work as a stockboy at the first supermarket in the black area, over on Central Avenue. Finally, after I'd been doing that long enough, I wanted to be a cashier, so I went to the manager and asked him for a chance. "Well," he said, "you've got to know all the prices of everything in the store." I told him, "I already do." He gave me the job, and I went on to be one of the fastest cashiers they ever had in that market. There were black people who were janitors and boxboys, but I strode in triumphantly as the first to handle the money.

I think the reason why I did so well working then is like everything else that's filtered down through my life. I just couldn't stand to do things halfway. I always believed: Whatever you do, do it well and do it right—give it the best that you have in you. That even goes for digging a ditch. Dig it right! I've tried to make that philosophy a trademark of my life.

Soon after I got the cashier's job, my mother went down and got the application for the post office and had us fill it out. Civil service jobs were the best thing for our people in those days. Lo and behold, I scored way up in the nineties on the doggone thing, so they called me, and I went to work at the post office. I went there in about 1936, so that would make me about twenty-two, wouldn't it?

But my youth wasn't all work. School and, later, sports took a lot of my time. And I was practically raised at the YMCA. I went to school at Wadsworth Grammar School, McKinley Junior High, and then on to Jefferson High School. At Jefferson High I was elected the first black student body president and was editor of the school paper, along with being a member of the Scholarship Society. I especially enjoyed music appreciation class and French—took three semesters and loved it!

I never got involved in sports until one day my high school track coach, Harry Edleson, held this 880-yard run for the gym class. I was scared to death of that race, just scared, but I got out there in those old tennis shoes and trailed on back. I don't know what, but something happened. When I got over on the backstretch for the last lap, you talk about Sea Biscuit! I ran over and around people to come on and win that thing.

After that, Harry said, "Emmett, you've got to come out for track." "No!" I said. "I'm too busy. I have too many other activities going." Besides, I was scared of track anyway. So sure enough, Harry waited for his time, and I was late for gym class one day. "All right," he said. "Either you come out for track, or you spend a week coming here at six-thirty in the morning and sweeping off the sidewalk all around Jefferson High School."

Needless to say, I went out for track. I ran the 100, the 220, and the 120 hurdles and one day went over and picked up the shot put and threw it farther than the number one guy did. Then I went over and broad jumped. I ran wild. That was Class B, of course, but it was still a feat. I went on to Los Angeles City College and then to Chapman College where I got a B.S. degree. I tried to run the 440 at City College, but in those days they had a lot of 9:8 to 9:9 sprinters there, and I couldn't crack that team. I played baseball at Chapman; since I was sports editor of the college paper, I was assured of a good press.

Those were great days. I think I developed my basic characteristics during that time. Who can explain why I ran for student body president as a black or later chose to become an umpire? I'd say it was because of my mother and the fact that I'm a Sagittarius. My mother was a secretary for a black newspaper, The *California Eagle*, for many years. She was quite an active person, and I know I got my ambitious traits from her. As a Sagittarius I'm an extrovert, and I can't let grass grow under my feet. At times I'm blunt and outspoken when I shouldn't be. I want to get out and do things. Even now I feel like I want to do a little more, but I guess all in due time.

When I was in college, I used to play with a semipro team in Highland Park called the Mystery Nine. The mystery, of course, was how I managed to be the only black face on that white team. Our uniforms had a great big question mark on the front as a gimmick. I played center field, but that long throw from center was a bit rough for me because I didn't have the accuracy required. So I moved to second base. We mostly played on Saturday and Sunday, and in the winter the wintering pros would come in and play with us. I couldn't throw or hit as well as the other guys could, so I usually rode the bench for the big games.

Then, one Sunday, the regular umpire didn't show up. After waiting fifteen to twenty minutes they came looking for me. I had taken batting practice, showered, and retired to my customary spot on the bench. But they carried me kicking and screaming out behind the pitcher and told me to umpire, notwithstanding the fact that I was dressed conservatively in green slacks, two-tone shoes, a green sport coat, and, I think, a green shirt.

Well, pandemonium ensued. But a strange thing happened. By the seventh inning they *loved* my umpiring. They would take up collections during those games, and the collection that Sunday was extremely heavy. Thenceforth the team decreed that I should umpire. I guess they thought I had added something to the game.

I went out there and worked about three Sundays before word came out from the city recreation department that they couldn't use me anymore because I hadn't joined the umpires' association. They told the club, "If that clown thinks he can umpire, have him come down here and fill out an application," not ever thinking I would. They didn't know me too well. I'd already bought a little $1.75 umpire's cap, and I wasn't about to lose my investment.

Bright and early Monday morning I went to the recreation office and said to the little secretary, "I would like to have a baseball umpire's application."

She looked at me like I was crazy. "Say that again, sir?"

"I'd like a baseball umpire's application."

She stuttered and stammered, didn't know what to say. Finally, she got the director of recreation. He came out and took me in back and tried to dissuade me, but after half an hour or so he found out he couldn't. He finally said, "All right, if you're willing to go out there and take it, I guess I'll have to back you."

That's the way I got started. But before I could go any further, along came the war. It was about '42 or '43 when I went into the Navy. I went first to the Great Lakes training station, then to Memphis, and finally down to Corpus Christi. I almost got killed down there in a hurricane trying to rescue a PBY. Nobody else would take a rope and swim out there and tie it on, so they could pull the thing in. My YMCA training stood me in good stead that time. The commander of the base heard about my feat and gave me the job that I was originally sent down there to do—be a postal clerk. I also ran the baseball team on the base. That was the black team in those days.

After the war I came home and went back into umpiring seriously.

I really got into it. Old Bill Lopez got me into the high school system. Then I started umpiring in junior college leagues, and then moved up to UCLA, Southern Cal, and the college circuit. That's where I learned the fine points of the art. Ernie Stewart, the former umpire, was one of my idols. I worked with him in the college games around Los Angeles. I learned the major league strike zone from Ernie. Too bad he got fired; he got caught in a vise. I admired the hell out of the guy.

Well, before you knew it, the umpiring mushroomed so that I was busier than hell. I had my own office in the Payroll and Finance Division of the main post office. They used to lock me in a cage every morning with about $200,000 in currency and stamps; by eleven o'clock I'd have to have the books balanced, so umpiring wasn't so tough. Anyway, it soon got so that the phone was ringing more for me to go umpire somewhere for $2 a game than for post office business.

Unbeknownst to me, Rosey Gilhousen, Kansas City's chief scout, was trailing me in that college circuit. The upshot of it was that he arranged a tryout for me with the Class C Southwest International League. They had to go through the National Association of Professional Baseball Clubs, which is the minor league system, back in Columbus, Ohio. George Trautman was the president then. They rigged up a four-game tryout for me, but they had to put it outside the continental limits of the United States.

I'll never forget it. It was a series between Tucson and Mexicali during the Fourth of July weekend in 1951. I was really hot to trot for this one. When I got to the border, the Mexican guards looked in the car (you know how they look perfunctorily because they're not going to turn away those American dollars). I said, "Me umpire."

They looked at each other for a second; then one fellow reached down and picked up a broken beer bottle and said, "You umpire? The last umpire leave here pretty queek because of this!"

The next crisis came when I got to the ball park. The two white umpires refused to work with me. So we had to hold the game up until the ball club sent up to El Centro, eleven miles from Mexicali, for another umpire. They played Latin music over the PA system to entertain the fans during the delay. They finally got the father of one of the umpires now in the National League, Doug Harvey's dad, to come down. He was doing semipro ball in El Centro. They got him down there in a hurry. I worked all four games behind the plate, and he worked the bases for me. It was really a rousing series. The Mexicans ate it up, and they had a full house all three nights. No problems.

After I worked that four-game series, I went back to my job in the post office. But I knew that I'd gotten my feet wet in what I really wanted to do. After having that success, I knew umpiring was for me. Sure enough, about a week later Les Powers, the president of the league, called and asked if I'd care to finish the season. Shoot, I ran into the postmaster's office, got a leave of absence for three months, and took off.

When I went into the league to work those last three months, the other umpires wrote the National Association office and said that they couldn't work with me because I couldn't stay in a decent place. In those days things were segregated, but it was different for me. In Las Vegas and El Centro I got out there and just hit those motel strips and told my story. I told them that I couldn't go out there and work at night unless I had a decent place to stay, and I'd usually find a real nice place.

I remember calling upon the finest all-white motel in El Centro. I approached the owner. "Sir, I am that barefoot and uncultured Negro man you have been reading about. I wish to seek lodging in your handsome establishment."

The fellow stared at me curiously. "If you got enough nerve to come in here and talk like that, then you got a room." With that he led me to the finest suite in the place. The man knew style when he saw it.

Finally, a supervisor from the National Association office came out to El Centro because of all the letters from the other umpires. (It was so bad that I think the office heard whenever I went to the bathroom. Later the same thing happened in the majors, too.) I didn't know him, but somebody told me that his name was George Johnson, a former umpire, and that he was in the stands. He didn't come down and introduce himself the first two nights. The third night he did. He said, "Where are you staying?" So I took him over to my motel. "Why, those sons of bitches," he said. "They're down the street in a fleabag, and here you are in a decent motel." Then he asked, "Where do you eat? They said you couldn't eat anywhere in town here." I said, "Come on. I'll take you right across the street to this beautiful Chinese restaurant!" He just shook his head. The next day he called the other umps together and said, "I'd like to show you how an umpire goes first class."

I never had a problem finding a place to eat. It was just one of the little extra things I had to do. Like in Vegas, I went downtown to one of the restaurants where they said the owner was a ball fan. I went into his office, and after we had talked awhile, I told him my problem. He says, "You come on in here and eat. I'll notify everybody." I made my own way. I had to in those days.

I always wondered, though, why it was that a league with towns like Tijuana and Mexicali and Juárez had to have dressing-room facilities that were so poor. In Tijuana the umpire's room was next door to the urinal. The wall wasn't all the way down to the ground, and those fumes used to float over into that dressing room. It got so bad I wouldn't dress in there. I dressed in the hotel. In Mexicali it was a little bit better, but over there you had to fight the crickets in the summer. They came in swarms, and you had to get a broom to sweep them out. El Centro was the same way. And the temperature down there was about 115 degrees during the day. Fortunately we played night games, when it went down to about 110 degrees. It sure made the digesting of beer great in the evenings.

Well, I wound up the year working the play-offs and the next year got a contract for the season. The postmaster was under political fire at the time, and I couldn't get that leave of absence again. So I had to make the decision which everybody has to make in his life sometime. How many men go to their graves without ever doing what's in their hearts? I resigned and gave up fifteen years' seniority to be an umpire. I've never regretted it. I've lived a lifetime in baseball. I sure have. But it almost didn't turn out that way.

After I resigned from the post office, I was up in Las Vegas one day and got a call from the president of the league. "Come back to Los Angeles. The league has folded." Folded! Well, I drove back home. In those days there were fifty-seven leagues, so there shouldn't have been any problem placing six or eight umpires. The president was able to place the other guys right away, but not me. So I went down to Ensenada, Mexico, and looked at the senoritas for a while. Then one day the president called me at the hotel and said, "Come on back, I got a job for you." I went back and then struck out for—guess where—El Paso, Texas, in the Arizona-Texas League.

Texas turned out to be a good thing for me. I was supposed to be going to relieve a gentleman who was retiring from the profession because of poor health, but that son of a gun had enough strength to stay on long enough to usher me behind home plate that first night. He was probably expecting to see some action. I don't know what the word was in El Paso, but when I arrived, there were two policemen outside the park, and by the second or third inning there were fifteen.

El Paso was playing its perennial enemy, Chihuahua. I didn't know it, but they had been fighting like cats and dogs before I got there. Hell, the first inning I had to go to third base to make a call on a fellow American, Barney Sorrell, playing for Chihuahua. The batter had hit a single to right-center, and of course, the right fielder came in and made the long throw to third. Well, I pulled out and I'm down there.

It was a close play. Even before I could get my arms up to a safe position, I heard all the stuff that Jackie Robinson used to get way back in 1946. I took it, made the call, and started back to the plate. I had gotten halfway to home when I hear this raucous voice: "Ashford, why in the hell don't you go back to California? We don't want a nigger here trying to do a white man's job." I turned around, and the shock was compounded when I saw it was another American who was leaning over that little fence in El Paso and shaking his fist at me and telling me to go back to California. Well, I am very seldom at a loss for words, so I gathered myself together and said, "If you'll kindly go home and put some shoes on and come back, then we'll discuss the matter."

The next crisis arose about the sixth inning. Marvin Williams, who was a fabulous home-run hitter in that area, was up to bat. He just couldn't cut it in the majors, but he sure was on a tear around that league. By the time I got there he already had forty home runs, and his Mexican owners were giving him hatfuls of pesos, suits, and everything else. He comes up with two outs, and he knows the opposition is going to try to get him out the best way they can. So with two men on and the count two-and-two, they threw a bill-of-the-capper, and before I could say, "Ball," the catcher was in my face, the pitcher was on his way to the plate, and the manager, who played second base, had beat them both in. You talk about Custer's Last Stand! That was it. I knew it.

Finally, I said, "All right. I know where I am. I know what the score is. If this is the last game I ever work, it's going to be worked my way. If I have to go out of here, I'm going out with my boots on. So be it!" Then I said, "I'm going to get some balls, and if any of you guys are still here, you won't have anything but a forfeit and those fifteen policemen you brought in." It worked; they played the game. The next morning, the El Paso press was extremely generous. They called it a great display of guts and courage and damn good umpiring.

Well, I went back there for two or three more series. During my final series they announced it would be my last game in El Paso. Those fans stood and gave me a standing ovation. Now that was 1952! Those fans taught me a lot. They gave me the basis of a good career. I found out from them that a good job well done is worth more than all the soapboxes you can conjure up.

My next stop was at the Class A Western International League. I almost didn't get in. I have heard that they had to remove the president in order to get me in. He had publicly said, "I'm not going to have any nigger umpires in my league." Clarence "Pants" Rowland

and Bob Brown, the new president from Vancouver, took care of that, and I went there in 1953. How was I accepted? Great! That was a good league in those days. There were ten teams stretching from Victoria and Vancouver way over to Calgary and Edmonton. Lewiston, Spokane, Yakima, Salem, the tricities—oh, what a beautiful league to drive in. I had just bought a new car, so I enjoyed the driving.

We worked a two-man system there, and I never had any trouble with partners, except my first, a Dutchman. He had the bad habit of calling me "boy." After a game one night in Victoria he started to tell me about something that I'd done wrong. Well, that's something you don't do. Even at a higher level, you don't come in and criticize another umpire. If he asks you, fine. But after he's had trouble, he usually doesn't want to hear about it. So I came into the dressing room, and he jumped on me. I had just had enough of it when he came out with "Boy. . . ." I whirled on his ass, grabbed him by the throat, and jammed him up against the wall. I said, "If you use that word 'boy' on me one more time, I'm going to knock your teeth down your throat and out your asshole. I mean it." He knew from the look in my eyes that I did. I said, "Is that clear?" He said, "Okay, all right, all right." That's the only time I think that I ever got violent. I'm a peaceable man, until aroused.

After a year in the Western International League, I got called up to the Pacific Coast League. When I got that call, I felt I was getting close, that I had a chance for the majors. Pants Rowland was responsible for calling me up to the Coast League. I spent twelve years there. Later he was responsible for getting me to the majors. Before the twelve years were up, though, I was really getting discouraged. Guys I had taught and helped at the direction of my president were all going to the majors. I had heard that they were going to take me up in 1960, but then somebody leaked the story. I don't know what happened after that, but I think somebody up at the top said no. Well, six years later they still hadn't called me up. I was disappointed, but I was making friends and learning to adjust to situations that built the confidence I would need later.

I had to learn to handle the pressure. I know there were times in those first years, when I was by myself most of the time, that just being alone caused pressure. If I had trouble or got into a jam in a game, then the pressure or the tension would get to me. Then, the next day before I went to the park, I'd get out and walk. That would loosen me up; it helped get my mind off whatever had happened the night before.

Because I was so much alone, I had to learn how to live with the rest of the world. My circle of friends became different from the other umpires because I had to make my own way. But I didn't come to town and have to go to the ghetto to enjoy myself. I stayed downtown and went to the theater and the opera. I just love some opera—know the librettos of a few. I loved Latin dancing, too. There were times some of the other umpires said, "He thinks he's white." Well, I didn't act like one. I met and associated with professional people. I made a host of friends; many of them were attorneys and doctors who invited me to their homes and nice functions. I'd meet with the lawyers for lunch in Spokane, and, shoot, in Vancouver, I think I could have run for office. And with my fraternity connections from college, I eventually didn't have any problem with being lonely. I had a good time. Thank heavens I had that foundation in the Coast League because I ran into all the same problems when I got to the major leagues, and I was able to handle them.

I spent the last three years in the Coast League as umpire in chief. That was a good experience. As the boss I never had much trouble with the staff. I know there were a few who mumbled, but not many, not even the guys I'd been promoted over. I always tried to handle things tactfully.

One time this umpire had a slow call, a real slow motion. The broadcasters couldn't call the strike over the air because he would wait so long before coming up with his right hand. I handled it the way I usually did when working with my staff. I didn't say much. I just went out there and did it right. My philosophy was don't talk, do it. That usually worked.

Some of the fellows I worked with in the Coast League are in the majors now and doing a fine job. I remember Dutch Rennert. One night, shortly after coming into the league, he had a bad game, and I stayed up with him till five o'clock in the morning going over things. I get cards from him and he still calls me Chief. Dutch is a very good umpire—and one of the most vocal!

While in the PCL I spent the off-seasons officiating football and basketball. You know, I was the first black referee in those sports on the Coast. I started in high school basketball and worked the PAC Eight from 1950 to 1958. And for twelve years I did football for high schools, junior college, and small colleges; never did make it to major college football—I quit because it bored me. Football was difficult for me to work because I couldn't report until late September, and by then the season was half over. I got tired of just dropping a handkerchief with nobody knowing who you were until they ran the films on

Monday morning. Besides, there was simply no challenge for me in football; it just got boring.

But basketball was a challenge. Baseball and basketball are related in the matter of quick judgment, but basketball is more strenuous because you have to make judgments on the run. My determination as a baseball umpire to see everything carried over into basketball. That's why I was so much in demand. I *hustled* and made calls with *motion*. (Some of my detractors accused me of showboating, but notice the emphatic gestures referees use today. I was twenty years ahead of my time.) I outran the players; that's how hard I worked. I'd have to change shirts at the half—one would be wringing wet. I used to run to midcourt, pivot in midair, and then backpedal to the basket so I'd be there when the players came down. (I learned my backpedaling from Bill "Bojangles" Robinson, the old tap dancer.) That hustle carried over into the majors. When I first went up, I used to run out to the outfield and stand out there next to the fielder while he caught the ball. After watching me that first year, Dick Young of the New York *Daily News* wrote, "How in the Hell can a 51-year-old man run that fast?"

By the end of the 1965 season in the Pacific Coast League I had just about had it. I was something of an institution in the PCL, but after twelve years I was plenty discouraged. After fifteen years of umpiring, I figured I was licked. I had worked about 2,800 games, and I thought I wasn't ever going to get called up. Maybe it was different when Jackie Robinson came in as a player. Branch Rickey took Jackie and put him out there on *his* team. Sure, people cussed him and everything else, but there was nothing anybody could do about it. Now here I come along, some twenty years later, and I'm *running* things. I'm the *boss*. I thought maybe they weren't ready for that yet in the majors. I was almost ready to quit. I had already enrolled in this real estate school when I got a call from Dewey Soriano, who was then president of the Pacific Coast League.

"Emmett, what are you doing?"

"I'm standing up."

"Well, you'd better sit down. I've just sold your contract to the American League."

There was silence. Then Dewey said, "Emmett, where are you?"

I finally said, "I'm up here on the ceiling."

Then I sat down, and we talked, and oh, it was one of the greatest feelings I ever had!

I was somewhat surprised about its being the American League. I had always thought that if I would go up, it would be to the National League. It's not generally known, but Leo Durocher was a voice crying out in the wilderness for ten years, trying to get the National League to call me up. Somewhere along the way I had heard some rumors about the American League, but I had just tossed them off. But somebody knew something. I had always used the National League-style inside chest protector, but after that call I went out and bought one of those American League balloons and slept with it. That winter I sneaked down to Long Beach on Sundays and worked the Long Beach Rockets' games, just to get used to it.

After the news of my appointment got around town, boy, my house was just like Grand Central Station. With the media coming in and calls from all over the country, it was quite a thing. Strange thing was, though, a lot of the same people who came up there slapping me on the back were the same ones who said I was crazy when I resigned from the post office. A lot of them had written me off and hadn't helped me one bit. It's a hard thing to say, but most of my support came from the white set, except for one of the black sports editors. When I went to the major leagues, here came those same people saying, "I knew you'd do it! I knew you'd do it!" Bullshit. I stuck it out, worked hard, and finally made it.

After a long winter's wait I worked the opener in Washington, D.C., on April 11, 1966. Johnny Stevens was my senior umpire. The Indians beat the Senators, 5–2, before the largest opening-day crowd [44,468] in Washington history. It was the biggest thrill of my life.

But I had trouble getting into the stadium. The Secret Service was out in force because Vice President Hubert Humphrey was going to throw out the first ball. They had set up command posts at all entrances to the parking lot and more where you went down underneath the stadium. I arrived with my wife in a cab. At the first stop the driver told the Secret Service agent, "I've got one of the umpires here."

"Who are you trying to kid?"

"That's right. I've got one of the umpires."

He said, "There are no Negro umpires in the major leagues."

I said, "Well, there will be a Negro umpire in the American League if you will let me into the park."

That agent looked at me with disbelief. Finally, he went to this folder where he had all the rosters and started thumbing through it, looking at me all the while like I was a spy from the Congo or a minister of an African nation dissatisfied with his relief money. After he read the last page, he said, "Okay." But he still couldn't take his eyes off me. That same thing happened twice more before I got to the umpire's dressing room, and with me holding my black bag all the time.

I eventually made it, got dressed, and walked out on the field. I looked around and thought to myself: After all these years, here I am. I was the wandering minstrel of baseball who finally made it to Broadway. Tears came to my eyes. It's quite a feeling—no one can quite describe it. I trotted down to third base and waved to my wife up in the owner's box. I only had one call all day, when Vic Davallio slid into third far ahead of the throw, but I'll never forget one guy writing: "He only had one call, but the footwork was better than the call." (I was just getting in position, that's all.) After the game Joe Cronin said, "Emmett, today you made history. I'm proud of you."

That was a thrill, but just as exciting was my first time behind the plate three days later in Baltimore. Aside from being a little sore in my posterior riding that jump seat in those cabs, I was ready. Even the hazing I got from the older umpires didn't bother me. I was working with John Stevens, Bob Stewart, and Bill Haller. They weren't a happy bunch after seeing me work in Washington. They just weren't used to my type of work. Consequently the hazing they gave me was just natural. Any new umpire coming in, white or black, is going to get the rookie treatment. But I had to be able to ward off a lot of extra things because of my style and my being the first black. Fortunately I always recognized them for what they were, roadblocks, and kept going.

Anyway, there we were on Sunday in Baltimore. They had a full house because the press had written a big article about Emmett Ashford making his debut behind the plate. Well, I'm rubbing up the balls, which the home plate umpire does, and my partners are telling me all these tales about Baltimore—how they didn't like blacks and all kinds of stuff calculated to get me worked up. But they didn't know me very well. Shoot, I went out there with a vengeance, just like I had done in the Coast League working with two men. I had to do the same thing. I literally had to stuff my guts back inside me and go out there and do my job every night. No, they didn't know that I'd been conditioned before.

The worst had happened twelve years before during my first season in the Coast League. The senior man in the league tried to screw me all season. Every time I looked around he was telling a lie here and a lie there—telling the players I was doing this or that. We worked the last game of the season together in Tacoma, where he tried to screw me up one last time. After the game, when we were dressed and standing outside the park, I told him, "Go back and tell the Ku Klux Klan that you have *failed*." Like I said, I was conditioned. I was ready for that game.

Whitey Ford was pitching for the Yankees. He was in the twilight of his career, and poor Whitey was wasting balls six inches outside. Some of the umpires were obliging him. Let's face it, they were still the Yankees of old—Mantle, Maris and all the rest. Well, they soon knew how *I* was calling them. (Clete Boyer later took me off to the side and said, "Emmett, you call a hell of a game. Don't let those guys screw you up." And Clete had a hell of an eye.) We had a tie ball game going into the sixth inning, 1-1. Andy Etchebarren was catching. A pop fly headed for the box seats, and Andy ran over there and dove into the box, hoping, as he told the press later, that somebody would put the ball in his glove so he could take it and act like he'd come up with it. "But," he says, "you know what? I looked up, and there's Emmett right in there with me!" I did it—dove right in there with him. The fans went crazy.

I really put everything I had into that game. Afterward, the boss, big Cal Hubbard, came into the dressing room. Being a southerner, he was entitled to his opinion—which I had heard wasn't complimentary. I knew that he'd heard a few thousand lies about me from other umpires and because he had followed me all through spring training. Well, after that game he hugged me. Cal and I became very good friends. Later, when some of the other umpires were getting set to organize against me, he quelled the uprising.

I think most of the problems I had with umpires were not technically a matter of race, but a matter of my different kind of style. I was not exactly without color. Every umpire has his own style. I can walk into a ball park, and with the home-plate umpire's back to me, I can still tell you who it is by his movements. Every umpire has his own characteristics, but I was a totally different article. I never went to an umpiring school because they didn't accept blacks in those days. So I developed my own style of officiating. I didn't think about it; it just came. When I first started umpiring out there behind the mound, I started putting some oomph into it and hamming it up a little bit. Later, when I did basketball, I did the same thing. It just came out. It's my personality. I'm an extrovert, and I couldn't help it. I guess you might say I'm just a natural-born ham.

I toned my routine down some in the majors, but I still did what came naturally. Some people didn't like my color on the field and called me a clown or showboat. Dick Williams called me a Hollywood hot dog. That was expected, so it didn't bother me one bit.

After umpiring in the sticks for fifteen years, I didn't care what they called me just so long as I stayed in the majors.

Sure, I was a showboat. For twelve years that was my routine in the Coast League. My clowning was a meal ticket for the league. People came to see me *and* the game. My picture was featured in the scorecards.

Look, just because umpires dress in blue doesn't mean we're presiding at a funeral. Baseball is and always will be fun, and nobody enjoys a ball game more than I do. I was a kid once, and I've never forgotten it. Everybody should have a little "boy" in his heart. I enjoy life.

Television didn't bother me one bit. In fact, I loved it. The same with the instant replay. Yes, all my running and hustle were part showmanship. Remember the days when I worked second base, how I would run and broad jump the mound? Well, one day in Detroit I was at third base when Norm Cash came running out of the dugout past me heading for first base. He ran to the mound and tried to broad jump it and tip his cap at the same time. He wrenched his back trying that.

I didn't even mind the ribbing from the fans. I had a different outlook on it. It never bothered me to hear "Three Blind Mice." I'd just take it in the context it was presented. Often, when I started for home plate, they'd come on with "Pomp and Circumstance" or something like that. The organist at Dedeaux Field at Southern Cal would play "Tea for Two," and I would give them a little soft shoe. The fans ate it up. Everybody's got to sell it, whatever they're selling.

Now, I know some of the jealousy I caused was because most umpires had never had a crowd react to them like that. All of a sudden here I came, and I go out and get the crowd all pumped up. The fans loved me, like Ron Luciano today—a showman and a damn fine umpire. I was the only umpire they ever paid to see. Well, the other umpires didn't care for that too much. When it got so the fans would erupt when they announced my name before the game, they would say, "Oh, now what the hell is this? I'm an umpire, too. He just blew two plays last night." Well, I worked like hell with all that in mind. I knew that I was not going to succeed unless I was 99.9 percent right. I had to be that.

I will say this, though, in defense of an animated style of officiating. The clearer a decision is made, the fewer problems you encounter. If the man is out, let everyone know beyond a doubt that he is out. Maybe my style was a little pronounced and unusual, but all I ever asked was to be judged on my competency. I proved that with all my antics I was a capable umpire.

I had a couple of crises early on that first year in the league. The first one came in a Washington-Baltimore game. The score was tied in the twelfth inning when Russ Snyder tripled for the Orioles. But he missed first base, and when the Senators appealed, I called him out. Nobody raised a fuss. They didn't even after the next batter got a single. Then there was the time I called out Tommy Tresh of the Yankees on a third strike with two of his teammates on base. Tommy started to argue, but I kept saying, "Now, Tommy, now, Tommy." He just couldn't get mad at me because I calmed him down.

The first player I ever ejected was Eddie Brinkman, the shortstop for the Senators. Mr. Brinkman threw his cap down very hard and had to exit. The second was Alvin Dark, a gentleman from Louisiana who managed the A's. Mr. Dark and I had an ethical conversation, and I was compelled to eject him. But he was right. I blew the play.

I realized that I was in a special position as the first black umpire in the major leagues. When I got called up, Dewey Soriano said, "The only reason Emmett hasn't made the major leagues before this is that he's a Negro." It wasn't easy being an umpire, let alone being a Negro umpire. But since the game is the ballplayer's bread and butter, all he wants is for you to make the right calls. He doesn't care if you're white or black, Eskimo or Indian. In turn, I worked like hell. I was an *umpire*, not a black umpire.

Still, I've always had to confront the issue of race. I realized I was black, so I tried to walk around possible trouble situations as best I could.

I remember an incident with Leo Durocher during an exhibition game in Arizona one year. A hitter took a half swing, and I called it a ball. Leo came roaring out of the dugout like the lion he is, vigorously disputing my call. To comply with the regulations on such matters, I consulted with Billy Williams, the umpire at first base. He agreed that the batter had not taken a full swing. As I returned to the plate, Leo was yelling, "What have we got? What have we got?" I stuck my face up against his and replied, "It was not a strike, and you got it in black and white—him at first and me at the plate."

Fans and players alike were extremely fair. Even though players have been boiling mad at me, there was never a racial slur. And if the letters I received can be used as a yardstick, the fans liked me.

I got hundreds of letters every season, and there were only two that were critical. One was scrawled on toilet tissue from a small town in Louisiana. It said, "They should throw people like you and the

NAACP into the river." The other was from a young girl in Baltimore. She wrote, "Mr. Ashford, you always have been my favorite umpire, but after the call you made yesterday I don't like you anymore." I don't remember the particular call, but that letter hurt.

Umpiring. It's the most jealous profession in the world. I came in wearing cuff links because of a habit long before baseball, and the cameras used to focus on the cuff links when I walked on the field. The other umpires didn't like that. It didn't help either that the Angels and Athletics used to call the commissioner and get permission for me to make special trips to umpire their games. I remember when Charlie Finley moved to Oakland and opened his new park. He got me out there for his opener, and I worked the plate. I had just worked the plate the night before in Baltimore, but I jumped on a plane, flew out there to Oakland, and worked his inaugural game.

Then sometimes, like in Boston one time, the fans tried to mob me. Gosh, they almost tore my shirt off that day. By the time I got dressed two of the umpires had run off to the airport and left me alone. One of them stayed behind and gave me a lift, though. One time I got left and had to ride the Railway Express wagon with the gear to the airport. Then, when I got to the airport, I had to start signing autographs. That's another reason why the other guys didn't like to be around me. They weren't recognized. Hell, I couldn't hide anywhere in daylight.

I guess you could say my style was a combination of laissez-faire, initiative, hustle, a sense of timing, and good judgment. I had exaggerated motions and a good voice. As one writer said, I was "animated." I never tried to model myself after another umpire, but when I was in the minor leagues, I sort of idolized Al Barlick. He was a great umpire who did practically the same things I did. He had the loud voice and good motion, too. I always knew when to put it on and when not to. When the game was serious, I was all business. But when it got to be one-sided, you know, I perked it up a little bit.

I think baseball needs its proceedings spiced up once in a while. That's why allowing the rhubarb is a good thing for the game. From my experience, having officiated most sports, there has to be one where we can go back to our good old days of democracy and free speech. We've got that in baseball. The rhubarb is a tradition as old as baseball, and I hope we're going to keep it.

Of course, sometimes rhubarbs are staged. It might be for the benefit of the fans or for the players. Ralph Houk has a set routine—jaw at you nose to nose and belly to belly; throw his cap down; kick dirt and cap on the way back to the dugout. That's strictly his act. I've had a couple of experiences where the manager thought enough of me as an umpire to send somebody over before the game to let me know we were going to have an argument. It happened once in Oklahoma City with Grady Hatton's club. The trainer called me outside my dressing room before a game and said, "Emmett, Grady's got to shake up his troops tonight, so he's going to pour it to you a little bit." He sure did, but at least I knew it was coming; they respected me enough to warn me.

Most of the time the rhubarbs are serious—they're not just trying to pump up their troops; they're really trying to change my mind or at least trying to get the next one to go their way. Then I used to grit my teeth and say, "If he was out, dammit, he was out!" I didn't give a good goddamn what they said. Of course, there was a line which the manager couldn't cross. He couldn't use direct profanity, get personal, or delay the game. Those three things. Now, you know it's no tea party out there. You're going to hear a lot of "Well, I'll be a son of a bitch," "Well, I'm a dirty bastard"—that type of thing. But when they say "YOU," then they are gone.

There were times when guys came out there wanting to get thrown out. It might be hot as hell. I'd tell them, "It's a hundred degrees today, and you're gonna sweat as long as I am." Or you might get some guy who is zero for four against, say, a Nolan Ryan. He might want out, but I wouldn't throw him; I'd make him stay there and suffer. Lots of times a manager will come out there just because he has to stand up for his player, even at times when he knows the player is wrong. It's just a part of a manager's job. But most of the time the arguments in the major leagues are genuine. By and large, the players don't bother you unless they feel you have really missed one.

I had one rhubarb that was no fun at all. It was the only time I was ever physically attacked by a ballplayer. It happened when I was working winter ball down in the Dominican Republic. That was 1964, the year the Cardinals won the World Series and then cut Julian Javier's salary by $3,000. The local newspapers had just released the story, so when Julian came to the ball park that night for the first game of the winter league play-offs, he was in a rage. We had a full house. Baseball in Latin America is something else: music, excitement, *electricity*. When they say, "Hang them from the rafters," down there they mean just that. The aisles were filled, and they were literally sitting in the rafters.

The first time Javier came to bat the pitcher was Larry Miller, then with the Dodgers. He threw the pitch Javier didn't like—a slider knee-high on the outside corner. I called it a strike. Javier stepped out and looked at me and then got back in the box. The second pitch was the same. I called it the same way, "Strike two." So he stepped out again and said, "Why you call that pitch on me? You know I don't like that pitch." I said, "Julian, why do you think he's putting it there?" I thought I knew him well enough to say that, but that night he was in this awful state of mind. So we got into this long, nonsensical argument—and with the full house that we had and both dugouts looking on, I knew that I had a powder keg on my hands.

I said, "All right, Julian, get back in the box. Don't make me call for the pitch." There is a rule that gives you the right to call for the pitch and, no matter where it is, call a strike. Well, he leaned on his bat and crossed his legs (it's his home country, not mine). "Oh, you're going to call for the pitch, eh?" Then he said, "I dare you."

I thought: "Oh, shit." But I told Miller to pitch, and he threw it right down the pipe. Strike three. I gave it the good old Ashfordian style, *"Strike three!"* But it was strike four which echoed around the world. When I lifted my mask to remonstrate with my friend Julian, he clipped me with a left to the jaw.

I staggered back, my mouth cut and bleeding. Now I was mad at him! While I do not advocate violence, I initiated my own version of the Charge of the Light Brigade and resorted to fisticuffs in retaliation. I got him a couple of licks with my mask before the players tore us apart. A hush fell over the stadium because I, too, was a favorite down there. They called me Pata Ditas, "Little Kicks," and they said I was the fairest umpire ever to come to the Dominican Republic. Also, I was the dictator Trujillo's favorite umpire—not that that meant anything. But Javier was a national hero. One guy jumped on top of the dugout and yelled, "You are a black Yankee, but still go home."

I did not go home. Nor did I quit. The other umpires wanted me to take off, but I said, "Hell, no. Get me some ice." I put some ice on my lip, got a towel, and went on back to work for the last eight innings.

When I got back to the hotel after the game, the league president called; Tatro Desano, the owner of the club, came up with a fifth of scotch; and Javier called crying because he was suspended. Well, the act was beginning. The next morning they had a meeting. They had about six more meetings, and as is the way with our Latin friends, politics took over. By the time we got to Javier's hometown of Santiago, ninety miles up in the interior, they had figured out some excuse to lift the suspension so that he could play. Of course, he had to apologize publicly on television and in the newspapers first.

So here we were again, with another jam-packed house and me behind the plate. When it came time for Javier to bat, he didn't go to the batter's box. He walked out straight to me and stuck out his hand. Well, what could I do? I couldn't be a lesser man, so I shook hands with him, and the house went crazy. Politics and inter-American relations, I'm telling you.

That was one time my working hard to get that outside corner got me in trouble. That's got to be the toughest pitch to call. I remember one time Mickey Lolich had a no-hitter going for about five or six innings, and he was throwing that roundhouse curve. It would come around sharp and hit the plate right at the outside front corner. Mickey told the press later, "That ball is a strike, but they haven't been calling it. Emmett's the first one to call it."

The crossfire that some guys throw is also tough. By the time the pitch gets to the catcher it's a foot outside. You don't worry about that. You watch the ball when it crosses the plate. Don't try to go around the catcher's head, like some guys make the mistake of doing. By that time it's already crossed the corner. You've got to catch it as it crosses that corner if you're going to be able to give the pitcher that pitch.

I used to psyche myself up for every pitch because I knew I had to be 99 percent right, and I had to be consistent. Some catchers give you better shots at the ball than others by getting down low, but you always have to adjust behind the plate. I got to the point where I would do anything to see that plate. I hardly ever talked behind the plate because it takes away your concentration and makes you open psychologically to the catcher. You always have to be ready for anything, be open-minded. You've got to coordinate dancing knucklers, diving breaking balls, and ninety-mile-an-hour fastballs that never come down the middle of the plate. All the while with an aching back and legs. You call maybe 225 or 250 pitches a game, and you just have to bear down to make sure the game is decided on its merits; even if it's a ragged game, they're going to jump on you if you miss one. Pressure? Tension from total concentration? I got so tight I couldn't eat for at least two hours after working that plate.

Of course, you must be confident. An umpire's got to have a certain amount of cockiness, but he can't become arrogant. You've got to have that certain degree of confidence in yourself which comes from a knowledge of the fundamentals, the mechanics, and the rules. Now, when I came up, I knew the rules by heart. That's not to say a good umpire has the rules out in front of his eyes for nine innings, but he has to have them in the back of his head where he can use them when he has to. In certain situations you have to be able to recall the rule instantly. It has to be second nature.

There are three other attributes of a good umpire that I always emphasize—integrity, perseverance, and dedication. You've got to persevere through the low pay in the minors. The biggest change from the minors to the majors comes on the first and the fifteenth. You have to dedicate yourself to become competent, and you have to have the integrity to gain the respect of the players. You have to top all that off with one word, "hustle." Hustling can get you out of some tough situations. I might miss one sometime, but instead of creating an uproar, a player would come up and say, "That's one for you, Emmett," or "You missed that one, Emmett." But they respected me enough not to come out and give me a hard time about it because they appreciated the way I worked. Then it took tact, good judgment, and good old common horse sense, too. And under it all, if I hadn't had a sense of humor, I never would have made it.

No, not everyone can be an umpire. Beyond everything else I've said, umpires are born. Very few are made. You've got to have something in you that's just instinct. The scouts and guys that had been in professional ball told me when I was on the playgrounds, "You've got it, kid." When I go out to see another umpire, I can tell whether he's got it or he hasn't. There is an intangible something that tells you that this guy can do it. Maybe it's the way he carries himself, his motions, or his sincerity. You can tell.

Of course, it takes a little bit of a different personality today. In the old days you had a different type of umpire, a completely different breed. You don't find the Reardons and the Magerkurths anymore, just like you don't find Gas House Gangs. Times have changed. I don't think I could have come in with the hammer and tongs that, say, a Beans Reardon or Bill Klem used to display. I came in with more of a "speak softly and carry a big stick" attitude, and I think the players and fans appreciated me for that. In the old days umpires used to sneak out the side door with their collars up around their necks. Now, thanks to those old guys and to the Major League Umpires Association, an umpire walks with a little dignity. It's a noble profession now.

Yes, it's tough to make it to the top, but I'll always remember what my mother used to tell me, "Emmett, no matter how full the bottle of milk, there's always room for cream at the top." Of course, I had some help getting there. I am grateful to those who supported me, especially Joe Cronin, who took the bull by the horns and had the guts to call me up when it wasn't the popular thing to do. Jackie Robinson had his Branch Rickey; I had my Joe Cronin. I am also thankful for those people in the baseball hierarchy and the people at court, so to speak, who hung in for me and, when the time came, spoke in my behalf. Also, the people who supported me when I made it to the majors—players like Clete Boyer, Mickey Mantle, Brooks Robinson, Harmon Killebrew, Boog Powell, and Paul Blair. And, of course, managers like Ralph Houk and Gil Hodges. They tried to get Gil Hodges to discredit me, but Gil said, "That man is a good umpire. Period," and I'll never forget it.

I hope that I am remembered as a good umpire. Because, without any braggadocio, I *was* a good umpire. Regardless of my detractors, the ballplayers will tell you that I was a damned good umpire. Sure, I put it on. But I had a job to do every night, and I did it well.

It was an honor to work the 1967 All-Star game in Anaheim, but getting into the 1970 World Series between Baltimore and Cincinnati was the culmination of my dreams and career. Unfortunately the Series only went five games. Had it gone one more game I would have worked the plate. The reporters and fans were anticipating that with great eagerness, but maybe it's just as well it didn't happen—the World Series would never have been the same.

I retired after the Series. Trying to top the exceptionally good year and the thrilling events of the World Series would have been superfluous and anticlimactic, hence the decision to depart on top. Besides, there is a retirement age of fifty-five, and I had had an extra year of grace. I hated to quit. It's just a shame I couldn't have worked longer. But a man must go on to other things.

Still, the first two years of retirement were traumatic. After twenty years of umpiring, it becomes a part of you. I guess I've never really left baseball. I've kept my hand in it. I eased out, kicked the habit so to speak, umpiring three years in that Alaska amateur summer league, teaching collegians like Randy Jones the professional strike zone. I'm now the commissioner's West Coast representative, and I've traveled all over the world as an ambassador of goodwill for baseball. I've been to Canada, went to Europe for the Air Force in 1970, and in 1977 did a two-week tour of Korea conducting clinics.

My five-year tenure in the majors was one of satisfaction and gratification at having conquered the biggest challenge in my life and in some measure opening the door for black umpires. I feel proud having been an umpire in the big leagues not because I was the first black man but because major league umpires are a very select group of men. But the greatest satisfaction I've gotten is the feeling of accomplishment in doing what I set out to do in the first place when they said it couldn't be done. I only wish it had happened sooner, but there's no point crying about it. It took a long time, sure, but it also took the covered wagons a long time to get across the plains.

Baseball has been wonderful to me. If you think umpiring is a thankless job, you've been informed correctly. But it has its rewards. I had the privilege of leading an entirely different life from before, a life that a lot of people would have enjoyed living. I've made lifelong friends. Most of the people I met in baseball are still my friends, and they're a different breed, not phonies. You know, it's surprising, but even the guys that I made calls against have the warmest handshakes now. It's like a friend told me: "Emmett, what you want to happen in baseball is to have people like and respect you. Not only respect you, but have them like you, too." I think I've accomplished that.

AFTERWORD

When *The Men in Blue* appeared in 1980, I was asked repeatedly why I wrote the book. It was a reasonable question inasmuch as my previous publications dealt with the American Revolution and I had just completed a study of the Ku Klux Klan in Utah. It was also a difficult question to answer simply and directly.

I entered graduate school in 1963 sincerely but naively hoping to combine a passion for baseball with a professional interest in American history. Inspired by the civil rights movement that would finally end racial segregation in the United States, I announced my grandiose intention to write a master's thesis on the integration of baseball as a prelude to a doctoral dissertation on the integration of professional sports in America. Pointedly advised that sport was not an acceptable subject for serious historical research, I pursued another love—early American history. But in 1977, burned out mentally by numerous publications and presentations occasioned by the bicentennial of the American Revolution and emboldened by the professional security afforded by promotion to full professor, I finally opted to follow my heart and do a book on baseball.

Why umpires? I had always been interested in sports officials, probably because so few fans knew anything about the rules and the running of the games they followed so intently. My appreciation for umpires increased when, after discovering that I could no longer throw or hit a good curve ball, I tried amateur umpiring, only to find out I couldn't call one either. More importantly, the topic afforded an interesting perspective from which to study baseball history as well as abundant research opportunities because so little had been written about umpires other than newspaper articles excoriating them for blown calls. The lone history of umpiring, James Kahn's *The Umpire Story* (1953), was incomplete and unreliable, while the two autobiographies by umpires, Babe Pinelli's *Mr. Ump* (1953) and Jocko Conlan's *Jocko* (1967), failed to address important historical questions. (Cynical colleagues regarded my concern with umpires a natural extension of my earlier research on such social pariahs as revolutionaries, Loyalists, lynchers, and Klansmen.)

I began to research the history of major league umpiring since 1871, but was soon troubled by an inadequate "feel" for the subject, especially before 1950, the year my interest in baseball moved from casual to compulsive. Oral history had become an increasingly popular research methodology among modern American historians, so I decided to interview several former major league umpires to obtain firsthand an insider's sense of umpiring and umpires. I soon discovered that there were few "old-time" umps still around: far fewer umpires than players ever reached the majors, and they both began and ended their careers at a significantly older age. On Opening Day 1977 Beans Reardon was the lone surviving umpire who had umpired in the 1920s. Six were still alive who debuted in the 1930s, and of the ten umpires who reached the majors in the 1940s only five had done so before the end of World War II.

Interviewing these "historic" men in blue suddenly took on special urgency. Locating most of them was much more difficult than I had expected. Numerous letters were returned marked "Address Unknown" and countless telephone calls were made to people who had the same surname as my quarry, but eventually I found everyone on my list. Meanwhile, I became increasingly aware of the potential importance of the interviews and began thinking about the possibility of doing a collection of oral autobiographies in the manner of another academic, Larry Ritter, a professor of finance whose edited interviews with players, *The Glory of Their Times* (1966), pioneered the genre. That complicated matters: a private interview was one thing, speaking for the record and possible publication was quite another. Initially, most of the umpires were hesitant about granting an interview, and several declined. But I persisted, knowing that umpires traditionally shunned publicity, were defensive about their calling, and were suspicious of interviewers because of frequent bad press. Several had heard about (but not read) Lee Gutkind's *The Best Seat in Baseball, But You Have to Stand!* (1975), a chronicle of one crew's experiences during the 1974 season, and were understandably worried about betrayal of confidence and unduly creative writing. Ultimately, they consented, intrigued, I think, by the idea of talking with a history professor instead of a sportswriter. Only Al Barlick, whom I regard as one of the best umpires in history, refused—vociferously and adamantly.

Over the next eighteen months I traveled from New Jersey to Florida to California interviewing umpires. I found them without exception eager to tell their stories. They quickly understood that I truly considered them important figures in baseball history and was more interested in historical issues than anecdotes. Each seemed genuinely grateful for the opportunity to tell his story as he saw it, and talked with feeling and frankness about much more than I had ever anticipated. They spoke, I sensed, not so much to feed personal egos as to speak sui generis about umpiring.

There were disappointments along the way. Tom Gorman, my first interviewee, telephoned shortly after I returned home to tell me he had decided to do his own book, *Three and Two!* (1979). Augie Donatelli and I were saying good-byes in the parking area of his condominium in St. Petersburg when he learned that a fellow arbiter would be in the book. He glowered and thumbed himself from the project with an emphatic "if he's in, I'm out." His family and I knew that our pleading was in vain, and that Augie would not change his decision. I suspect he knew he kicked the call, for he was delighted when his "chapter" subsequently appeared in *Baseball History* (1989) a few months before his death in 1990. Most regrettably, the Umpire-in-Chief called out three men—Bill Grieve, Cal Hubbard, and Hal Weafer—before I could interview them.

It was an enormously enjoyable, yet challenging experience. I carefully researched each man's career, but then, instead of reconstructing the events, found myself trying to get the actual participants to recall them. At first I was frustrated: why couldn't they remember everything major and minor? Were their remembrances reliable? Did the interviews have any real historical import? I finally realized that the value of oral history lies in the "subjective" representation, not the "objective" documentation, of the past, and that an ump's personal sense of his life and career was at least as valid as a scholar's impressionistic reconstruction of the story. Still, belief in the traditional canons of historical scholarship prompted me to check, insofar as was possible, every game incident recalled by the umps. The most vexing task was determining the date Joe Rue was "garbaged" in New York (1940). He had identified "Rizzuto" as one of the principals, so I began reading newspaper accounts of Yankee home games in 1941, the year Phil joined the team. Nothing. Nothing in 1942 either. Rizzuto then left for military service, and I began reading pre-1941 game accounts. I eventually located the game and found Rue's account to be accurate in every detail save one: The player in question was not Phil Rizzuto but Marius Russo. He had misspoken. Or had I heard wrong?

Impressed with both the accuracy and the compelling substance of the interviews, I tried to turn disjointed comments into a semblance of unified life stories, and sent off the completed manuscript with keen anticipation. Rejection followed rejection as sixteen publishers decided that there was no market for a book about a bunch of umpires. I had heard from all but Viking Press, so I sent off a follow-up letter of inquiry. The letter came to the attention of Corlies Smith just as he was preparing to leave the office, headed for Yankee Stadium. Cork picked up the manuscript, perused it during the game, and decided to give the umpires their day in print.

Much has changed since the book's publication fourteen years ago. Most significant, six of the men in blue have died:

> Emmett Ashford, March 1, 1980
> Lee Ballanfant, July 15, 1987
> Bill McKinley, August 1, 1980
> Beans Reardon, July 31, 1984
> Joe Rue, December 1, 1984
> George Pipgras, October 19, 1986

They are missed, but I am grateful that their stories are now part of the annals of baseball history. I am also pleased that two more umpires, Al Barlick (1989) and Bill McGowan (1992), the finest arbiters of their generation, have been elected to the National Baseball Hall of Fame.

Recent developments have made this book even more a history of a bygone era. As symbolized by the American League's abandonment of the "balloon" in favor of the inside chest protector championed by the National League, there is no longer any significant difference in umpiring styles between the two leagues. The success of the Major League Umpires Association has utterly transformed the status of umpires. The strike of 1979, which occurred while the book was in press, resulted in a greatly increased salary schedule ranging from $22,000 to $55,000 depending on years of service; the four-year contract signed in 1991 called for a pay scale of $61,000 to $175,000 and provided for three weeks of paid vacation during the season. And, like the Major League Players Association, the MLUA has moved from a collective bargaining agency to a powerful force in the administration of the game; greater job security and higher salaries have affected the behavior and attitude of umpires as well as players. The financial lot of the minor league umpire, while proportionally far below that of his major league counterpart, has also improved substantially, and he no longer endures humiliating working conditions or is subjected routinely to physical abuse and extreme verbal vilification. Although only three of the twelve umpires in the book attended an umpiring school, it is no longer possible to become a professional umpire without formal training. Today's umpires are also better educated and more "professional" in their demeanor: The Gas House Gang is long gone, and so are mavericks like Beans Reardon, Lee Ballanfant, Shag Crawford, and Emmett Ashford. The umps of *The Men in Blue* labored on the periphery of the game, their work seen only by the crowd at the ballpark; today's arbiters occupy center stage, their work seen daily—and repeatedly when controversial—by millions of television viewers.

On the other hand, some things remain the same. The confrontations, controversies, rigors of the road, lack of understanding and respect persist; today's umpires endure most of the age-old problems endemic to umpiring, but are much better compensated for it. Debate over individual umpires' strike zones continues unabated. The title of the book is regrettably still apposite as major league umpiring remains an all-male guild. Also disconcerting is the fact that it took twenty-three years after Emmett Ashford retired in 1970 for another black, Chuck Meriwether, to join the American League's staff. Meriwether is only the third currently active regular major league umpire of African American descent.

My most enduring memories of writing *The Men in Blue* are not about baseball or umpiring, but about people. Joe Rue roaring with laughter at remembering the time he got bowled over on the base paths by Johnny Lindell. Ernie Stewart awash in tearful emotion after talking openly for the first time in thirty years about how Will Harridge destroyed his career. Jim Honochick boasting about his visual acuity during our interview and later telling me how he received far more recognition from playing the role of a "blind" umpire in a single beer commercial than during twenty-five years umpiring in the American League. Emmett Ashford speaking softly in a voice alternately tinged with pride and pain as he recalled his fight against racial discrimination. And I'll never forget how Beans Reardon's tough-guy facade crumbled as we shook hands after the interview. "Come on," he growled amiably and led me into his den. He wanted to show me a pencil sketch of Norman Rockwell's famous painting of umpires that would later adorn the dust jacket of *The Men in Blue*. "That's the original drawing. Rockwell gave it to me," he said proudly. He showed me other memorabilia, balls and bats, photos and plaques, each one evoking a smile of pleasant remembrance. As I started to leave the room, he barked gently: "Here! Take it." He handed me a photograph of three umpires having a discussion at the mound with a Boston Braves pitcher. "That's me,

Babe Pinelli, and Larry Goetz—the best damn crew of umpires there ever was." And the player? "Ahh, some sonofabitch." The photo adorns a wall in my study.

The Men in Blue did more than provide me with fond memories and new friends: it changed my life. The preparatory research convinced me that sport was both a legitimate and important topic for historical study, and the interviews provided the inspiration to pursue it. In particular, Emmett Ashford's rhetorical challenge—"How many men go to their graves without ever doing what is in their hearts?"—gave me the courage to effect a career change. I joined the North American Society for Sport History and the Society for American Baseball Research, and began a new career teaching and writing about the history of sport in America.

I had hoped *The Men in Blue* would give readers a better understanding of the history of major league umpiring as well as an appreciation that umps are people too. After all, it is less a book about umpires than the collected autobiographies of men who happened to have been umpires. Unlike many who reach the highest level of sport, these twelve men were not defined *by* their job. If anything, *they* defined umpiring. Judging from the comments of numerous readers, including amateur and professional umpires, I think the book succeeded on both counts. It was especially gratifying to hear from several who decided to attend an umpiring school after reading the book. One so inspired, Perry Lee Barber, thanked me because "your book, Conversations with Umpires, changed my life." She was correct to emphasize the gender-neutral subtitle, for it conveys both the nature and substance of the book, but her appreciation was misdirected: we are all indebted to twelve special umpires for their contributions to baseball—the game and its literature.

Larry R. Gerlach
1993